T0277495

# LOST BUT FOUND

## An Upcountry Life

### ROBERT KIMBER

Camden, Maine

**Down East Books**

An imprint of Globe Pequot, the trade division of The Rowman & Littlefield
Publishing Group, Inc.
4501 Forbes Blvd., Ste. 200
Lanham, MD 20706
www.rowman.com

Distributed by NATIONAL BOOK NETWORK

British Library Cataloguing in Publication Information available
**Library of Congress Cataloging-in-Publication Data**

Names: Kimber, Robert, author.
Title: Lost but found : an upcountry life / Robert Kimber.
Description: Camden, Maine : Derrydale Press, [2023] | Includes
  bibliographical references. | Summary: "Robert Kimber has led a largely
  rural life as a farmer, writer, and woodsman. The essays gathered in
  this wide-ranging collection reflect a lifetime of adventures and
  misadventures. Kimber writes of canoeing and fishing, stubborn sheep and
  old tractors, and the joys of roaming the woods with his dog"— Provided
  by publisher.
Identifiers: LCCN 2023017367 (print) | LCCN 2023017368 (ebook) | ISBN
  9781684750948 (cloth) | ISBN 9781684750955 (epub)
Subjects: LCSH: Farm life—Maine. | Natural history—Maine.
Classification: LCC S521.5.M2 K555 2023  (print) | LCC S521.5.M2  (ebook) |
  DDC 630.9741—dc23/eng/20230602
LC record available at https://lccn.loc.gov/2023017367
LC ebook record available at https://lccn.loc.gov/2023017368

♾™ The paper used in this publication meets the minimum requirements of
American National Standard for Information Sciences—Permanence of Paper for
Printed Library Materials, ANSI/NISO Z39.48-1992.

# Contents

# Sandy's Painting: A Preface

*From the editor: For fifteen years, from 2006 to 2021, Robert Kimber wrote a quarterly column for* Northern Woodlands *magazine. The volume you hold in your hands collects this extensive run of short essays as well as many highlights from previously published books and other magazines. His final column for the magazine, titled "Sandy's Painting," was a farewell in its original context. It does a second turn here as an opening preface for this anthology of his work.*

This column sets a milestone for me. Exactly fifty years ago, Rita and I pulled up stakes and moved from Cambridge, Massachusetts, to Temple, Maine. The number 50 as such doesn't strike me as ominous, but when I consider that half a century added to my age in 1971 makes me eighty-six now, then maybe I should be taking stock and checking my priorities.

As octogenarians go, I have little to complain about. Granted, I do have some memory slippage, ditto for hearing loss, also for decline of muscle mass, physical endurance, and attention span. I've been known to fall asleep in movies—a sure sign of advancing dotage, I'm told. Although I'm still able to do the work and have the fun I've been accustomed to these past fifty years, I'm finding it's taking me longer and longer to do less and less. I love writing, but I've always been slow at it, and now the slowest snail could leave me in the dust.

For well over a year, I've been meaning to go through my files and to assemble a new book of essays—some previously published and some not—but, given my increasing inefficiency, I haven't been able to find the time and focus I need to make this prospective book a reality. To help me find that space, I've decided to stop writing this "Upcountry" column. In 1999, Steve Long had invited me into the *Northern Woodlands* family, first with a feature on axes and a couple more features in subsequent issues. Then, in 2006, Steve suggested I take over his "Notes from the Puckerbrush" page and call this new column "Upcountry" after my book by that title.

The art that accompanied Steve's column was a pen-and-ink drawing of a rushing stream, and it appeared with my column for several years until Dave Mance asked if I could suggest a change. I could, because our neighbor and one of our closest friends, Sandy Gregor, had done a beautiful oil painting of Titcomb Hill in Farmington for the dust cover of *Upcountry*. Along with being a gifted landscape painter, Sandy had been a newspaper reporter, run our local Seniors Plus, worked in a nursing home, and hosted with her husband innumerable neighborhood Thanksgiving dinners. Years ago, she had carried our tiny newborn son, Greg, around in a wicker basket, and we babysat each other's dogs.

Then suddenly, in her fifties, this strong, lively woman was out of breath going up stairs. Metastatic breast cancer. That summer she asked her son Matty and me to take her for a canoe outing on twelve-mile-long Flagstaff Lake for a full view of equally long Bigelow Mountain. Matty and I made Sandy comfortable in the canoe with cushions and a backrest. She had her camera and kept busy with it, along with exclaiming how lucky we were to have picked this sweetheart of a day for our outing.

A week or two later, Sandy gave me a little scrapbook with photos and notes from our day on Flagstaff. I know I felt it then to be a precious gift, and I still do now.

At Sandy's last birthday party, at which Rita, Greg, and I were the only guests with her and her partner, Greg was about to leave for nearly a year's work teaching English in Brazil. Sandy broke into tears and said, "I may never see you again."

The rest of us assured her she would, but she was right, and we were wrong. Now she is gone, but before she left, she decided she would rather give us her painting of Titcomb Hill and see it hung on our living room wall rather than leave it to us in her will. She wanted it to go from her hands to our hands, from her heart to our hearts.

So when Dave asked for an illustration for my column, Titcomb Hill was my instant choice. Sandy's focus as a painter matched mine as a writer: we both loved this western Maine hill country. Sandy's brush captured the perfect close-up melding of the farm buildings into their hillside with the long view out across the valley and onto the blue mountain hilltops in the distance.

How can I capture in a few lines here the richness of these last fifty years? How do I express the immense gratitude I owe *Northern Woodlands* for letting me write four times each year on any topic of my choosing: the antics of my friend Wes's dogs, the ingenuity of gray squirrels despite their miniscule brains, catching no trout in some remote unnamed pond with my friend Steve, celebrating the arrival of spring by drinking tea with my beloved Rita on our porch steps.

Perhaps it is apt to simply say thank you, readers. Thank you, one and all.

# Lost But Found

In the summer of 1955, when I was twenty years old and just beginning to find my way around in the woods of northern Franklin County, Maine, I popped out of the brush one Sunday afternoon onto a high granite ledge and saw one of the sweetest views I've ever seen in my life. Looking off into the distance, I felt as if I were standing on the prow of a great stone ship plying a motionless course through the swells of forested hills. In a satiny blue sky, fair-weather clouds scudded along on a northwest breeze and sent shadows racing over the hills. To the east rose the twelve-mile skyline of the Bigelow range: Cranberry Peak, the Horns, West Peak, Avery Peak. To the south and west, ridges and peaks both named and unnamed rolled off as far as my eye could see, the light green of the hardwoods mingling with the dark of black growth in endlessly shifting currents until all color blended into the hazy blue of the summer horizon.

The ledge plunged about three hundred feet straight down, and at its base lay a small pond looking every bit like its image on the topo map. A triangular cedar bog poked back along the inlet stream; the outlet, wide at first, snaked its way into the woods across from my lookout, narrowed, and disappeared around a bend. The far shore shone bright with the luminous green of birch leaves, the white of the bark visible here and there through the foliage.

But I have to add that my first feeling on stepping out onto that ledge was not the near euphoria I would feel a few minutes later as I sat there, taking in the glory I'd been lucky enough to stumble upon. My first feeling was relief, for young and green and inexpert with map and compass as I was, I'd gotten myself lost; but when I saw that little pond that so unmistakably matched up with a pond pictured on my topo map, I was found. Now I knew I'd be out of the woods in about an hour. I'd even make it back to my father's camps on Big Jim Pond before supper. No one but me would be the wiser.

But what I had found that afternoon was much more than just my route out of the bush. I'd found one of those rare places on this earth that we recognize instantly as home, places where the heart soars and cavorts, playful as a raven, yet also finds utter repose, places where we rejoice to live and might hope to die.

Over the next two decades, I returned to my ledge often. It never disappointed, not in rain, not in fog, not on wind-torn January after-noons when the sun low in the southwest cast long shadows on the snow-decked pond below and gave off no heat. Now, I live sixty miles away and go back there seldom. But this last summer, my brother, Bill, visited me here in Temple, and we drove north of Eustis to fulfill a long-postponed filial duty. We carried our mother's and our father's ashes with us, not knowing exactly where we would leave them. The moment we reached Big Jim Pond, we realized that was not the place. All the camps but one are gone now; the camp yard has gone back to the alders. This place was no longer my parents' place or our place.

And then I thought: Of course, my ledge. On the bulldozed logging roads that now lace the whole region, we drove as close as I thought we could get, then set off on foot, picking our prickly way through raspber-ries in a now abandoned yard, then heading up a rutted skidder track. I wondered whether my ledge, too, had been transformed; but parapet that it is, it had remained inviolate.

Breaking out of the woods, we found the identical scene I had come upon nearly half a century ago. The same breeze ruffled the bright blue of the pond. The same clouds skimmed across the sky. Elated with the beauty and rightness of this place, teary-eyed yet gleeful as kids with Fourth-of-July sparklers, Bill and I poured our parents' ashes out over the edge of the cliff, powdering it white and sending plumes of finer ash off over the treetops. The rains would come and wash the ash down to the forest floor below where it would mingle with the roots of fir and moosewood and bunchberry, of trillium and Canada mayflower.

Here, it seemed to us, if our parents' souls had wandered lost, they now were found. Here, in sky, hill, pond, branch, blossom, and leaf, was all I could ever wish them of the resurrection and the life.

# Big Jim

In the summer of 1955, the year my father quit his job with the Bankers Trust Company in New York City and bought Big Jim Pond Camps—the year, that is, when my father took a flyer and did what he had always wanted to do, which was own and run a hunting and fishing camp in Maine—he discovered after just a couple of months at Big Jim that substantial as the place may have looked to the casual eye, it was as tender and vulnerable as a newborn baby, in need of constant coddling and attention if it were not to succumb to the heat, humidity, rot, rust, and decay of Maine summers, the crushing weight of winter snows, the rank growth of alders that kept marching, marching against this tiny beachhead of cleared land, threatening to engulf it if they were not constantly beaten back.

Take the main lodge, two stories high, built of full logs, nobody knew when exactly, but a long time ago, around the turn of the century. Downstairs: one big, open room, forty by twenty-two feet, the guests' dining room. Upstairs: eight little bedrooms, supposedly for the help, but so stifling hot in the summer and icy cold in the fall that neither my parents nor any previous owners had ever asked a cook or waitress to occupy one of those rooms. Then, sticking out the back, an addition that housed the kitchen and sticking out the side of the kitchen, the back dining room, where the owners and the help ate.

This whole gangling structure perched on a narrow shelf of land between the water and the hill that rose steeply behind it and every other building at Big Jim. All eight guest cabins, also built of full logs, stood within just a few footsteps of the shore. If that potbelly of a hill had ever added a few inches to its girth, it would have pushed Big Jim's lodge, camps, shower house, ice house, woodshed—every last stick—out into the pond.

Rain and snowmelt poured down the hill in the spring, soaking the soil, rotting the camps' underpinnings, tilting them ever so slightly year after year toward the water. Don Yeaton, Big Jim's year-round caretaker, and I crawled under the lodge, drove blocks and shims between sagging foundation posts and the joists to keep the floor from bouncing up and down like a trampoline. We replaced rotting posts and sill logs, first in Camp Four, then in Seven, then Three, then Eight, then started all over again.

The roofs were covered with green roofing felt. Pine needles collected on them, held the moisture, rotted the felt, which expanded with the heat, contracted with the cold, pulled at the nails that held it down. We climbed up on the roofs with gallon cans of black roofing tar, smeared the leaks, hoped the black goo would hold this roof together until next year, when we'd get around to laying a fresh layer of green roofing felt.

I tried to convince Don and my father that the camps needed standing-seam metal roofing or—second best—asphalt shingles, something permanent, or good for twenty years anyhow. But Big Jim didn't have either a lot of time or a lot of money. Green roofing felt was a lot cheaper, a lot quicker and easier to lay.

I realize now that the impermanence of those roofs was just right for Jim Pond. Big Jim's camps were, after all, *camps*, temporary dwellings, not as permanent as a house, not as impermanent as a tent, but somewhere in between. You make camp, and you break camp. Camps are not forever, much as I may have thought they were.

That first summer and the next and the next one after that I worked with Don at Big Jim, then over the next decade a few more summers plus a couple of autumns and winters, too. Don had gone to work washing dishes in a lumber camp when he was twelve. He'd been just about everything a man could be, both in the woods and out: lumberjack, river hog, teamster, guide, game warden, millwright, truck driver, 'dozer operator, plumber, rigger, mechanic. During Prohibition, he'd hauled pack-loads of bootleg whiskey across the Canadian line to a rendezvous point he kept mum to the end of his days. At forty-two he enlisted in the Navy, was assigned to the Seabees, and built airfields in the South Pacific. He had come to Big Jim when he got out of the Navy in 1946 and stayed on ever since.

Like my father and like the century, Don was fifty-five years old; his hair was graying, his square-jawed face permanently tanned and creased from a lifetime of sun and wind. A handsome old devil, but dressed in a white shirt, he looked, he said, like a crow in a milk can. He walked at a steady, mile-gobbling gait, never pushing, never puffing, never tiring, rocking slightly side to side, a metronome ticking off the miles. Game wardens and bootleggers learn how to pace themselves. He went on occasional benders but knew how to pace them, too, indulging only at slack times, only after hunting season was over at the end of November and before it was time to reopen for ice-out and the first spring fishing in May.

That Don was something of an old rascal made him all the more appealing in my eyes. I got his life history only in hints and tag ends, never enough to make a coherent story.

"There was times when I was drivin' truck," he told me, "when I'd stop for a drink, and when I come out again, I'd be so drunk I'd see three roads in the headlights instead of one. I'm not proud of that, but it's the truth."

Married twice, divorced twice. He never went into the details but did sum up the essential point in very few words. "There's many a man has left a good woman to marry a slut," he said. "I ought to know. I done it myself."

End of story.

The hardest thing he had ever done in his life, he said, was visit the widow of one of his Seabee buddies to give her a few snapshots he had of her husband and tell her, as best he could, how her husband had died.

I loved Don Yeaton. I trotted around at his heels, a happy puppy. In me, he had the ideal right-hand man, an apprentice eager to learn and equipped with the nearly inexhaustible energy of a twenty-year-old college kid. I wanted to know everything he knew, do everything he could do, hunt deer, build log cabins, trap beaver, maybe even go on an occasional bender.

Don was Big Jim's genius loci. Owners could come and go, but without Don, the place would falter, stagger and die. There would be no firewood to burn. No truck, tractor, chain saw, generator, or outboard motor would run; no toilet would flush; no shower would shower. Without Don, we wouldn't have had a shower at all. He built the shower house the first year he was there, a neat little full-log build-ing with Big Jim's traditional green roof. In back, partitioned off from the two shower stalls, he concocted a Rube Goldberg hot-water system out of an old wood heater stove and a boiler he salvaged from the Strat-ton dump.

Every Wednesday evening and on Saturdays, when we worked only half a day, Don went in to Stratton to visit his lady friend, Virginia. Before he left, he visited the shower house. He went in still wearing his dungarees, a faded green Dickies work shirt, and his old Navy fatigue cap turned cockeyed on his head, the bill of it sticking out over his right ear. He came out again scrubbed and combed, outfitted in clean khakis and a sport shirt.

"Shower's the only fit way for a man to take a bath," he said.

I understood him to mean that a man shouldn't settle into a tub and sit there in his own muck. A man needed to stand under a cleansing downpour, preferably warm, and sluice his grime on down.

All Big Jim's necessities and luxuries Don provided.

***

Unless our guests had unusually keen eyes, they saw nothing of Big Jim's flaws. They saw instead a Maine sporting camp looking just the way a Maine sporting camp was supposed to look: cozy, woodsy, but with a touch of rustic elegance about it, too. The lodge stood at the far right of the yard, with the camps strung out to the left of it, a mother mer-ganser with her ducklings trailing obediently behind. The two peeled spruce posts supporting the gable roof over the front porch of the lodge, bleached nearly white by the weather, looked almost Doric and added a classical note to the place. For all our clientele knew, the underpinnings of the camps were as unshakeable as Gibraltar, the roofs tight as the tightest drum. Ask any of our guests, and they would say that Big Jim offered not just the image of solid comfort but also the reality. In their experience, the floors under their feet didn't as much as quiver. Not once, even in the most ferocious, wind-driven downpours, did a drop of water seep through onto their heads or pillows.

On the screened-in porches, Big Jim's guests could settle into a rocking chair at five in the afternoon, safe from the blackflies, and sip their gin and tonics as the wind began to die over the water, promising a perfect evening for trolling. They could take in the glory of the pond stretching out in front of them, about a mile across, Norway Point off to the right, named for the stand of Norway pine on it, and straight across, where the Northwest and Northeast Inlet streams came down out of the hills, the island, round and domed and densely covered with spruce and fir.

Rolling away on every side, hills upon hills: Jim Pond Mountain, Farm Hill with that big rockslide on it, Antler Hill just to the left of it and quite a bit higher, and beyond them, on and on, all around Big Jim in every direction, hills and mountains, ponds, lakes, rivers, brooks, some with names, many without: Kibby Mountain and Snow Mountain, Pickle Hill and Picked Chicken Hill; Hathan Bog and Spencer Bog and Hay Bog Brook; Big Island and Round Mountain ponds and Felker and Baker and Douglas ponds; Spencer Stream and Kibby Stream; the Moose River and the Dead River.

Not the wilds by any means but timberland, forests that had been cut before and would be cut again. Still, peaks enough to climb, ridges enough to run, valleys enough to explore, waterways enough to fish to keep a man going a long time and, in the middle of it all, Jim Pond Township itself, much of it uncut since the 1920s, the loggers' old winter roads only a network of footpaths now that Don and I swamped out and blazed fresh each year for hikers in the summer, hunters in the fall.

\*\*\*

Big Jim Pond lies about a mile and a quarter east of the Dead River's North Branch. Maine Highway 27 runs west of the river, parallel to it, and often in sight of it on its twenty-five-mile route from the tiny village of Eustis to the Canadian line. In 1955 there was no bridge across the North Branch that connected with any road leading to Big Jim Pond Camps. That lack of a road connection with the outside world meant that everybody and everything that came into camp had to travel a complicated path. Our guests drove down a narrow woods track to our parking area and boat landing on the west bank of the river. There, they called into camp on a crank telephone (five short rings was our number) and most likely got my mother, Jean Kimber, who would be in earshot of the kitchen phone and who would then dispatch either my father, Frank Kimber, or Don or me, whoever was handiest, to climb into the Model A Ford beach wagon and go pick them up.

The call could just as well be from the grocery wholesaler who delivered cartons of canned peas, corn, carrots, beets, peaches and pears, quarters of beef and pork, slabs of bacon and tubs of lard to the boat landing, or from the guy who brought the bottles of propane that lit the gas lamps in the kitchen and fueled the ancient gas stove the cook could resort to if he needed some quick heat and the wood range was already tied up. All this stuff, plus an endless procession of five-gallon cans of gasoline to keep Big Jim's machinery running—even the washing machine was powered by a little one-cylinder, lawnmower-sized gas engine—plus toilet paper and typewriter ribbons and postage stamps, every last toothpick or pencil, crossed the North Branch in our ferry, a big green scow hitched to an endless rope that ran through pulleys anchored to trees on either side of the river.

All that fuss—having to haul all our supplies across the river and then into camp in the Model A, having to do the same with our guests and their gear, then having to do it all in reverse again when they left after a week or two—was a price both we and our clientele gladly paid because the North Branch of the Dead River was Big Jim's moat. On its far side, you parked the overstuffed plenitude of your bulgy Buick sedan. On this side, you climbed aboard the lean austerity of our 1932 Model A beach wagon, a vehicle never matched for elegance before or since, the body and doors all wood, all painted green, the roof built like a canoe with light ribs and planking covered with heavy canvas painted black, no glass in the windows, wide open to breeze and sun: a rolling verandah, a motorized surrey with no fringe on top.

Over there, you left the *Ed Sullivan Show* and the House Un-American Activities Committee behind to set off over here on a road that wasn't a road at all but a buckboard track on which the Model A Ford had replaced the buckboard. Big Jim in 1955 was still halfway between horses and horsepower, not caught up with—no, not overwhelmed by—a world ten years after Hiroshima. This road-not-a-road was a mile-long bower, the canopy of red and sugar maples shading us, keeping the soil cool and damp and hard in the two tracks under the beach wagon's wheels. No dust ever rose here, even in the driest of summers. On this side of the river, we had most of Jim Pond Township to ourselves, six miles by six of woods where no bulldozer blade had cut through the forest floor. Over here, time ran slower than it did on the other side of the North Branch, and even if you had never been to Jim Pond before, you knew, just minutes into your passage through that leafy tunnel, that you were heading for a place that would prove an oasis for the eye and heart and soul.

***

Don, my father and I each had our dreams for Big Jim. Not that any of us ever talked about them. Real men didn't talk about their dreams, but I knew all three of us had them anyway.

Mine, a pipe dream. I dreamed Big Jim would live forever. If no young man believes he will ever die, no young man believes the world he has been born into and fallen in love with will die, either. I expected that Big Jim's moat would never be bridged, that the trails that had once been loggers' winter roads would not become logging roads again, that the lease the owner of Jim Pond Township granted my father each year would continue to be granted year after year, on into perpetuity. I had still not experienced, on my own hide, change and the fragility of human arrangements.

My father's dream: To hold his own, to break even, or at least even enough that he could hang on here, to keep waking up every morning in his camp set back on the hill a little ways and look out, over the roof of the lodge, onto the water and the hills beyond, to go out in his Rangeley boat any evening he liked after supper to troll for togue and landlocked salmon or, on wind-still nights, to cast a fly to rising trout. To never ever again climb aboard the 7:23 that had carried him every morning from our commuter town in New Jersey to Hoboken, to never again work from nine to five in the real estate division of the Bankers Trust Company, where he had dealt with deeds and mortgage papers all day. He had his dream, a good part of it anyway, and dreamed only of keeping it.

Don's dreams became projects. If you indulged in dreams alone, you had nothing to show for it. If you indulged in projects, you had a shower house, running water, and flush toilets in all the camps, a root cellar dug into the hill, shored up with timbers and planking and equipped with two sets of tightly fitting, insulated doors. It could be forty below outside, but inside you could keep carton upon carton of canned goods, jars of pickles and fruit juices, barrels of potatoes and carrots and beets, and nothing would freeze.

In that first summer, which was a time for Don and his new boss to feel each other out, he didn't push hard. He eased my father into the idea of projects.

"You know, Frank," Don said one night after supper, "I think it'd be worth our time to add a screened-in porch to that little housekeeping camp over in the cove. It's awful miserable havin' to cook and eat inside a stuffy little camp in hot weather. If we screen in the deck that's already there, folks can sit outside in the cool of the evenin' and enjoy their supper. Make the place a lot more comfortable."

It just so happened that sometime in the spring, before my parents had even arrived at camp, Don had cut and peeled the fir we would need for the corner posts and rails of that porch and for the plates and rafters of its roof, so the work went quickly. In three days we were done, a mini project completed, not a full-scale construction job, just an upgrade, an improvement, but something new nonetheless; something that hadn't been there before was there now. We swept the porch clean, raked up the sawdust and wood chips, picked up the scrap ends of screening and roofing felt, gathered our tools and put them in the boat, stepped back to admire our handiwork.

"There, by the bejesus," Don said, and we climbed into the boat and headed back to camp for supper.

*** 

We had to spend most of our time, of course, not on projects but on the relentless, routine work that kept Big Jim functioning: the woodpile, for instance. Big Jim cooked and baked on a wood range, so even in the summer I hauled wheelbarrow loads of wood from the big drying shed back of the ice house to the kitchen woodbox twice a day. But come fall, especially the final weeks of deer season in late November, the demand for firewood increased five-, six-, tenfold. The hunters in each guest camp kept a fire going from the time they came in at dusk until bedtime, which might not come until a poker game finally broke up at midnight. The huge heater stove in the main dining room had to be roaring by five in the morning if the place was going to be warm enough to keep coffee from freezing in the hunters' cups at breakfast. When the season closed at the end of November and my parents went south to a house they had built in Daytona Beach, Don moved into their camp for the winter—the roomiest camp at Jim Pond and the only one, apart from the main lodge, with a kitchen—and he needed enough wood for both heat and cooking to see him through until May.

All told, Big Jim gobbled up twenty or twenty-five cord a year, wood that we felled, dragged into the wood yard with a 1940 Cletrac crawler tractor, then bucked up with a brutishly heavy old Homelite chain saw. Any stick that cracked open easily, neat slabs popping off it with one whack of the axe, we split small enough to fit into the cook-stove fireboxes. Any lumpy, knotty, twisty-grained stick that didn't yield instantly would wind up in one of the big, boxy heater stoves. When the pile of wood got so high we couldn't see over it, we'd load as much of it onto our 1939 Chevy truck as the body would hold, haul it into the camp yard, pile it in the drying shed that was open to the air on all four sides, then go back for another load and another until all of it was in. Then we cut some more.

Every morning after we had driven the Chevy out to the wood yard, Don would say, "Well, Robert"—he always called me "Robert," which he pronounced something like "Rahbut"—"it don't look as any-body's done a goddamn thing out here while we was gone."

Nobody had, and we would set to it for another day.

Young and green as I was, I thought twitching whole trees out of the woods with the Cletrac and working them up into a small moun-tain of sweet, clean stove billets that shone in the sun was just plain fun, though I had sense enough not to say so.

Don, who was neither young nor green, did not emote about the work, either. He just did it the same way that he walked, neither hurrying nor dawdling, just doing what needed to be done at a steady pace, knowing that the next jag of wood to fell and buck and split and pile would be there this afternoon if we didn't get to it this morning, tomorrow if we didn't get to it today.

In spare moments during the workday—before breakfast in the morning, during the hour lunch break, after our five o'clock supper in the evening—I fit in all the little jobs a chore boy would have done if we had had one. I tended to all our guests' needs. I made sure their cabins were supplied with firewood, kindling and old newspapers for tinder. First thing in the morning, I built a fire for Mrs. Fyte, who suffered from arthritis, so she wouldn't have to get up in a damp, cold camp. I took a bucket of hot water to Mr. Reese, who, unlike most of Big Jim's male guests, wanted to shave every day. If it had rained during the night, I bailed out our fleet of Rangeley boats tied up at the dock, waiting for their passengers like patient horses at the hitching rack of a saloon. I checked the bait traps and filled bait buckets for anyone who wanted to troll shiners. If Mr. Thorpe wanted to cast a fly on the river in the evening, I drove him down there in the Model A, pulled a canoe off the rack at the boat landing, and paddled him to the best pools upstream and down. If both Mr. and Mrs. Thorpe decided the next day that they wanted to visit the homestead museum of the famous opera diva Lillian Nordica, who was born and raised in Farmington, I again drove the Model A down to the river and ferried them across, and when they came back after dark in the evening and called on the phone to be picked up, I picked them up, all with a smile I didn't even have to fake.

At noon, just before lunch, when Don and I came back from the woods dripping sweat, I ducked into the dank, delicious coolness of the ice house, where Don had stored, under a thick blanket of insulating sawdust, the hundred and fifty blocks of ice he had cut out of the pond in February. I scraped away the sawdust and horsed two or three of those blocks onto a wheelbarrow, carted them around to the back side of the kitchen, lugged them up a set of stairs onto a small landing, and slid them into the ice compartment of the walk-in icebox that kept Big Jim's quarters of beef and pork, its milk and butter and eggs and cheese, from souring and spoiling. At cocktail time in the late afternoon, I revisited the ice house and lopped a breadbox-sized hunk of ice off one of those big blocks. In the kitchen, I washed the ice, attacked it with an ice pick, and then delivered little wooden buckets full of chipped ice to all the occupied camps.

Big Jim ran on wood and water, fire and ice.

\*\*\*

By the time I got back to Big Jim in June of our second summer, Don had convinced my father that what the camps had been lacking for their entire history was a lounge. Don had planted that seed back in early September the previous summer, when we had nobody in camp for a few days and my father and mother, Don and I were sitting in the red Adirondack chairs on the porch of the main lodge pretending we were our own guests lazing out there, enjoying the absence of bugs and the bright, clean air with a nip of fall in it.

"Somethin' me and Otho never got 'round to was buildin' a lounge onto the west end of the dinin' room," he said. "An afternoon like this one's perfect for sittin' out here, but in a few weeks with cold fall rains comin' on, it sure would be nice to be able to just walk into a room next door with a fire goin' in the stove and some books and magazines to gawk at."

Otho Record had owned and run the camps from sometime in the late '30s until he sold to Wayne and Peggy, the young couple who had lasted only two years and who had sold in turn to my father. Over the several years my father had come to Big Jim as a guest, he had gotten to know and like Otho, so Otho's opinion added some extra weight to Don's own.

"Well," my father said, "Otho spoke often about wanting to do that, but what with building the bathrooms onto the camps and running the water to them and all the other things you and he did in those years, it's no wonder you didn't get around to it."

"Could have a poker table in there, too," Don added. "Now the boys have to crowd into one camp or another for a game. No question, Frank. It'd add a lot to the place."

"Let's see how things pan out this year and what kind of season we're likely to have next year," my father said. "I agree that some kind of space here in the lodge for people to get together in after a meal would be a nice thing to have."

Don, I was sure, had carried the day.

***

And indeed our project in that second summer was cutting and peeling camp logs so they could dry for a year and be ready to build with in our third summer. In the winter, Don had scouted out and marked about forty tall, straight fir a foot and more at the butt, also some smaller ones for floor joists and rafters. Just a week after I arrived in June, we went out after those trees with two axes, a two-man crosscut saw and two spuds.

"Aren't you going to take the chain saw?" I asked.

"Don't want to horse that brute around all day," Don said, which was his way of saying he preferred to cut those trees by hand: no ear-splitting racket, just the sweet sound of a sharp axe chunking out a notch, the steady rhythm of the saw rippling back and forth, spitting sawdust out of the kerf. We felled two trees, then split up to limb them and peel the bark.

You trim off every branch close to the trunk, getting rid of as many lumps at this first stage of the game as you can. Then you run the corner of the spud lengthwise down the trunk, slicing through the bark so you can tuck the front of the curved blade into that cut and start rolling the bark off, first down one side, then the other. When you're done, you have a snake lying out straight as a string and glistening gold in the sun, shed skin lying in tatters on either side. But in no time at all, the sap that imparts that sheen to a freshly peeled softwood will dry out and leave the log still clean and fresh but without the glow that seems to be an emanation from the heart of the wood. No matter how clean the logs are when the camp is finished, or whatever preservative or stain you might buy to protect them, they will never again look the way they did in those first few minutes; and if anyone should ever find a way to keep that glow from fading, we would have a building material fit for the City of God.

As it was, Don and I had building material quite fit enough for a lounge at Big Jim Pond Camps, a pile of logs dragged into the camp yard with the Cletrac and stacked up on skids to keep them out of the muck and snowmelt of the next spring. And when, in our third summer, we had gotten ahead enough on the woodpile and put new roofing paper on two camps, we dug the post holes for the foundation of the lounge, set the posts and laid the three stringers that would carry the floor joists.

***

There are any number of ways you can build a log camp, but in Don's universe the only right way was to notch the bottoms of the logs at the corners so that each new log straddled the one below it. Any rainwater that got driven into the joint could not collect there to rot the wood but would roll off the rounded surface.

Not all projects required the right way. For the shower house and the bathroom additions on the camps, Don and Otho had used the much quicker and easier method of setting corner posts on the sill logs, cutting the logs for the walls square at the ends to fit snug between the posts, then spiking them into the posts. But this lounge was a different story, a showpiece. It had to have some class. And then, though Don never said so, he probably saw it as his swan-song. He was fifty-seven; Big Jim wasn't likely to need another new building in his time, so this one should be a masterpiece.

Building with logs isn't what you'd call fine woodworking, but we came as close to that standard as axes would let us get. We scribed the exact shape each notch should have onto the log with a compass, rolled the log up, then took turns, first Don, then me, carving the notches out with the axe and hewing off any lumps or curves in the log that kept it from settling down snugly on the one below it. We might roll a log back up three, four, five times to shave off just a little more wood along the length of it or to clean the notch out so that it fitted the log below tightly.

When Don was satisfied, he'd grin and say, "Just the cock for dolly," and we'd spike that log in place.

***

In late September we finished the lounge, the floor varnished and gleaming, a couple of bookshelves built onto the wall just inside the entrance from the dining room, a Franklin stove in the far corner, a green sofa against the back wall with end tables for drinks and magazines at either end, a big hooked rug on the floor, a couple of rocking chairs, a view of the pond from a picture window we concocted out of three big sliding windows Don had salvaged from the wrecking of an old hotel in Lewiston and, in the middle of the room, a snazzy octagonal poker table, complete with a green felt playing surface and little sunken compartments in front of each of the eight players' stations for chips, drinks and ashtrays.

The weekend after the lounge was finished and furnished, Don brought Virginia into camp late Saturday afternoon for a little celebration. The fall foliage was at its peak, the maples across the pond flaring up red and orange against the green of the softwoods; fair-weather clouds scurried across a blue sky.

I'd built a little fire in the Franklin stove and opened the doors up, as much for atmosphere as for warmth. We settled into the green couch and the rockers, my father and mother, Don and Virginia, and I, and made fairly short work of a fifth of Canadian Club, classy booze my father had bought a couple of weeks ago at the state store in Farmington and tucked away specially for this occasion.

Sitting in this room built of clean logs, its rafters and roof boards overhead still so new they seemed to rain light down on us, I let my head drift off on the fumes of that good whiskey, picturing a future I thought all but assured. In it, all five of us would keep gathering in this room Don had been itching to build for years. Don would keep going out to see Virginia every Wednesday evening and Saturday noon; they'd keep dancing at many another hunters' ball—how many more I couldn't guess, but many more. What the practical arrangements might be to make all that possible, I did not trouble my woozy head about.

"Fall is so beautiful," Virginia said. "Just look out there. I love the fall, but it's so sad, too, because you know what's coming right behind it."

\*\*\*

The other project going on in the summer of 1957 was not ours. It was the bridge across the North Branch and the bulldozed road that would run a mile downstream from the bridge to meet up with our buckboard road.

That year, the new road went no farther. The jobber built a small camp at the junction of the new road and the buckboard road, and that winter two men with horses cut birch that a mill in Dixfield would turn into spools for the Coats and Clark thread company.

We had to admit the new road had its advantages. Our guests could drive themselves into camp and drive themselves back out again. We could drive our Mercury station wagon to Stratton or Farmington, load it up with groceries, hardware, roofing paper, gas cans, anything, and everything, and drive the stuff right to Big Jim's back door. Delivery trucks could drive in, too. We soon had, up on the hill back of the kitchen and next to the guides' camp, one of those huge propane tanks that looks like half an airliner fuselage. Never again would Don and I horse hundred-pound gas bottles into the green scow at the river, then into the Chevy truck or, in the winter, haul them in behind us one at a time like sleds.

Once we had hewn the rafters for the lounge and were ready to put on the roof boards, a truck from Jordan Lumber in Kingfield drove right down to the porch of the main lodge, and we had our roofing boards delivered within twenty yards of their final resting place. A week later, when the roof was up and papered, the same truck came back again with the finish boards for the floor.

Now, who in his right mind could complain about that?

\*\*\*

My college years were over; my ten *Wanderjahre* just beginning: drafted in 1958 for two years, stationed in Germany, graduate school, a teaching job in Berlin. I didn't get back to Jim Pond for an extended stay until the summer of 1968. In the few visits I'd been able to make in the previous decade, I could see the continuing changes the road was bringing to both the camps and the surrounding territory.

That it made life easier at Big Jim any fool could see. Because the Fotters' grocery store in Stratton was only a twelve-mile drive door to door now, my parents could make frequent, easy runs to buy perishables there and no longer needed all the cold-storage space the big walk-in icebox had provided. Two used gas refrigerators my father was able to pick up and the propane tank that could be refilled at a moment's notice took care of the camps' refrigeration needs, also relieving Don of cutting and storing ice in the winter. His only winter responsibility now was to keep the roofs shoveled clear of snow so they wouldn't cave in. The ice house, with its insulating sawdust, was obsolete; so too was our old, cantankerous sawmill now that we could get lumber delivered right to pond's edge. The sawmill had all but disappeared, the shed roof caved in and the timber framing rotted out from under the tracks and the log carriage. Young poplar were springing up in and around the wreckage.

And of course the bulldozer had continued on its march, following many of Big Jim's hiking trails, making wide gravel roads of them and extending the reach of the road network. Hunters and fishermen could stay in Stratton or Eustis and in an hour's drive or less reach parts of Jim Pond Township that would have been inaccessible before the bridge and roads went in. Big Jim's clientele shrank. Because more and more people could easily get into more and more of the area, fewer felt the need to stay at a sporting camp on the township. Also, many guests who had been coming to camp year after year were aging and dropping off Big Jim's mailing list. In my father's first years at camp, he had hired a cook for the entire season, May through November. Now he and my mother did the cooking and waiting on tables, only hiring a woman to help with kitchen and cabin chores if business turned out a little better than expected.

He and Don were both sixty-eight, far from decrepit but sixty-eight nonetheless. Don allowed as he was slowing down. Come deer season, he still guided hunters from dawn to dusk, some old customers he had guided for years on end and who remained loyal to him and to Big Jim, but now, instead of sitting up with his party for a few drinks in the evening, he headed straight for the guides' camp and bed the minute he finished his supper.

Virginia, who had worked for the local telephone company as an operator in the Stratton office all the years we had known her, had been offered a better job in the company's headquarters in North Anson and had moved there.

\*\*\*

The next two years I spent teaching in the Boston area, where Rita and I met and married. In the summer of 1971, we moved to Maine, not to Jim Pond but to Temple, a small town near Farmington. We bought an old farm with a rickety house on it that demanded all our time to make it livable for the coming winter. Our weekend trips to Jim Pond were few.

In late July my father called us to say the main lodge and the ice house right next to it had burned to the ground. Don, sleeping in the guides' camp right behind the lodge, had wakened to the flames and raced out to Eustis to summon the state forest service tank trucks. The forest service team had come in as quickly as they could, but by the time they arrived, the buildings were already a total loss. All the firemen could do was wet down the guides' camp and Camp Two, both of which were quite near the blaze, and prevent the fire from spreading into the grass and trees.

The only explanation for the fire anyone ever came up with was spontaneous combustion in that great mound of old sawdust in the ice house. The conditions were ideal: some dampness left over from the melted ice, just enough air for oxidation. Once we had stopped storing ice, we should have shoveled that sawdust out, carted it off down one of the new logging roads, and thrown it to the winds. But none of us had thought to do that.

\*\*\*

Two summers later, the family company that had owned Jim Pond Township for generations sold it. The new corporate owner didn't want a commercial camp on the land and would not renew my father's lease for the next season.

Oddly enough, or perhaps not oddly at all, this sudden end to Big Jim Pond Camps did not hit any of us as a catastrophe. My father and Don were both seventy-three. Big Jim was about the same age, and, by the time the township was sold, the camps had long since ceased to be a going business. My parents came up from Florida later and later each spring and left a little earlier each fall. The only clients who came, even before the fire, were few and far between, mostly old friends for whom Big Jim remained an oasis for the soul and who were content simply to be there. Once the lodge had burned, Big Jim was just where my parents spent their summers, where Don continued to live and where a handful of couples might turn up in the course of the season for a few days.

My father sold off everything movable on the place—boats, motors, the stoves and furniture in the camps. Friends of mine in need of housing but with little money took down three of the cabins, numbering the logs as they worked, carted them away on lumber trucks, then reassembled the cabins on their own plots of land. You make camp and break camp, and sometimes somebody else makes camp again.

With the exception of the owners' camp, the remaining buildings were bulldozed and burned. Now, thirty-five years later, the alders have taken over the camp yard.

My father had owned and run Big Jim Pond Camps for eighteen years. I suppose, from most perspectives, his venture at Jim Pond was a failure, even a crazy enterprise from the word *go*. How could a man who had worked in real estate law for much of his life buy a place where he owned a set of buildings but not the land underneath them, where the fate of the business hung on the annual renewal of his lease?

Well, the lease always had been renewed year after year, decade after decade. My father had been more than willing to go in on those terms. Life was not forever, and if Big Jim wasn't, either, too bad. Four, seven, eleven, or however many years doing what he wanted wasn't so bad a deal. As it turned out, he got eighteen.

I never thought of my father as an adventuresome man, but he had been brave enough to take the chance he took. He had also managed his assets just carefully enough to get him to the end of his days. He died at eighty-one, felled by a heart attack in his Daytona Beach house. He and my mother must have been living on not much more than their Social

Security checks. His bank account was down to only a few dollars. He owned only the house, its furnishings, and his car.

\*\*\*

Don had died shortly before my father, in a house in Eustis where his mother had lived out her last years and that he had inherited from her. The newspaper report of his death said he had been trying to repair a gas heater and it exploded on him, that he had been found lying face down on a heating grill. But Tommy Lamont, who worked for the state forest service in Eustis, told me when I saw him a couple of months later that the newspaper report was wrong. Don, too, had died of a heart attack.

"He was a good man," Tommy said—somewhat defensively, I thought—as if he knew, as I did, that whatever Don's failings had been, they were as nothing compared to his goodness, and that nowhere near enough people knew how good he had been, that all they saw in him was an old ne'er-do-well woodsman with a woodsman's persistent hankering for whiskey.

My father may have owned Big Jim Pond Camps, but the only one of us who had truly earned the right to call Big Jim his own—because it was his work that kept the place from falling down, his work that brought in the wood and the ice and kept the roofs from caving in year after year when my parents weren't there and I wasn't there and he was the only person there, holding this small part of the world up on his shoulders—that only person was Don.

His funeral in Farmington was a routine affair. He was a veteran; a flag draped his coffin; a few older men whom I didn't know but assumed were there from the VFW attended. So did Virginia, who had come over from North Anson.

The minister, clearly called in on a rotation basis, knew Don not at all and went through his rote service: "O death, where is thy sting? O grave, where is thy victory?" And that was that.

I'm never quick on the uptake. I always think, long after the opportunity has gone by, of the clever argument or quick-witted response I should have thought of in a discussion days earlier. I knew at the time that this service for Don cheated him, did him no honor or justice at all. But I could find no words to speak at the moment, so Rita and I left and went home, and when I said to her what a sad, empty fiasco that had been, she said, "Don would have laughed."

Maybe. Laughed or snorted.

But whatever he would have done, he was Big Jim. He still is. And these words are just some of the words I couldn't find to say for him that day.

# A Kitchen with a View

Rita and I tend to make major life-changing decisions on impulse; then we'll dither over trivia, like buying a new can opener.

"The old one still works, doesn't it?"

"Yes, but I've never liked the handle on it."

"Well, before we rush into something we'll regret later, let me do a little comparison shopping."

But offered the prospect four decades ago of spending our meager life savings on a one-hundred-acre Maine homestead and a wrecky old farmhouse, we reached agreement in a matter of minutes.

On a cold, windstill February afternoon under an immaculately blue sky, we circled the house once on snowshoes and wandered along the course of Temple Stream, winding its way through the bottomland fields.

The exterior walls of the house were festooned with cracked, dangling clapboards; inside, the previous owners, preparing the way for a total renovation, had torn out the walls and ceilings—plaster, lath, and all. A few ancient light fixtures dangled overhead from runs of BX cable. In the kitchen, a lone cold-water pipe stood sentry over the sink. A bleak prospect.

But when we went over to the kitchen windows, which look northwest up Temple Stream's valley, we forgot the bleakness of the indoor scene behind us and reveled in the glory of the outdoor one before us.

"Lovely, isn't it?" I said.

"Yes," Rita said. "Beautiful."

And that was that. We were sold.

Now, before we go any further, I have to add that our view is neither spectacular nor panoramic. There are hilltop locations in our neighborhood where the whole spread of Maine's western mountains—all

23

the four-thousand-footers from Saddleback to Bigelow—seem to fill the horizon. Not so here on the Temple intervale. Hills rise right up on either side of this little valley, and Spruce Mountain, which closes off our view and the end of the valley, is only about four miles from our kitchen and twenty-six hundred feet high. Small potatoes as Maine mountains go.

So our view is a modest one, not made for the wide screen. If I lived on a high hill with a 180- or 220-degree view, I might get to thinking I was monarch of all I surveyed. Down here in this valley, where the hills begin at my doorstep and then roll away to the northwest, climbing a little higher, ridge by ridge, I feel instead like a fellow citizen living in close company with those hills and with the trees that cover their sides, the squirrels and deer and bear that roam them, the brooks that rise and flow among them. Our small-scale view discourages megalomania and makes our kinship with this place vividly clear to us.

Because those kitchen windows we first looked through were only two and spaced nearly three feet apart, the first improvement we made was to install a third window between the existing pair. We contemplated a picture window, but then realized it would have been a breach of style for this traditional one-and-a-half-story Cape.

On one level, the new window was a stupid move because the north wind comes roaring down this little valley in the winter hard enough to play our metal roof like a steel drum and drive snow in through the smallest cracks. In our first winter, we often woke to find mini-snowdrifts on the sills of our triple kitchen windows, and we would quickly discover other practical failings of a nineteenth-century farmhouse, like the loose rock foundation that admits ready access to both rodents and heavy rains. But we were not about to let a few drafts lessen our enthusiasm for our view. We fell in love with this place for its beauty and accepted its little failings into the bargain.

By now, we have eaten approximately 43,800 meals seated at the long table we placed up against those windows. Month after month we take in—with breakfast, lunch, and supper—the gradual shifting of the seasons. Minute by minute, we watch the summer sun drop behind the hills and paint the underbellies of the clouds crimson, then deep purple. The wolf pine growing just to the right of the house, a big tree when we came here, towers over us now and, lit by the winter's rising sun, flings its shadow far out on the snow-covered hayfield. On clear, crisp days in the fall, Spruce Mountain seems close enough to reach out and touch. In mist and drizzle, it's a ghost mountain hardly visible at all. In the spring, with the windows open, we've heard the pile-driving *oonk-ka-chunk* of a bittern in the marshy ditches of the hayfield, and sometimes caught glimpses of wood ducks paying brief visits there.

Now that I think about it, it's really not impulse we act on, but instinct: an inherent capacity to choose what matters most to us, to pay heed to the heart and the gut. We probably could have chosen more practical places to live, but not any other with just this view from the kitchen.

# A Fine Woodworker

When Rita and I left the fleshpots of Boston and Cambridge and moved to Temple nearly forty years ago (forty years!), we made that move with the blessing of our friend Molly Gregory. Molly lived in a modest little apartment she had constructed for herself in the barn of hospitable friends in Lincoln, Massachusetts. Underneath the apartment, on the ground floor in the barn, she had a fully equipped woodworking shop, and outside the barn she had built a smaller barn where she kept a Jersey cow and a flock of chickens. She also had a black poodly mutt officially named Griselda but whom she usually addressed as "Grum." Grum adored Molly, and so did we, though had we even hinted at such a notion, Molly would probably have made one of her many funny faces and said something like, "Oh, gawrsh, don't be so silly."

Although she had grown up on a farm and wound up running the farm at Black Mountain College, where she had gone to teach in 1941, she was, first and foremost, a woodworker, the very best of several first-rate ones it's been my good luck to know. She could do it all, from designing and building a house to fine cabinetmaking to intricate carvings for a church altar. And along with everything she knew about woods and their properties and tools and their uses, she had an artist's eye, which she had developed to a high level working with Josef Albers at Black Mountain. Whatever she built, whether barn or sideboard, had clean, simple lines and seemed just made for whatever setting it was in.

Knowing that Rita and I had bought an ancient farmhouse we would have to practically rebuild from the sills up, Molly recruited us to apprentice with her on a couple of renovation jobs, one of them constructing a new living room to add to her own apartment. In retrospect, I wonder if she hadn't invented that job as much for our benefit as for her own so that we'd get a little more practice in framing and putting up drywall.

When the time came for us to make our final run to our new home in Temple, Molly gave us three house-warming gifts: a superb Spear & Jackson panel saw, a black cherry cutting board we have used practically every day of our lives ever since, and half a dozen of her chickens to provide us with breakfast eggs in our first year and stew meat in our second. So with a couple of cartons full of chickens in the back of our VW Beetle, we moved to Maine. Molly had of course unknowingly given us still another gift: When we knew we would soon have a child to name, we didn't have to peruse any lists at all. If the baby was a girl, she would be Molly; if a boy, Gregory, and so he turned out to be.

But then fifty-five plus twenty makes seventy-five, and ten more makes eighty-five. Molly had to give up the barn, the Jersey cow, and her "girls" (the chickens) and move to a retirement home where she was not allowed to keep any animals but managed to anyhow. She built a small-scale fire escape, not for herself but for her cat, Sophia, who used that unobtrusive structure to leave and enter Molly's second-story room day or night, unseen by other residents or the staff. Sophia occasionally brought red squirrels along, too, some alive, who would often find refuge in Molly's closet.

Work, she believed, was one of life's great privileges, and unable to run a table saw in her new home, Molly turned to sewing gorgeous quilts and painting her own Christmas cards and note cards in watercolors. They usually had barns and cows and chickens in them.

Molly could, in short, turn old age into art, the approach of death not something to waste time fretting about. Often faced with tough problems, she had always solved them elegantly. Once, when she'd been installing a set of classy and expensive kitchen counters and cabinets, a knot broke out of the middle of one of the counters. What to do? She made an inlay in the shape of a leaping dolphin, converting a disaster into a beautiful decorative detail. "If you can't hide it," she said, "feature it."

The other night, cleaning up after supper, I realized that a crack that had started in Molly's cutting board was getting longer and deeper. Soon the board will break apart. Molly died two years ago at ninety-three. I can't ask her to repair that board with her inimitable touch, but what I can do is remember what she told me. I'll laminate a contrasting strip of wood in between the two halves of that board, featuring the break that can't be hidden. And then I'll make sure Molly's cutting board is one of the things our son, Gregory, takes away from this house when our time for leaving comes.

# Meanders

When Rita and I moved to Temple, Maine, in 1971, we had a swimming hole on the place. We didn't know that when we signed the contract to buy this old farm of a hundred acres. We'd seen our future home only in winter, in February of that same year, a hard, cold winter with lots of snow. We had explored the wreck of a house, careful not to fall into the cellar where the previous owners had torn up the floors. They'd torn out the interior walls, too. They were intent on total renovation.

We looked northwest out the kitchen windows. The view was lovely: a field of snow on our place; then the tree line marking where we ended and our neighbors, the Mitchells, began. The dear, prudent Mitchells, thinking ahead many years ago, had planted a white pine plantation on their land. We saw the green patch of that maturing pine, a hayfield between the pines and the road, and the Mitchells' house beyond the field, a house much like ours, an old, white, one-and-a-half-story Cape. We liked the view, so we bought the place. A torn-up, falling-apart house, but so what? Location, location, location.

Temple Stream flowed through our land. It was no more than fifty yards from our back door to the stream, so we put on our snowshoes and walked the stream, first northwest to the end of the property, then back to where we'd started, then southeast to our property line that way. We realized there was a big backwards S-curve in the stream right in back of the house, but not until we took up occupancy in June of that summer and saw that S-curve freed of its cover of ice and snow did we understand what a treasure we had snowshoed over back in February.

Much of Temple Stream's course, up in the hills, is steep and rocky. If you're rambling around up there on a sticky summer day, you'll find little pools among the smooth, water-worn rocks, oases of calm in the rush and noise around them, where you can strip off your sweaty clothes and dunk yourself. But down here in the valley, before the stream hits Temple village, tips downhill, and races off in another rush of whitewater, it meanders through the floodplain; and thanks to that meandering and its looping curves, we had a swimming hole just a few minutes' walk away from our kitchen door. The water at its deepest was just over my head; the pool was just big enough that you could swim in it, not far, of course, but a few strokes. It was big enough to be a *swimming* hole.

What a treat it was after tearing out rotting old sills in the house and putting in new ones or loading hay bales all afternoon to head for that deep bend in the stream, the coolness of the water, the shade of a big, billowy-branched red maple on the outside of the bend, the sunlight filtering in through the leaves, the little sand beach the stream had deposited for us on the inside of the bend, the sweet privacy of the place. The stream was too low now in mid-summer to interest canoeists, too low for the trout fishermen who come through in May and early June. We had it all to ourselves. The heavy screens of alders meant we could be blessedly, unworriedly naked there, Rita and me and our boy, Greg, who bounced and splashed in our arms as a tiny tyke, then later took his own first paddling strokes in the swimming hole, joined by our friends, their kids.

Whatever mix of sweat and grunge we carried on our skin and in our hair we sloughed off. We arose from the waters rejuvenated, born anew, no blessings of any preachers required.

Rejuvenation, I've since learned, is not only what we experienced nearly every summer day in our swimming hole but also a technical term in physical geography, "the state of a river when its energy has been revitalized, thereby leading to an increase in its erosional capacity."

Temple Stream is subject to frequent revitalizations of its energies: spring floods, winter floods, sometimes several a year. Rejuvenation is what keeps meandering streams and rivers meandering.

So the inevitable happened. The force of the water kept undercutting that big maple until the tree did what it had to do: pull out of the bank and crash down, form a dam where silt built up and up, filling in the swimming hole, shunting the current aside, sending it off on its patient, meandering work of reshaping this stretch of Temple Stream for the who-knows-how-manyeth time.

Sending us meandering off, too, in search of a new place for our summer afternoon swims, a pond—as it has turned out—where moose feed in the outlet bog, loons yodel, and kingfishers dive for their supper. Temple Stream keeps moving on and changing, and so do we.

# Deep Cold, Deep Snow, Decent Winter

Some people may think a winter with mild temperatures and not much snow is a good winter, but they are mistaken. Any winter worth its salt has deep snow and deep cold and, therefore, good skiing. By skiing, I don't mean the downhill kind that relies on gondolas and T-bars and big squirt guns that make fake snow even in a warm, lousy winter. Nor do I mean the kind done at—what do they call those places?—touring centers, I think it is, places where a guy goes out in the morning with a trail groomer and makes a nice wide swath for skate-skiing and cuts side-by-side tracks for folks who like to ski in a rut.

Forgive me if I sound opinionated and curmudgeonly on the subjects of skiing and good winters versus bad, but I am opinionated on these subjects and might as well own up to it. Skiing—the kind that matters for people of my persuasion—is cross-country skiing, and essential to skiing across country is snow covering not just a few trails on a mountain or in a touring center but snow everywhere, a *whole countryside* covered with snow. Not any old snow will do, either. Not just a few piddling inches that leave every rock and root and stump sticking up to gouge and shatter skis. No, there has to be a lot of snow all over the place, a couple of feet to settle into a solid base that buries those rocks and roots and makes the rough places plain.

Cross-country skiing is not about the thrills of schussing down big hills or the cardiovascular benefits of skiing 'round and 'round in big circles on prepared tracks. Far be it from me to denigrate aerobic exercise or, for that matter, to suggest that wedeling your way down a mountain at breakneck speed isn't fun. The point is simply that cross-country skiing, while by no means lacking in downhill thrills and healthful exercise, is primarily about exploration, hence the need for plenty of snow in all those nooks and crannies of your local geography that you haven't found yet or that remain messily forbidding in spring, summer, and fall.

In a decent winter, the hummocks and black sucking muck of the Great Dismal Swamp, for instance, are transformed into white velvet under your feet. An old twitch road the dense foliage of July has kept hidden from you is visible now, and when you follow it up out of the undergrowth down here in the valley, sometimes losing it as you climb up onto a hardwood slope, then finding it again, sometimes guessing by lay of the land where it should go, when you keep following it and ski over a long, low ridge only a couple of feet high, then you know you've found another old stone wall you hadn't come across before, and then there's a depression in the snow about three or four feet deep and too rectangular to be anything but manmade, and on the south side of it are a couple of huge old sugar maples much older than any of the beech and red maple and ash and yellow birch nearby. So your skis and a good deep snowpack under them have let you find still another old cellar hole, another abandoned home on what is a lovely site indeed, a gentle south slope with a small stream nearby providing water, those big maples shading and cooling the house that once stood here in the heat of summer.

All right, you may say, have your snow, but why do you want it so bloody cold? What's the point of that? Two reasons. Sustained daytime temperatures hovering between zero and ten above make for powder snow and keep powder snow powdery after it's fallen. One of the great joys of a stretch of cold weather is that one wax job on your wooden skis, if you're still lucky enough to have a pair—green wax on the shovel and tail, blue under your feet—will give you, for as long as the cold snap lasts, the smoothest, silkiest, glidingest ride you can hope for.

More important still, all those brooks and streams and rivers you need to cross in your explorations will be frozen solid enough to let you cross, solid enough, too, to let you follow their paths on the ice, skimming along among the boulders of a mountain stream, stopping to check out the mink tracks at an open lead, the fishy-smelling otter scat on a flat rock.

So revel in that cold and snow. Count your boreal blessings while you can. In New England, you'll have to retire those wooden skis and resort to your old, plastic, non-waxable beaters soon enough. If winter comes, spring—with its thawing and freezing, its glare ice, mudholes, and corn snow—can't be far behind.

# Sheep in the Parlor

Sheep came into our lives the way just about every other creature on our place has come: unplanned, unpremeditated, flung our way, so to speak, by the forces of benign rural chaos. It was mid-summer, our second on the tumbledown, overgrown old farm we had bought in western Maine. Rita was working in the garden; I was peeling split and curled clapboards off the front of the house in plain view of all who passed on the road. Among the passersby was our neighbor Leo Rioux, who at the time was still running a small dairy farm two miles up the intervale. His truck screeched to a halt, the gears complaining bitterly as he shifted into reverse and rumbled into the driveway tail-end first.

The body of the truck was filled with assorted forlorn livestock.

"What this place needs," Leo said as he leapt down from the cab, "is a couple of sheep."

There were exactly two sheep on the truck. One was a black-faced, black-legged, gray-muzzled, round-bellied, bony-hipped old ewe that stood braced squarely on all four feet and looked me straight in the eye, her head tilted pugnaciously to one side. "Let it be understood right now," she said, "before negotiations go a step further, that this lady takes guff from nobody."

Her companion was an immense wool ball, dirty white all over. He was so round and woolly that it was hard to locate his feet and head, much less his eyes, ears, and mouth. But even though I had trouble telling one end of him from the other, I did get the impression that he was young and good-natured and would be happy to roll around our place like a huge fleecy bowling ball, knocking down anything in his path.

"I can give you an awful good trade on 'em," Leo said. A lean, dark-haired man, Leo spoke and moved with a quick authority that was hard to resist. He was already unloading the sheep before I had said a word.

"How much?" I managed to blurt out.

"Twenty-five for the pair."

Rita had heard Leo's truck arrive and had come up from the garden to join us. She falls for anything fuzzy and four-footed, and I could see a familiar, almost narcotic glaze form over her eyes. If she had said anything, it would have been "Aren't they dear?"

"What am I gonna do with sheep, Leo?" I said. "I don't have any fencing. I don't have a shed. I don't know anything about sheep."

"You can send me a check," he said, and climbed back into his truck.

As he turned onto the main road, I took a closer look at the old ewe. The reason she had looked at me with her head tilted to one side was that she was blind in one eye.

"Hey, Leo," I shouted.

But he was already gone, his hand waving out the window of his truck.

And, as Rita said later, if she's healthy, so what? The lack of one eye didn't slow the Old Lady down at all. I hate to think what she might have accomplished if she'd had two.

Because we had no fencing, I thought it would be clever to tether the Old Lady. Not only would that keep her under control (along with, presumably, her son, whom we christened the Oaf), but it would also enable us to use our new sheep to battle brush and grass. The sheep would gobble up everything within the radius of the Old Lady's tether; then I would move the stake. I could already imagine our neglected old farm gradually being restored to trimmed beauty, one overlapping circle after another.

But the Old Lady had told me she would take no guff, and she had meant it. She pulled up the tether stake and went where she pleased. When I used a stronger stake and drove it deeper into the ground, she tangled both herself and the Oaf in the rope so thoroughly that the struggles of each to get loose would topple the other. A hideous bleating and blatting followed. When I ran to their rescue, the Old Lady always looked on the verge of strangulation, a purplish tongue lolling from her mouth. Purple, of course, was the natural color of her tongue, but I didn't know that then, and she knew I didn't know it. She was not above cheap histrionics when they served her purpose, and her purpose was to have the run of the place. After two or three melodramas at the stake, she got it.

One of the most ancient and persistent misconceptions humankind is given to is that sheep are stupid. The longevity of that delusion attests not so much to the witlessness of sheep as it does to our narrow, self-serving ideas of intelligence. We tend to think animals that learn to do what we want them to do, and like us into the bargain, are smart. Sheep are ineducable and don't give a damn about us; therefore, we conclude, they are stupid. Granted, they are flock animals and prefer to rush into disaster as a mob rather than seek safety as individuals. But we humans are hardly immune to that kind of behavior ourselves.

I suppose it is true that sheep are not particularly skilled at abstract reasoning, but then they are rarely called on to solve abstract problems; and whatever they may lack in rational powers they make up for in character. Or such has been our limited experience of them. We have never kept many sheep, our flock ranging from a minimum of three to a maximum of sixteen. Then, too, this odd little line we have developed by sheer accident may be atypical. The Old Lady, the mother of them all, clearly had a strong dose of Suffolk in her. The mate we found to keep her company after the Oaf went into the freezer was a brown, rangy, aquiline-nosed, well-behorned ram who was covered with something closer to deer hair than to wool. Indeed, he looked something like a cross between a deer, a goat, and a sheep. The neighbor from whom we got him advised us that his lineage was Barbados, more or less. We called him Rambaud.

The following spring the Old Lady produced twins, as she would right up to the spring she quite literally turned up her toes and died. With sheep strength up to four, the Old Lady decided she would make a bid for total control over the place. The summer before, with only the Oaf as her ally, she had been content to win her freedom to roam the farm at will. But now, backed by an athletic mate and two daughters who had inherited her brains and his brawn, she decided it was time to move out of the old chicken coop I had converted to a sheep shed and take over the house.

Her campaign started on the porch. When it was time for the midday siesta and cud chewing, the Old Lady and her crew would head for the back porch and rattle up the steps onto the shaded deck. Santa's eight tiny reindeer never made such a clatter.

If I was at my desk, I would race outside yelling, "Scram! Beat it!" and herd my visitors off. But they would come back, and the scene would be repeated. If we were away for a couple of hours we would come home to find a woolly welcoming committee waiting for us on the porch. Judging by the amount of manure on the deck, they had moved in the minute they had seen the car pull out of the drive.

"I don't think they'll ever learn," Rita said.

"Of course they will," I'd say, shoveling and sweeping the boards clean. "If I keep booting them off this porch eight or nine times a day, they'll get the point sooner or later. No animal is that stupid."

After several weeks it began to dawn on me that in this particular duel of wits, I was not faring well. The sheep were having a lovely time. What was it to them if they were kicked off a porch several times a day? The lambs, Marion and Muriel, thought the porch game particularly good fun. They enjoyed looking in the kitchen window to see what the people were up to, and if they saw me coming, they would tip off their parents. "Here he comes!" they'd say, and bound off the porch only to run back up again while I was shoving Rambaud and the Old Lady off.

The lesson finally sank in when, after what may well have been the 437th encounter, I overheard Rambaud say to the Old Lady, "I don't think he'll ever learn."

"Of course he will," the Old Lady said. "If we just persist he'll get the point sooner or later. No animal is that stupid."

The next day I erected a fence around the porch. It was a hasty, makeshift job, and it irritated me no end that I had to climb over a fence to get onto my own porch. But it did keep the sheep off. The usual procedure, I knew, was to fence the sheep in, not the shepherd. But I was pushing hard to make more of our house livable for the next winter, and I didn't want to take time out to fence in a sheep pasture.

The sheep took great interest in the renovation project. As I jacked the house up and tore out rotting sills, they would hang around and kibitz.

"If I were you, I'd put in another prop before I yanked that section out."

"There's dry rot in the bottom two feet of that corner post. Better splice in a new piece."

They were usually right, but that hardly made their advice welcome. The Old Lady was especially pushy, and more than once I had to postpone swinging an axe or hammer because, chewing away like a teenager with a mouthful of gum, she would stick her head between the tool and its target.

In an old farmhouse, one step leads to another. If you replace a sill, you'll be forced to remove some weathered, shattered siding beneath which you'll find shaky, splintered sheathing haphazardly tacked to randomly spaced studs. Faced with such prospects, folks even less compulsive than I are moved to rip out everything but the post-and-beam framing and start over again. So in one frenzied afternoon, I tore out the south and east walls of what had been the parlor. Because we were already late for supper with some friends, I cleaned up hastily, and we set off.

When we came home about nine o'clock, the sheep were comfortably settled in the parlor, the Old Lady with her knitting, Rambaud with his paper, the kids sprawled on the floor playing Go Fish. The two-foot leap into the wide-open building had been no obstacle. The Old Lady allowed that the room was pleasant enough but seemed rather bare of furnishings.

Over the next couple of days, the sheep kept leaping into the house to check up on my progress, ask endless questions, and stick their curious noses into every phase of the operation. Uppermost in their minds, though, was when the place would be ready for them to move in permanently. So it came as something of a shock to them when the walls went up without a ramp and a sheep door. They were miffed, and they were even more miffed when, after I had finished working on the house for that summer, I finally got around to fencing them into the field where I thought they should stay.

"Now," I thought, "I've done it right. My troubles are over." But as every neophyte shepherd soon learns, there is something that doesn't love a fence, and that something is a sheep. The Old Lady may have had Suffolk blood in her, but she must have had a strong streak of Houdini as well. In the spring and summer, when the pasturage was lush and plentiful, she was content to stay on her side of the fence. Our tiny flock had the run of a cleared pasture plus another four or five acres of mixed brush, grass, and alders beyond it. Two sides of this area were blocked off by my new fence; Temple Stream formed a barricade on the third side; and there were alders and a bogan, or marshy backwater, on the fourth.

All went well until sometime in September, when the choice food on the sheep's range had been eaten up and when the shortening days and frosty nights told them that the days of milk and honey were just about over. The grass on our side of the fence looked greener (it actually was greener). Memories of the good old days of grazing around the house and garden came alive (when it comes to remembering good eating places, sheep put elephants to shame). The Old Lady's ingenuity and spirit were roused.

Was there a place where the fence was not stretched piano-string tight? She would burrow under it. Was one of the twelve-inch gaps in the mesh more like thirteen or fourteen inches? She would stick her head through and lean and push until she had a hole large enough to wriggle through. In later years, when the flock was larger and the fence even weaker, she organized her troops into a phalanx and smashed through with brute force. If I had patrolled the fence carefully and reinforced it, she would bide her time, waiting until the ice in the bogan had thickened enough to let her cross. Then she would lead her band of guerrillas onto one neighbor's lawn, into another neighbor's strawberry fields. Smart she was, a smart old sheep. And her intelligence runs in the family. Her daughters, Marion and Muriel, are still with us; and they are every bit as clever as their mother was. Chain them, put them in a trunk, sink them in a pond, and they'll pop to the surface again inside of a minute.

In *The Sheep Book*, Ronald Parker introduces his system for evaluating ewes with these wise words: "If your flock is small, you may have some favorites that you are reluctant to send off for slaughter. At the very least you may not be very objective about culling if you have an emotional attachment to some of the animals. To prevent this pitfall you can rank your ewes numerically." Parker then suggests assigning percentage points for desirable characteristics: profligacy, 30; lamb raising, 30; health, 10; fleece, 10; and genetics, 20. You then set a minimum acceptable score, say 70 or 75 percent, and cull any ewes that fall below it. Each shepherd can adapt this system to his or her own needs. My own scale goes something like this: On the plus side are profligacy, 25; lamb raising, 25; health, 35; omnivorousness, 5; taste of lambs produced, 10. On the negative side, obstinacy, -25; escape and evasion, -25; intelligence, -25; meddlesomeness, -10; ability to make a sentimental fool of the shepherd, -15. I then add the plus and minus percentages together, and any ewe who falls between 20 and -20 percent I keep. The Old Lady and her daughters all scored a perfect zero.

If your flock is small, in other words, your supposedly stupid sheep may well make a dummy of you. Mine have been highly successful at that, running roughshod over whatever minimal business instincts I have, though I am thankful that I can say we don't lose any money on our sheep. We have ample pasturage for our small flock and more than enough hay for winter feed. Our animals have been remarkably healthy and hardy for what I suspect is a combination of reasons: uncrowded living conditions, happily haphazard crossbreeding, and complete freedom of expression. Costs for medical supplies and veterinary services are low, and grain cost is our only real outlay.

But if sheep are not a serious business proposition, why keep them at all? Well, if you have a taste for lamb and if you ever have a chance to eat lamb chops at my house, you'll know one good reason. The difference between the lamb we raise and what we can buy in the store is the difference between ambrosia and a Big Mac.

And then there are the lambs in their first few weeks and months, those lanky-legged, airplane-eared little creatures who bounce into the air as though propelled by four pogo sticks. There is perhaps no other young animal that touches us more with the sweetness, brightness, and glee of new life. And then, of course, in the depths of winter when Rita and I are feeling a little dull, it's nice to know that we can always invite Marion and Muriel up to the parlor for a little tea and intelligent conversation.

# Trees and Dendrons

I've always been grateful that, in the great melding and merging of tongues that produced our beloved English language, we came out of it all with "tree" as the word we use for a tree. Tree is a light, airy word altogether fitting for those magnificent plants that rise up into the sky to be dappled by the sun and ruffled by the wind. It rhymes with "glee" and "free" and "see" and "be." What would Joyce Kilmer ever have written if the Greek word for tree rather than the Middle English one had emerged triumphant in the process of natural linguistic selection? He never could have penned those thumping iambic tetrameter lines that etch themselves so indelibly into memory that we can't rid ourselves of them even if we want to:

> I think that I shall never see
> A poem lovely as a tree.

He would have had to make do with some messy, imperfect rhyme instead:

> I think that I shall never send on
> A letter lovely as a dendron.

"Dendron" has ominous alliterative associations: dengue, dungeon, doom, dead. Dendrons, by the sound of them, ought to be citizens of an evil nation in a science-fiction saga, allies of the Klingons in Star Trek.

The aversion I feel to this word may explain my reluctance to take up the study of dendrology but in no way excuses it. Indeed, all this self-erected obstacle has done is expand the range of my already formidable ignorance. I take some pride in knowing by name most of the trees in my home territory, but beyond that I know next to nothing about them. And what little I do know is impressionistic stuff, miles wide of hard science. I know, for instance, that no matter how grand and dramatic the brilliant foliage of fall may be, the pastel waves of greening poplars and the blush of red-maple buds washing over the hills in spring make the far sweeter sight.

Along with that panoramic feast for the eye come the little close-up miracles that transpire on branchlet and twig. Rita and I take the same walk each morning to follow day by day the slow-motion emergence of leaf and flower, a process as touching to the heart and dazzling to the mind as the birth of a lamb, the pipping of a chick. If the child is father to the man, then each tiny leaf of red oak and white ash, even in its first unfolding, is the clearly recognizable parent of the oak's bristly adult leaf, of the pinnate ash frond to come. Infant red maple leaves, bronzy and iridescent, are as tightly clenched as a baby's fist. Open them up and, just like a baby's hand, they will curl softly back around your fingers. Beech leaves swell out of their slender, lanceolate buds and leave wispy husks behind like shed snakeskins.

Our shadbush flowered on May 3 last spring, a week or so earlier than it usually does, and ushered in a bonanza of tree florescence. A roadside white ash sprouted a cloud of reddish cheerleader pompoms—male flowers, I think (staminate, that is). At any rate, stunning. A white birch was so heavily festooned with catkins it looked like a benign arboreal Medusa, adrip with tiny, red-spotted yellow snakes.

And the sugar maples. They practically disappeared in their own deluge of yellow flowers. Yellow pollen, yellow flowers everywhere: in the driveway, in the rivers and streams. I quit fishing one afternoon because I had to clean my line and fly after practically every cast. The flowers clogged the hook and formed a yellow gob around the surgeon's knot in the leader. I've never witnessed a flowering quite like it. Or maybe I just haven't been paying careful enough attention in the past. Maybe several maple flowerings every bit as wondrous as this one have gone by me, and I've been oblivious. Maybe if I'd been attending to what was in front of my face, I would have seen what was plainly there to see. Folks who have looked and seen noticed long ago that sugar maples in a given area have heavy crops of flowers and fruit one year but then may show no flowers at all for the next two or more years. Then again, there are maverick maples that refuse to go along with the crowd and flower whenever they damn please. I've always had a soft spot in my heart for trees and critters and people who go their own way, and I wonder what motivates those individualistic maples.

I've just picked up a copy of the old standard dendrology text by professors Harlow and Harrar, also two silvics handbooks put out by the USDA Forest Service. Maybe I'll learn from them what makes those offbeat maples tick. And if I stick with dendrology long enough, I may eventually even see a dendron lovely as a tree.

# Raising Rocks

We always look forward to the wild perennial crops of spring. Maple syrup comes first; then, later, the fiddleheads, the dandelion greens, the wild onions, the pepper root. The syrup takes some work to bring in, but the plants come so easily—with just a little cutting or digging—that they might as well be growing on that Big Rock Candy Mountain where, as the song has it, "the handouts grow on bushes."

One of the most dependably bountiful of these crops, though hardly the most palatable, is rocks, not rock candy but just plain rocks. No matter how many we turned up and weeded out of the garden last year, we turn up just as many this year. Our pile of rocks—in assorted sizes from baseball- to football- to basketball-size—just grows and grows. These are the easy ones to harvest. They can be dug up with fork or shovel and tossed aside. Others are more formidable, like the ones that keep rearing their heads through the grass a little more each year until I finally realize that trimming them back with a lawnmower is futile. Because these specimens keep getting larger and more intrusive each year, they are clearly not ledge, so we know we are dealing with free-floating agents, which means they can be moved and removed. But what we can't know and don't find out until we try to excavate them is how deeply rooted these shoots of granite are.

Wanting to avoid serious shovel work, my friend Wes proposed leveling off with a sledgehammer a rock that kept raising its muffler-destroying head in the middle of his driveway; and knowing I was an old hand at rock raising and rock busting, he invited me to join him in this project. What better way to spend a few hours on a sunny May afternoon, I thought, than pounding on a rock, so I loaded my sledge-hammer into the car and, for good luck, a shovel and crowbar.

We began by digging away the dirt to see if the grain of this rock had some crack or flaw that would yield to a few well-directed whacks. We saw nothing that gave us much hope, and indeed several minutes' work with our sledgehammers produced nothing but a few tiny chips and a couple of spoonfuls of powdered granite.

"A tough customer," I said.

"Just the kind of challenge that brings out the best in you," Wes said.

"The best in us," I said. "We're in this together."

"Well, yes, but, as always, I defer to your age, experience, and wisdom."

"Age, experience, and wisdom call for a backhoe," I said, "but only a wimp would take that route. A little more shovel work and some crowbar leverage applied at strategic points and that rock will come flying out of there."

"Right, flying," Wes said.

By the time we had the whole top of the rock clear and a few of those strategic leverage points exposed, we also had a pit nearly as wide as the driveway. We now knew this rock was a good three feet in diameter. Knowing, too, that mere crowbars would not give us a big enough mechanical advantage to move it, we found some eight-foot two-by-fours in Wes's garage and started prying, raising one side of the rock a few inches, stuffing blocks underneath it to hold the elevation we had gained, prying again to gain a few more inches—a truly Sisyphean task, for every time we thought just one more pry would send the rock over the top, it would escape our control and go tumbling back down, taking our elaborate scaffolding with it.

"Okay," I proposed, "we'll use our two-by-fours as skids and haul this thing up and out with my old Subaru."

Wes liked that idea, but all we could find for hitching rock to car was some feeble rope that broke before the rock showed the slightest sign of moving.

"I don't suppose you have a logging chain," I said.

"No, I don't," Wes said, "but I'll bet Dennis does."

Wes's neighbor Dennis is one of those enterprising geniuses who settled in rural Maine in the 1980s and taught himself how to do everything: log with horses, graft apple trees, build houses, dig wells, you name it. Then he decided he'd go to law school. He works now as a public-service attorney for Legal Services for the Elderly, providing a wide range of no-fee services for elderly clients.

So while Dennis regaled us with tales from a lawyer's life in rural Maine, I wrapped his chain around our rock and skidded it off to a place of honor under a maple tree at the edge of Wes's yard. We jiggled it around a bit with the crowbar so that it showed to best advantage, looking like not just some old rock dug up out of the driveway but a modest monument celebrating the fecundity of New England rocks and how much fun three guys can have harvesting one on a May afternoon.

# Citizen Scientists

I n 2011, the Maine Department of Inland Fisheries and Wildlife, Trout Unlimited, and Maine Audubon put their collective heads together and launched a program just made for my friend Steve and me. Called the Brook Trout Pond Survey, this program's goal is to identify previously undocumented wild and native brook trout populations in remote Maine ponds.

Our state contains 97 percent of the known native brook trout lakes and ponds left in these United States. Maine's fisheries biologists are understandably determined to protect those waters already identified as clear, cold, and unsullied enough to support native trout populations; but they are determined, as well, to find out which of Maine's lakes and ponds not yet surveyed also contain wild native trout.

Maine has about fifty-eight hundred lakes and ponds greater than one acre in size, hundreds upon hundreds of which the fisheries biologists, given all their other duties, would need at least half a century to get around to surveying. The solution? Enlist fishermen and fisherwomen to go to these ponds and see if they find any evidence of trout (and perhaps even catch a trout). If they do, the department's biologists can follow up with a bona fide scientific survey, the results of which can be used to write management plans governing these waters.

This program provides Steve and me and others of our ilk with benefits of no small importance. First, we gain the honorific title of citizen scientists. Second, and far more important: Now, when we go off for a day or two of searching for remote little pockets of water, we are not indulging some prepubescent hankering to just mess about in the woods. No, we are responsible adults on a noble mission. We are venturing out to find creatures not only of great beauty but also of iconic value to humankind. Native brook trout have come down to us from a pure, primal, unpolluted world. They are holdovers from Eden. To lose them here in Maine—their last stronghold in our country and in a time that is already, on so many fronts, an age of extinctions—would be a failure of will and foresight no self-respecting Maine angler would want to be guilty of.

So what we are talking about is a sacred duty and no less so because it's great, though often strenuous, fun. Steve and I sift through the list of ponds that the survey offers up each spring to find those farthest from any road, in the deepest swamps, and in the highest, ruggedest hill country. Equipped for foul weather and the possibility of spending an unplanned night in the woods, we carry an ungodly amount of stuff: rain gear, a change of clothes, matches, tinder, headlamp, maps, compass, pocket knife, food, fly rod, reel, fishing vest. Then, because it is all but impossible to cast flies from the shore of most woods ponds, and because you can't cover the water of even a fairly small pond from shore anyhow, you need some way to get out into the middle and paddle around. With the likelihood of finding a boat stashed away on one of these back-of-beyond ponds at about zero, you have to take a belly boat along, a device descended from an inner tube but now, in its present, more highly evolved form, an ungainly rig that looks like a legless, inflatable easy chair. You also need a small pump to inflate your belly boat and, once you're launched in the thing, a pair of swim fins to propel yourself around. And, finally, if the water is cold enough, which it almost always is, you need your stocking-foot waders on to avoid hypothermia. Carrying all this gear calls for a huge pack that just loves getting caught in the alders or the spiky branches of a fir thicket. We bushwhack, we wallow, we thrash, we stumble uphill, we tumble down, we've been known to mutter mild oaths. The trials we have to endure in the interest of citizen science are by no means trivial.

But the rewards are not trivial either. We have the satisfaction of performing a socially valuable service; we see on every trip one more corner of this delicious world of ours; and if I come home skunked and Rita asks me where the fish for our supper are, I don't have to say, "I didn't catch any." I can say instead, "Making all due allowance for the limitations of my scientific competence, I am sorry to report to you that there are no trout in Unnamed Pond No. 2,648."

I mean to get a book out of these expeditions, too: *Bob and Steve's Guide to Fifty Barely Accessible Troutless Ponds in Maine*, a surefire bestseller. And the best part of it is that we have at least thirty more ponds to go.

# Bailey

S everal months after our neighbor Sandy had lost her calm old German Shepherdly mutt, Pokey, she decided she would not go to the Franklin County Animal Shelter for her next dog but would get the first purebred of her life. So one evening in the summer of 2007, she came to our place for supper and to introduce us to her new eight-week-old Springer, whom she soon named Bailey.

I have yet to meet a puppy that couldn't reduce me to dithering, doting idiocy within a minute and a half, but this guy worked his magic in about fifteen seconds: those paws still a bit too big for the rest of him; his gorgeous tricolor markings; his silky ears; his ambling, roly-poly gait as he explored our kitchen, cleaned up the cat's food, snuffled in every corner and crevice, nibbled on my fingers, gazed at me with his soulful brown eyes that said, "No matter how many of your slippers I chew to shreds and how often I pee on your floor, you will love me now and forever, won't you?"

"Yes," I said, "yes, I will. I promise, now and forever."

Sandy's household and ours have a long history of mutual dog-sitting. If we went away for a weekend or a week or more, Sandy would take our dogs in; we did the same for her. When our last dog, Lucy, died nine years ago, we didn't rush to get another dog, and we soon found that Sandy's dogs were with us so often, as Sandy's work required her to be away more and more frequently, that we never lacked for canine company.

Rita and I looked forward to that relationship continuing with this new little tyke, but we soon found, as did Sandy, that sticking to vows of eternal love for Bailey was going to be a tough job. As he grew into rangy adolescence, he became more and more of a handful, chewing up boots, vaulting onto furniture, jumping up on anyone and everyone he met. The prospect of a walk sent him leaping and spinning into the air, ricocheting off walls and doors like a furry squash ball. Once outside, he would race off, taking those great springing leaps that give Springer spaniels their name. In his first winter, he would chase and catch snowballs for as long as your arm would last. Like a fielder spearing a long fly ball up against the left field fence, he would race out under a tossed snowball and bound straight up into the air to snag it.

Guiding and disciplining all that youthful energy was almost too much for Sandy, who is no weak sister and as strong in spirit as anyone I know. At one low point she said to us, "He has me on the ropes. I just may have to take him back to the breeder where I got him."

But she didn't, because, as exasperating as Bailey could be, there was not a mean molecule in his body. Every nutty thing he did, he did out of ebullience, buoyancy, joie de vivre. His heart leaped up with love of the world—and for Sandy—and he just had to leap up with it. At night, he would curl up with her on her bed and never disturb her once all night. He began to mellow a bit, and she knew that he would become the perfect dog: spirited, devoted, easy to live with.

But then Sandy was stricken with a debilitating illness, and as strong a person as she is, she could no longer care for a young dog who needed lots of exercise and outdoor time to be happy and healthy.

Rita's first thought, and mine, was that we should take him, but then we had second thoughts. Rita's knees, both surgically repaired, would not respond well to collisions with a fifty-pound Springer racing at full tilt. And Bailey grew up on a dead-end dirt road traveled by only a few cars a day. The road past our place, though hardly a major thoroughfare, is paved, and cars pass often enough and fast enough to be dangerous for a dog as naïve about traffic as Bailey is.

We consulted with Nina, who runs a magnificent gourmet food shop in Farmington and is also our local patron saint of animals and animal lovers. She knew just the right person, a man in his forties who lived on a back road with fields and woods outside his door, a certified dog lover with perfectly sound knees who would like nothing better than roaming the hills of western Maine with a lively, affectionate Springer.

Bailey has not written often since he moved in with Craig, but we hear through Nina that Bailey and his new master are ecstatically happy together, a report that makes Sandy, Rita, and me, whose love for Bailey told us to give him up, ecstatically happy, too.

# Baffling Beavers

Whenever the interests of animals come into conflict with the interests of human beings, I'm inclined to side with the animals. There are just too many instances in which animals have gotten the short end of the stick. So even with species like beaver, that are no longer threatened and are even thriving in environments considerably altered by humankind, I tend to accommodate animals and let them have their way.

Then, too, where beavers are concerned, I've always had a particularly soft spot in my heart. Anyone who imbibed a Yankee work ethic with his mother's milk, as I did, can't help but think well of beavers, and it's not just their hard-working ways that recommend them. They have other virtues that make them model citizens. They mate for life, raise well-behaved kits, don't kill, don't steal, mind their own business, and don't covet their neighbors' houses or wives (though they are territorial and don't take kindly to invasions of their turf). And like all model citizens, they exert an influence for good that extends beyond their immediate circle and is felt by generations to come. The wetlands their dams create provide habitat for myriad other creatures, ranging from wood ducks to mink and muskrat, salamanders and crayfish, not to mention the woodpeckers that hollow out their nesting cavities in water-killed trees and feed on the insects drawn to the rotting wood. The list of animals that benefit from beaver flowages and meadows that remain long after the beavers have abandoned them goes on and on. And then one of the great treats of roaming the Maine woods is following small streams up into the hills and finding one abandoned beaver meadow after another, like the stepped terraces of some ancient Inca site in Peru.

Mindful of all these benefits beavers provide their fellow creatures both great and small—including us humans—I've done my best to stay on friendly terms with the beavers that live in the stretch of Temple

Stream behind our house. That has demanded some willingness to compromise, on both my part and theirs, because we have had our differences over the management of the drainage ditches in our hayfield. Unwilling to see that field turned into a beaver pond, I want to keep the ditches clear so the water that flows under Intervale Road through two huge culverts can continue on its way into Temple Stream. The beavers want the ditches dammed to give them water access to the alders, willow, and young birch trees growing along the ditches.

The solution we've arrived at is a tug-of-war conducted over the summer months. I tear a hole in the dam large enough to drain the water down to the level I want. That night, the beavers build it back up to the level they want. We go back and forth like this a few times until the beavers give up. I've always assumed, perhaps wrongly, that the beavers realize that it's a waste of time and energy repairing this constantly disappearing dam when they could be filling their winter food cache from more productive and more stable foraging areas closer to home.

This arrangement has served us well for the last four decades. Our friend Charlie, who does the haying on our place, has been able to mow and rake and ted and bale without sinking hub deep in mud and water, and the beavers, ever hopeful, have returned every year to have another go at colonizing this outpost.

But now it appears the game has changed. In the summer of 2011, Temple's road commissioner had to install heavy wire-mesh fencing on the far side of Intervale Road to prevent the beavers from plugging the culverts there and flooding the road. And after I thought the beavers on my side of the road and I had reached our equilibrium point last August, I didn't return to check on them again until well into October, when I found the dam had been raised to a height and thickness never achieved before. I may have been able to baffle my beavers up to now with our dam-wrecking and dam-repairing routine, but Temple's growing beaver population is forcing me, along with Temple's road commissioner, to come up with better means of coexisting peacefully with our beaver neighbors.

Fortunately, the resurgence of beavers throughout the Northeast has inspired a wave of effective beaver baffler designs dealing with my problem. The basic idea is to install a pipe long enough and of large enough diameter to extend through the dam, keeping the pool drained to the level you want to maintain.

I'll have one of these in place well before the leaves start turning this fall, and what I'll particularly enjoy about this project is that while it may appear to be baffling the beavers, what it's really doing is accommodating them.

# The Perfect Canoe

My infatuation with canoes began sometime during my grade-school years, when my father bought from our neighbors a neglected old wood-and-canvas canoe and reconditioned it. I remember him working in the cellar with a blowtorch and putty knife, carefully peeling off the boat's tattered red paint before he gave it a fresh coat.

We lived right across the road from a cove in the largest of the lakes that gave our New Jersey town of Mountain Lakes its name. As a little kid I could be fishing from shore for sunnies and yellow perch after a two-minute walk from our front door, and once my fishing buddy John Miller and I were old enough and strong enough to lug the canoe to the water, we could paddle all over the lake to fish other coves for big game—pickerel and bass—with our bait-casting tackle.

Unaware as we were of the fine points of canoe design, it was just our good luck that had given us this sturdy, capacious canoe. It provided not only a stable platform for John and me for our fishing expeditions, but was also roomy enough that my father, mother, brother, and I could all fit into it for weekend cruises on the lake.

John and I were also lucky enough to find abandoned in the brush alongside the one undeveloped pond in our town a water-filled old canoe with several broken ribs and as many gashes in its gray canvas hull. Our patches were only marginally successful, but wet feet seemed a price worth paying for a boat on the closest thing to a wilderness pond our town had to offer.

It wasn't until years later, when Rita and I—just recently married—moved from Cambridge, Massachusetts, to Temple, Maine, that my canoe education began in earnest. During our first Maine summer I had a chance to buy a used Old Town Tripper still good as new and at a modest price. Like the canoe of my boyhood, this one was red, stable, seaworthy, and capable of carrying heavy loads. What was radically different was the stuff it was made of: acrylonitrile butadiene styrene, better known as ABS or the brand name Royalex, a material that required next to no maintenance. That was fine with us. Rita and I still had our hands full patching up our old homestead.

But once we were settled into our Temple life for about ten years, I had the good luck to become a regular contributor to Blair and Ketchum's superb *Country Journal*. My first piece was "Choosing a Canoe," which covered hull design and the whole range of materials that had come into canoe building after World War II: aluminum, fiberglass, plastics.

My second stroke of good luck was meeting Garrett and Alexandra Conover at a canoe program at L.L. Bean. During a break, I struck up a conversation with them and learned that they ran a guiding service called North Woods Ways and specialized in using traditional gear—most importantly, their wood-and-canvas guide canoes designed by E. M. White in the late 1890s and built now in Atkinson, Maine, by Jerry Stelmok at Island Falls Canoe and Rollin Thurlow at Northwoods Canoe Company. Learning, too, that the Conovers would be guiding their first trip on the Churchill River in Labrador in August of that summer, I thought it likely that *Country Journal* would welcome an article on this trip.

So it was that after this brief conversation the three of us quickly came to the conclusion that we would get along just fine on a three-week trip in the Labrador bush, not to mention the four days of driving and train travel both going and coming home. And so it was, too, that the editors at *Country Journal* gave me the go-ahead.

In the telling of all this, it begins to take on the feel of a fairy tale for me. Suburban kid's quest for the perfect canoe takes him to the wilds of Labrador where he finds himself paddling one of the Conovers' E. M. White canoes, as perfect a canoe as he's ever had the privilege of paddling. Then he realizes as well that any canoe he's been in before was a step on the way and therefore perfect in its time and place: the leaky old hull he shared with John on Birchwood Lake, the neighbors' neglected canoe his dad brought back to life for his family, the Tripper he paddled with Rita during those early days in Maine and later with their son, Greg, as soon as he was old enough to wield a paddle.

Blessed are the travelers who take to canoes, for they shall see this world of the wild up close and will rejoice with their brothers and sisters of the trail. So it is only right and meet that I write these words for my lifelong friend John, for Garrett and Alexandra, and of course for Jerry and Rollin, builders of these aquatic magic carpets.

# Summer's Boomerang

Our friend Suzy had brought the boomerang from Cambridge when she came to visit in February. It was a gift for Greg, who was twelve years old at the time and not one to postpone gratification; but after the boomerang took its second nosedive onto the icy driveway and a few splinters flew from one of its red, laminated tips, he was willing to yield to parental advice and wait for softer days and soils.

By the time summer came, Greg was thirteen. The boomerang had been circling on the outer edge of our attention for several months, first fading, then hoving into view again in the catch-all clutter of our ancient Maine farmhouse where objects appear and disappear and reappear in tune with some mysterious seasons of their own.

Then, one evening in July, when Rita had gone off to play in her recorder consortium and Greg and I were home alone with the whole spread to ourselves, the boomerang turned up in his hand. "Hey, Dad," he said, "let's throw the boomerang."

It was a perfect night for it, windstill and just starting to cool off, and the barn swallows were out cavorting, swooping, circling in quick, banking turns that invited imitation and envy.

On our first attempts, the boomerang behaved more like a mole than a swallow, heading not for the sky but for the earth, where it would often bury one of its scimitar snouts in the turf. Chastened, we finally read the instruction label. Hold the boomerang as you would a sickle, the instructions said. Throw it overhand and nearly perpendicular to the ground.

My first toss lodged the boomerang high in an old apple tree. I fetched my canoe pole and knocked it down. Greg sent the boomerang on a gorgeous outward flight that ended in a fluttering descent into tall grass. Like hunters searching for a downed bird, we worked our way out in ever widening circles from the crash site. The light was fading. It took us ten minutes and three combings of the area before Greg finally kicked the boomerang free from where it was nestled into the grass.

But there was enough daylight left. We learned how. The boomerang sailed out over the chicken coop, started its banking, side-slipping turn over the apple tree, then swung back toward us over the garden.

"Yay!" Greg yelled. "We've got it!" And he would run to retrieve the boomerang. We weren't perfect. It would not come back to our feet, like an obedient dog, so that all we had to do was lean down and pick it up. It fell fifteen yards in front of us, ten to the left of us, twenty to the right. Wherever it landed we scrambled after it to try again and again.

It was almost dark now. Our white, red-winged bird flitted out into the dusk, always returning but always taking a slightly different path, flying at a slightly different angle. July will come back again, too, but never quite this same way. Greg will never be thirteen for another July; I will never be fifty.

There is just this one summer night with the veeries belting out their cascading evensong, the sky bright blue and white, then dark purple overhead and red in the west, this hush that holds our laughter and whoops of triumph in its hands.

# Rites of Spring

Astronomically speaking, March 21 may be the first day of spring, but in these parts, a more accurate description of the season would be something like "late winter starting to give some serious thought to verging on spring." Granted, the sun has been climbing higher and higher and gaining in authority for several weeks now. We may have had some perfect sugaring days with the temperature shooting up above freezing after nights in the twenties. We won't see the thermometer drop below zero again until next December or January. But despite all that, despite the softening in the air and the faint greening and reddening of the hills, there's still a foot or more of snow on the ground, and we can still get walloped with one or two more storms.

No, I won't know we've come to spring proper—that tipping point when all the vitality gathering in root and bud starts to burst out and when the warbler wave is just about to wash over us—until Rita says after lunch, as she's pouring boiling water into our midday teapot, "I'm going to take my tea out onto the porch steps."

Of course. The porch faces due southeast. It's gathering the heat of the sun the way a reflector oven captures the heat from a campfire.

Mugs of tea in hand, sunglasses perched on our noses, we two biscuits step outside and settle on the steps to bake, soaking up heat from the sun-drenched boards, where not long ago we were sprinkling rock salt against the ice of winter. Crows go hollering across the cloudless sky; a few patches of snow huddle up against the north sides of the chicken coop and sheep shed and garden shed, hanging on for dear life against the deadly heat. Already, on the higher ground above the garden where the snow has been gone for several days now, the grass is beginning to green up.

We grin; we clunk our mugs together in a wordless toast to the sweetness of this late-April day and to our respective lucky stars that brought us together and brought us to this place, where year after year we have celebrated the coming of spring with this same simple tea ceremony.

From the steps, we look out over the garden, which is still much too wet to start forking up. Green as some of the grass is, it won't need mowing for at least another couple of weeks. It hasn't been warm long enough to bring the flies out. "Celebrate, you foolish mortals," the world is telling us. "There'll be time enough to dig and sow and weed and mow and swat blackflies."

We take the hint. We seize the bounty that is ours for the taking. Rita unearths the parsnips and leeks she bedded down under comforters of mulch last fall. I dig up dandelion greens and crowns to eat steamed or raw in salads.

Our house stands high and dry on a knoll, but down where Temple Stream frequently floods our intervale fields, fiddleheads grow in wild profusion, more than enough for us and for any of our neighbors who care to harvest some; and once the purple nubs of asparagus shoots have nuzzled their way from darkness into daylight and reached edible adulthood, we're faced with an enviable dilemma: do we eat asparagus or fiddleheads tonight?

On May 5, Wes calls. The day is more than warm. It's downright toasty. "Don't you think we should open the camp up this afternoon?" he says. "I'll see if I can round up Bill and Drew, too."

That sounds like an invitation to participate in serious work, but it is not. It is, instead, a coded message, which means we'll take a few minutes to lug the canoe and kayak off the screened-in porch and tie them up at the dock; we'll put down the porch rug and the dog bed and bring out the two rockers and the table with its four chairs; and then we'll go for our ritual salute-to-spring swim.

That's just what we do. Our few chores accomplished, we flop into the water from which the ice retreated only two weeks ago. Snorting and yelping in that lethally cold water, we take a few frantic strokes out, ten, fifteen, twenty yards, maybe, then back to the dock and up and out into the heat of the sun, our hands papery white. We towel off, let the sun warm us through to the bone, then head back up to the porch where we change into our clothes and settle around the table to pop a few beers.

So much to celebrate: that loon just barely visible far out on the pond, the pair of Canada geese floating off the inlet bog, painted trillium, pink lady's slipper, yellow violets, friends crazy enough to swim on May 5. Spring in the North Country.

# Paddling with the Young Guys

W hen my friend Steve called in early May to ask if I would like to paddle Maine's Machias River in a couple of weeks, I of course said yes. How long it had been since I was last on the Machias I couldn't even remember. High time I went back again.

We had four days, only enough for the first forty miles of the trip. From its start in Fifth Machias Lake, the river heads north into Fourth Machias Lake, then swings southeast into nearly six-mile-long Third Lake. From the outlet of Third, it heads due south another seventeen miles—with Second and First Lakes forming just skinny ponds in the river—to our takeout where the river intersects Maine Route 9.

My only vivid memory of the upper Machias was of a small, idyllic island in Third Lake that rose high over the water and provided us with an airy, pine-shaded campsite and sun-warmed ledges as a swimming beach. The roughly ten miles from Fifth to Fourth Lake I remembered as an easy, occasionally riffly run where my partner and I had stopped now and then to cast a fly. The rest was a blank, but these two memories lulled me into thinking of the Machias as a mild-mannered river. Along with everything else I'd forgotten, I'd forgotten that "Machias" translates from the Passamaquoddy not as "Smooth Sailing" but as "Bad Run of Water."

Our companions would be rugged young guys in their late twenties: Steve's son, Ethan, who had recently settled in the down east village of Lubec, Maine, and his friends Brannin and Noah, two brothers who had grown up there. Noah would be my bow man; Brannin would paddle a borrowed solo canoe.

Brannin runs his own arborist business, and when Noah isn't off teaching skiing in Colorado, he often works with his brother. When we met them on Route 9, they had just come off a job and still had their chain saws and climbing gear in the back of their pickup, along with their food and a few six-packs of beer in shopping bags and tucked into a plastic milk crate—not exactly orthodox provisions or packing methods for a wilderness expedition in Labrador, but altogether acceptable for what I pictured as a little four-day riverine picnic.

Ethan, for a young man, is an old hand in a canoe, but Brannin and Noah—though they had grown up boating on Cobscook Bay and the Atlantic—hadn't done a lot of river canoeing. But again, I thought: No problem, not for this cinch of a trip. They were clearly bright, athletic, and adventuresome. If they had to learn, they would learn fast.

As it turned out, they had to and they did. When we set out the following morning from our campsite on Fifth Machias Lake, my memory of an easy-going run to Fourth Lake held true for the first five miles, but we soon hit a series of ledge drops that did that "bad run of water" translation justice, and even moved us to portage the last and trickiest drop.

Steve, who had done this trip within the last five years, remembered running this entire stretch without a second thought. So, was the water much higher (or lower) this time, making these drops more formidable, or were we becoming needlessly timid? In any case, Brannin and Noah handled it all with aplomb and obvious enjoyment.

On our traverse of Third Lake the next day, we could practically taste the sweetness of spring in the air: bright sunshine, rafts of geese, three moose cows and their stilty-legged calves wading the swampy shallows at the head of the lake. That little island was as beautiful as I remembered it where we stopped for lunch, a short swim in the still-icy water, and a long bake on the warm ledges.

Between Third and Second Lake, the bad in the Machias gets worse at Long Falls where, without any debate, we all agreed to portage. Next comes a mile and a quarter of drops that have remained nameless but that the *AMC River Guide* allows are "significant."

Quick study that he is, Brannin nonetheless had some trouble here. He ran up on a big flat rock, jumped out of the boat, and pushed himself off again like a kid on a scooter. Then a few hundred yards farther downstream, he flipped coming off a narrow chute, found his footing in the pool below it, lifted his canoe over his head upside down, plopped it back on the water right side up, piled his floating gear back into it, climbed back in, and headed out unfazed and grinning.

I loved paddling with these three young men. Whatever they lacked in finesse, they more than made up for in strength, energy, generosity, and joie de vivre. If the meek should inherit the earth, I hope they'll have some big-hearted, competent young guys like Brannin, Noah, and Ethan along to help on the unexpected Long Falls portage trail and to break out the cheese, sardines, beer, and good cheer when the day is done.

# In the Interior

## Your Not-So-Typical Suburb

Rita and I moved to Temple in June 1971, almost thirty years ago, twenty-seven years and three months ago, to be precise; and because I find I can't be very precise about much else, I cling all the more desperately to that small raft of precision. When, exactly, did the woods get around to taking over that narrow strip of hill pasture we decided to stop mowing several years ago? The evolution from grass to blueberries to young poplar snuck up on me and passed me by when I wasn't looking.

Whatever changes have come to Temple in the time we've been here have come that same way, slowly, in barely perceptible increments, and none have radically altered either the physical or social landscape. When I drive into Farmington, I count maybe four or five more houses than in 1971. There are a few more, too, on the back roads. But our population is still under six hundred; most of the township is still in woods; to the eye of just about any beholder, this is still a quiet little country village.

But in the eyes of the State Planning Office, Temple is a bedroom community, a "typical suburb." Any place where 85 percent of the employed adults leave town in the morning to go to work somewhere else is, I suppose, a commuter town. And any place where the 1990 census showed only three people out of a workforce of 266 employed in farming or forestry can hardly pass muster as a rural, resource-based village.

But I balk at the suburb definition nonetheless. I grew up in suburban New Jersey, and having decided to leave the suburbs behind, I find it depressing to think I've wound up back where I started. So I console myself with all the ways in which Temple has resisted suburbanization and so has remained, if a suburb, then a distinctly rural suburb.

For one thing, topography is on our side. The Temple intervale is a floodplain, and almost every other place in town is a very steep hill. You can fit a new house in here and another one there, but if somebody is eager to build a thirty-house subdivision, there are far more hospitable places to do it than Temple.

The pattern of land ownership is on our side, too. I can't give you percentages, but most of Temple's land area is still woodland, a patchwork of timber holdings both large and small; and timberland, whatever the management regimen, is still not a shopping mall. I can walk the ten to twelve miles from my place to Weld (another suburb) and not run into any other suburbs in between.

And then there is mindset. I haven't conducted a survey, but I'm making a strong guess that if I asked Templars to describe where they live, they would say they live not in the suburbs but in the country. And they'd like to keep it that way. In a survey the planning board actually did conduct about ten years ago, an overwhelming majority said they wanted to see the town retain its rural character; and Temple citizens have repeatedly indicated certain kinds of commerce and development just aren't a good fit.

When it became clear back in 1978 that the presence of a dining, dancing, and drinking establishment meant, among other things, that befuddled drivers would sometimes wind up stuck in snowbanks and come knocking on doors at 1:00 and 2:00 a.m., asking to use the phone to call a tow truck, Temple voted on-premises drinking out. One thing country people insist on is getting a good night's sleep.

Another example: When Hydro-Quebec contemplated running a high-tension power line through western Maine, a couple of possible corridors went through Temple, one of them through my back field. The engineering firm entrusted with designing the line sent PR troops out here to conduct a so-called informational meeting.

Temple did itself proud. One woman stood up and told it the way it was: "You want to destroy our beautiful town," she said, then burst into tears. Another citizen informed the suits up front that at that very moment someone was outside setting charges to blow up their cars. Still other voices, if I remember correctly, implied strongly that any agents of Hydro-Quebec seen snuffling around private property in Temple would be greeted with buckshot. During all those uneasy months, I considered various monkey-wrenching schemes myself and wondered how long it would take me to fell a pylon with a hacksaw.

But strong as Temple's sense of itself as rural and its desire to stay that way may be, it was not the fervor of our loyalty or the force of our buckshot rhetoric that kept the pylons from marching over these lovely wooded hills. Concerted and thorough as the protest was that western Maine mounted, it was ultimately economic factors that scuttled Hydro-Quebec's plans. Temple, Wilton, Weld, New Vineyard and all other small towns lucked out.

But being a chronic worrier, I worry about how much longer our luck will hold. In a world increasingly driven by urban and suburban interests, I worry that the lay of our land, traditional patterns of land use and our mindset may not be strong enough bulwarks to protect the things all of us here, old-timers and immigrants alike, treasure.

And just what are Temple's great treasures? Surely the beauty of its landscape, that long ridge of Spruce Mountain sloping off to the northeast from the peak of Mount Blue, the sweet symmetry of Potato Hill, the shaded pools and rapids of Temple Stream as it tumbles down out of those hills. A less obvious treasure is our social coherence. Not, of course, that Temple is in any way tightly knit. It is indeed typically suburban in having a diverse population who work and play and socialize in circles that rarely overlap. But separate as most of our lives are here and vehement as some disagreements may be, my sense is that, on the whole, a spirit of tolerance, cordiality, and even guarded affection holds sway, an attitude of "Well, old Tom may be nuts, but he's not a bad fella."

Rub elbows with just about anybody long enough, and your rough edges will wear off. Pretty soon you discover you've grown rather fond of old Tom despite his misguided ideas about politics. I never would have believed it, but after nearly thirty years here, I find I genuinely like several Republicans. "No matter how you've squabbled in the past," George Morse told me once, "if there's sickness or fire, you help out."

Will Temple look and feel just about the same after another thirty years? What bulwarks, if any, should be built to protect its natural beauty and sense of community? I don't know, but feel quite sure that whatever measures Temple may take, they will have to be homegrown and based on communal values, not on model ordinances developed by lawyers in Augusta.

The most useful economic, social, and environmental model I've seen hasn't come out of any office of community development but is located about half a mile from me, where a sign on the side of the road reads "W. A. Mitchell, Chairmakers." Arthur and Donna Mitchell live there and have a professional woodworking shop next to their house. They transform wood into high-quality chairs, an ideal value-added enterprise for Maine if there ever was one. Their business is small, thriving, unobtrusive, nonpolluting. They design and manufacture under one roof. They have six full-time local employees and no offshore labor force. They make a beautiful, useful product. They care about this town, where Mitchells have been living since 1803. They are thoughtful, generous neighbors. They go fishing whenever they get a chance.

What better model for a typical rural Maine suburb as it heads into the twenty-first century? W. A. Mitchell, Chairmakers, using local raw materials, employing local people, working to high standards of craftsmanship, rooted in the past, looking to the future, living in the present and, it would seem, having a pretty darn good time.

# The Great Garden Glut

Gardens can be fickle, overwhelming us with their bounty one year and producing little more than a few blighted tomatoes and wizened carrots the next. Most years fall somewhere in between, but I'm happy to report that here on the Temple intervale, "in between" has tended more often toward bounty than blight.

A few facts of topography and history for which we can take no credit have worked to make that so. Having a garden on an intervale is a great help. An intervale, as *Webster* tells us, is a chiefly New England term for bottomland, which is, in turn, low-lying land along a watercourse. Our house and garden sit on a knoll well above current flood levels but still down in the valley where the deluges of eons past have left behind a thick layer of rich, friable soil. A friend of mine who was helping me dig post holes, and who lives on a rocky, gravelly hillside, kept marveling that we could dig down through a good foot or more of dark, organic dirt before we hit the rocky, yellow layer. "No fair!" he said. "It's taken me ten years to build up a few inches of stuff like this on my place."

As for history, when we moved onto this old farm forty years ago we found, just behind the ell, what was left of a barn foundation. Next to that jumble of rocks was a patch of quite level land, measuring about fifty by fifty feet. Remnants of cow manure dumped from the now-razed barn had boosted the fertility of the soil to high test, making any composting on our part unnecessary for the next few years.

Add to those blessings, handed to us scot-free, the skills and savvy of a gardener like my wife, and the odds for consistently good yields are in your favor. Rita has not just one green thumb but two, along with eight green fingers as well. She likes to say she really doesn't know what she's doing, that she loses track of what she planted where from one year to the next, can't remember which variety those particularly productive tomatoes were, that her garden is a rather haphazard mess. But the harvest puts the lie to all her protestations. The garden starts feeding us asparagus in late May, early June, and the first lettuce follows close on its heels. Rita spends two, three, four hours in the garden almost every summer morning, preparing beds, planting, weeding. She takes on pests in hand-to-hand combat. On cool, misty mornings, she heads out to the garden armed with scissors for the slug hunt. She bends down, snips, looks, bends down again, cuts another slug in two. She can't bear to pour salt on them or drown them in beer. Even the loathsome slug, she believes, deserves a quick and honorable death.

All gardens bear the stamp of their creators, and this one is Rita through and through—not compulsively neat, not in clearly defined rows, but an evolved thing, a place where she fits this year's annual crops in around the ever-expanding asparagus and the constantly spreading poppies she won't tear up because they're so gorgeous in among the beans and leeks.

Her intuitions never fail her. Even in the worst of years—come a cold, wet summer, come drought and blistering heat—in the fall we always have some potatoes, carrots, and beets stashed in the root cellar; peas, pesto, broccoli, raspberries, and blueberries in the freezer; onions and garlic, butternut and acorn squash tucked into the corners of unheated bedrooms upstairs.

And then in those rare years like 2010 when conditions are ideal, when the snowpack is gone and the soil dry enough to work by the end of May, when June comes in warm and there's no chance of another frost, when there's plenty of sun through July and August and just enough rain to keep things watered but never sodden, and when that sweet summer weather persists into September and even early October, well, in a year like that Rita's garden outdoes itself. We eat bowls full of green beans for lunch every day; we bake zucchini bread every other day; we can cannerful after cannerful of tomatoes; we eat stir fries every night but still can't keep up with the summer squash and chard; the winter squashes grow leaves like elephant ears and send tendrils wriggling out under the lowest strand of the electric fence to stretch out and luxuriate on the lawn.

In a year like this past one, with Rita in charge, what you get is a garden glut, a tsunami of red lettuce and leaf lettuce and rattlesnake beans and cherry tomatoes, an abundance that stuffs the fridge to overflowing and nearly overwhelms all hands with blanching, freezing, and canning. It leaves me awed, dazzled, and eternally grateful for the genius of soil, sun, seed, water, and my wife. And mindful, too, of Mae West's famous dictum: "Too much of a good thing can be wonderful."

# Comfortable Winter Camping

Most folks invited to go winter camping will usually decline. Too cold, they say. They have visions of shivering all day, of cold feet and cold hands, of huddling around the pitiful little flame of a backpacking stove at dusk to heat some tasteless, freeze-dried glop, of wolfing it down before it freezes back to its freeze-dried state, of crawling into a cold sleeping bag inside an ice-cold tent to shiver through a night of fitful sleep only to get up shivering in the morning for one more day of shivering and cold feet and cold hands.

It need not be so. Winter camping can be not just comfortable but downright luxurious, provided, that is, you camp the way Maine guides Garrett and Alexandra Conover taught me a little over thirty years ago and have since taught dozens upon dozens, if not hundreds, of others since.

The key to the Conover system is toboggans—not the wide, six-foot-long kind you use for sliding downhill with the kids, but trail toboggans anywhere from eight to ten feet long and narrow enough to slide along on the packed float your snowshoes leave behind you. Toboggans let you transport what no backpacker could begin to carry— a cotton tent and a wood-burning stove. In those two items lies luxury. In the winter, days are short, nights long. How pleasant to spend those few hours from sunset to bedtime relaxing and eating supper in a warm tent. How equally pleasant to wake at five in the morning, touch off a fire in the stove, and wait until the tent is warm before you get up for breakfast.

A winter camping trip can be as strenuous or as laid back as you care to make it. You can load your toboggans so heavy you can barely move them and head off across northern Ontario or Quebec for a month, or you can load up light and go for just a few days near home. In late February last year, I joined some friends for a laid-back trip here in Maine. Five of our crew were old hands. Chris was new to the enterprise. He was willing to believe us when we told him he would not lose any of his toes, but he reserved the right to a little skepticism about the luxury business.

We had picked what we thought would be a pretty stretch of river to travel on, and we arrived at our starting point on the kind of glorious, sunny winter morning that could turn the most dour skeptic into a true believer. Soon we had our toboggans loaded and were headed upstream.

For the six of us, we had two three-person tents and two stoves. With nothing else to haul but our food, personal duffels, sleeping bags, and group gear like the cook kit and a couple of saws and axes, our loads were light; we breezed along, soaking up the sun and taking in the flocks of white-winged crossbills foraging in the spruce and a bunch of loopy slides some playful otters had left on the riverbank.

About 3:30 we pulled off into a sheltered spot to make camp. Dick and I took the axes and went in search of firewood; Chris and Tony set up one tent, and Roger and Tom, the other. By the time Dick and I had several rounds of dry, dead spruce back in our camp yard, there were some free hands to saw it up and toss the billets to us to split into stovewood and kindling.

When we had finished working up the wood and piling it handy to the tent doors, the sun was well below the treetops, dusk was closing in fast, and the temperature was dropping just as fast, finally settling at twenty below zero.

Roger and Tony had the stoves already cranking. We retired to the warmth of our respective tents, took off our mukluks and wool shirts, and settled back in our longjohns on the floor of Therm-a-Rest mattresses laid out on the tent ground cloth.

Dick, Tony, and Chris came over to our tent, where Tom was bartender and cook for the evening. He served up a concoction involving whiskey and lime juice for cocktails, followed by beef stew for dinner and Ben & Jerry's ice cream for dessert.

The next few days passed in much the same way, each of them as beautiful as the first, each starting off with pancake and sausage breakfasts, each with the bends in the river unwinding before us, each with time for a little side jaunt into a stand of huge old fir or up a tributary brook where we roused two moose from their beds.

And at the end of each day, always the warm tents, the gathering of the gang for snacks and drinks, the flow of talk—some antic, some thoughtful—the thick pea soup and cornbread, or the stroganoff and bannock. I'm almost ashamed to say how good we had it, we snowshoe sybarites.

No wonder Chris was a convert before the trip was half over.

# Country Mice, City Mice

Rita and I are country mice, through and through. So strong is our attachment to our old farmhouse and to this little upland valley in western Maine that Rita once said, "I think this place has gotten into my DNA."

"I'm sure it has," I said, in full agreement with her metaphor, if dubious of its biological accuracy.

But, that said, we are not above making occasional visits to the city. If we're feeling bold and feisty enough, we'll even take on New York, though not too often. Boston is more our speed. For one thing, it's a lot closer, just three and a half or four hours by car. For another, it's the unofficial capital of New England, maybe not politically but spiritually. Don't people in the northernmost reaches of Maine, Vermont, and New Hampshire all root for the Red Sox? Bostonians may be city people, but they're still New Englanders. We speak just slightly different dialects of the same language. And despite the crop of skyscrapers Boston has sprouted over the last several decades, it still feels more like a big village than any other megalopolis I know. It's got the Charles River and Frederick Law Olmsted's Emerald Necklace of parks winding through it. It has lots of ponds. It has cobblestones on Beacon Hill and streets that meander every which way. It also has old friends of ours who are roughly our age, which makes them old friends indeed.

In Aesop's fable of the country mouse and the city mouse—and in the many adaptations of it ever since—the country mouse goes to the city, drawn by the promise of fancy foods his city cousin claims are far tastier than any rural fare. Though we grant there's some good eating to be had in cities, venison tenderloin from the Maine woods and fresh kale from Rita's garden can hold their own against anything an urban five-star restaurant can cook up; so what we're looking for on our city visits is a different kind of nourishment, a connection with the

77

energy and imagination and productivity that critical masses of people engaged in shared pursuits can generate, whether in the arts, sciences, or whatever.

A case in point: On our last Boston visit, we stayed with a young couple who live in Jamaica Plain, just a block away from Harvard's Arnold Arboretum. After we'd arrived on a Friday afternoon, we walked over there and wandered around until dark among all the exotic trees on the arboretum's 281 acres. Despite the distant origins of those trees, the genera of many of them are familiar to any visitor from our northern forest: *Acer, Tsuga, Pinus, Quercus*. I've rarely, if ever, met a tree I didn't like, so I take particular pleasure in making the acquaintance of Japanese or Chinese or Korean cousins to our own maples, hemlocks, pines, and oaks, seeing how much alike yet also how different they are.

The creation of this extraordinary living collection of some thirty-eight hundred primarily woody plants from temperate regions around the world has been the work of many hands over many decades, but considerable credit for shaping the arboretum as a scientific institution as well as a park for the education and enjoyment of the public must go to its first director, Charles Sprague Sargent. Collaborating with Frederick Law Olmsted, Sargent chose to organize the plantings by family and genus. "It is hoped," he said, "that such an arrangement, while avoiding the stiff and formal lines of the conventional botanic garden, will facilitate the comprehensive study of the collections, both in their scientific and picturesque aspects." Over the next fifty-four years of his directorship, he had the satisfaction of seeing those hopes realized many times over.

A second case in point: The next morning we took a bus downtown to the Museum of Fine Art, where Rita and I had not been since long before the new Art of the Americas wing opened in 2010. Once there, we headed straight for an exhibit of photos by the great African American photographer Gordon Parks. This collection records Parks's return to his home town of Fort Scott, Kansas, in 1950 to find and photograph eleven classmates with whom he had graduated from the segregated Plaza School in 1923. If Karen Haas, a curator at the museum, had not happened across a single photo by Parks showing a young couple outside a movie theater, she might not have been moved to contact the Gordon Parks Foundation, which had the other forty-two photos from the series that Parks had shot on that assignment for *Life* magazine. Never published in *Life* or shown anywhere else in Parks' lifetime, this collection is but one of the thousands of treasures the staff of the museum has found and made available to us all. Get enough talented, public-spirited city mice together, and these are the kinds of wonders they can work.

I'm happy to report, too, that the restaurant in the spacious atrium of the new wing serves up a superb lunch, and unlike the mouse cousins in Aesop's fable, we could enjoy our meal in peace without being chased away from our food by a pair of dogs.

# A Slipping-Down Farm

There are many times in the year when I realize I am spread too thin, but right now, in mid-October, I feel like a last pat of butter that has been told to cover six more slices of bread.

I settle down after Sunday breakfast and draw up a list: Clean up garden and put it to bed. Convert five lambs on the hoof into legs, chops, roasts, and stew meat. Behead, pluck, and draw twelve chickens. Move this year's dry firewood from drying shed into wood room, thereby emptying drying shed. Cut, twitch, split next year's firewood to fill empty drying shed. Fix leak in chimney flashing. Bank north side of house. Take mowing machine off tractor. Put snowplow on tractor. Do not think about all the projects you were going to complete this summer and now have to postpone until next summer (that's a sure route to depression, a luxury you can ill afford). Sweep chimneys. Clean out stovepipes. Collect apples. Press apples. Bottle cider. Drink cider. Jack up garage and repile the rock piers so garage will not slide off them into swamp. Ask yourself for the eighty-seventh time why anybody put a garage on top of loose rocks piled in a swamp in the first place. Resolve to pour cement footings for the garage. Pray for rain so that you can curl up with a good book and do none of the above (except perhaps drink some cider that the neighbors have already pressed). Better yet, pray for snow that will cover up all your sins of omission until next April.

I look hopefully toward the skies, but they are bright and clear. I climb up on the roof with the chimney brush and go at it. From my roof, I can see out over most of our 136 acres, taking in both their glory and their ignominy at a glance. The glory is mostly God's, and I can take no credit for it: that fall melding of birch yellow, oak brown, swamp-maple red, sugar-maple gold, and evergreen green; the meanderings of Temple Stream flowing through our land; the hills rising up steeply on either side of the valley. The ignominy lies in all those things I ought to have done here but have left undone: the fence posts, heaved by the frost, tilting every which way; the sagging page wire around the sheep pasture; the legions of chokecherry and alders surrounding the fields, ready to overrun them the instant I lower my guard. When my wife, Rita, and I bought this place thirteen years ago, the fields were run down but free of brush. Today they are still free of brush and still run down. I've held my own but not made any headway. As for the hundred-plus acres of woodland, they have tended to themselves. The dense stands of fir that should have been thinned and opened up thirteen years ago are denser than ever. A stand of red oak that was mature thirteen years ago is overmature now.

Clearly, I think, sitting astride the ridgepole, we bit off more than we could chew. The acreage and my body weight are equal: 136 acres, 136 pounds. In the past, I might have considered that a fair contest. We're both junior welterweights. But now, pushing fifty and with several of my life's fondest projects still not started, I begin to suspect that I'm outclassed.

When we bought this place, it had been slipping down for years. It was then (and still is) known as the Dana Hamlin place, for Dana lived here from 1901 until 1968. We were lucky enough to know Dana, and he showed us pictures of the place when it was in its prime and he was in his. The huge old barn was still standing. The fields were immaculate. There wasn't an alder or a stalk of goldenrod in sight. That is the image I have of this place; that's how I think it ought to be. But I forget that Dana and his wife and a hired man gave their full energies to keeping it that way. I forget that in the last ten years of Dana's time here, when he was already in his eighties and clearly had no business being here but clung to the place out of a gentle, tenacious passion for it, in those years the barn sills went down, the alders, chokecherry, and hardhack took over the stream banks and the drainage ditches and the swampy areas where you can't mow with a tractor. Somebody could always be found to knock down the grass and bale it, but only somebody like Dana in his prime would patrol the stream banks and the swales with a brush scythe.

Then Dana finally sold to a man from a neighboring town who came out on weekends and days off to gut the house so that it could be renovated from the ground up. For three years nobody lived here, and when the new owner, who worked for the state, was transferred out of this area, we bought from him. The land had gone back further still; the house was a shell with rotting sills, rotting window frames, and holes in the walls big enough to throw a cat through. Local observers advised us to knock the house down, burn the rubble, and start over again. A friend who drove up with us from Massachusetts one April weekend to see our new home threw up her hands and said, "Why are you doing this to yourselves?"

There have been many occasions since when I have wondered myself. Even in the first flush of our infatuation with this place, we knew we did not want to be full-time farmers. Both Rita and I had years of literary training and work behind us. We couldn't simply abandon that, nor did we want to. We wanted some physical work and some mental work. We wanted to satisfy some (not all) of our needs for food, fuel, and shelter through our own physical efforts. For the cash we still needed, we would rely on freelance translating, writing, and editing. What we wanted, in short, was wholeness, an organic life. I almost blush to use those terms, because I and lots of other people I know have said and done some foolish things in their name. But I remain loyal to the ideas the terms represent. For all the romantic excesses the "organic life" may conjure up, it means some of the things I still think essential for a sane existence: work for the body, work for the mind, a place in the natural world and a place in the social one, some direct participation in the production of food.

We did not need 136 acres for that. Five or ten would have done nicely. But now that we've got the 136 acres, what do we do with them? In our early years here, the problem was not as pressing as it is now. The problem then was to rescue a nearly moribund old farmhouse, to clear away the brush and burdock so we could get in the front door, and to carve a garden plot out of the sod. We behaved then as if we had only five acres. We had our hands full to get the house and the grounds closest to it under some kind of control. We were thankful that a man up on the hill still had a dairy herd and wanted to hay the fields. That was all the thought and care we could give to them.

Our first ten-year plan is behind us, not all of it executed to perfection by any means, and the place is more or less livable. The house, given some reasonable care, is good for another hundred years. The sheep have not gotten onto the front porch for some time now. They stay on their side of the fence; we stay on ours. The tractor and the tools have their shed. The chickens have their coop. The garden grows. The blueberries grow. The raspberries grow. The fruit trees don't grow. We appear to be lousy orchardists.

We have imposed some order on our immediate surroundings. Within a radius of some two hundred yards out from our kitchen stove, there is clear evidence that somebody lives on this place. Beyond that, nothing is clear at all. It would seem logical that we should keep enlarging that radius until it reaches our outer boundaries. Someday, according to that logic, we should look out our kitchen windows onto lush green fields free of hardhack and swale grass. Someday we should walk through a woodlot of tall, flourishing, marketable trees with more on the way, a woodlot like the municipal forests of Rita's native Switzerland.

But all that calls for a major policy decision, a major commitment, and as I consider how I will ever meet that commitment if I take it on, I remember that Dana and his hired man worked full time on the farm and did not spend forty to fifty hours a week translating books. And if their example is not enough, I can turn to Thomas Jefferson's *Garden Book* (published in 1768), in which a correspondent named Thomas Boyne wrote to Jefferson: "It is my conclusion that the smallest farm needs two men. One may plow and sow and harvest and tend to the needs of stock. The other must needs be diligent in fence repair, battling building decay, preparing fuel and marketing the increase to advantage. If there be a boy as well, some advance may be made in clearing, cistern building or other forward tasks."

At a time when my farm is calling me to ever greater advances in forward tasks, I find that simply holding my own is about all I can do and is often more than I want to do. Time's winged chariot is doing its work; my second boyhood seems to be coming on prematurely. In my first boyhood, all I wanted to do was read, write, and run around in the woods. That's about all I want to do now, too. By the time you're fifty, you'd better know what your priorities are, even if they are regressive. Then, too, I have horrendous bouts of hay fever every June. And on top of that I'm convinced that my genetic inheritance must go back to a hunter-gatherer folk rather than to an agrarian one, which is to say I would much rather go fishing than hoe corn.

The solution many people have found to the problem of the slipping-down farm is to let their places go to hell. Fifty years ago there were forty-two working farms in the Temple Stream valley and on the hillsides around it. Dana Hamlin knew. He used to collect milk and cream from them and haul it into the railroad station in West Farmington. Today there are only two working farms nearby, and only four families (including ours) even bother to keep their fields open. Why not let the fields go back? Why not follow the example of many others who were far better, more talented, more devoted farmers than I? It is no disgrace to throw in the towel where better men have failed. And nature is smart. She will make her own good sense of my land if I do not.

That may well be, but I can't make my peace with it. Farms, it seems to me, are the closest analogue to the Creation we have. All our mythologies tell us that God or the gods made an ordered universe from incomprehensible chaos. Equipped with less than divine powers, we make smaller ordered universes out of the vast, teeming complexity of nature. Millions of animal species are more than we can handle, so we keep cows, horses, sheep, pigs. We cannot deal with the millions of plant species in nature, so we grow wheat, barley, oats, carrots, and peas. A farm is in nature and of nature but contrary to nature; it is our small gear that meshes with the greater one of creation. We have some influence, though hardly complete control, over the part of creation we have staked out as our own; but if we hold up our end of the bargain, if we stick by the land and keep our little wheel rolling, God (or the gods) will keep the big one turning, too.

To make a deliberate decision to let my own place go back, to let this one patch of land that I've taken on as my responsibility slip down even more, seems like breaking a covenant. Yet to neglect all those loud voices in my own head that say, "Stop! Enough!" would be a breach of another kind. What is organic about a life that ignores its own strongest inner promptings?

If I throw all the (dwindling) spare energy I have into making this place a model New England farm, it may be the better for it, but I will be the worse. And there is no doubt, as Thomas Boyne knew, that "forward tasks" call for extra energy. You need two men and a boy, or you have to work as hard as two men and a boy yourself. The first of those solutions I cannot afford financially; the second I cannot afford physically or psychologically.

The solution is a time-honored one in northern New England: you patch and make do; steady by jerks, you move ahead; you muddle through. Jack, who used to mow the fields, is cutting down his herd and doesn't want to hay our place anymore, but Charley, the only other dairy farmer left within ten miles of us, wants to lease the fields, plow them up, reseed them, build up the humus. We see eye to eye on the care of the soil. For the next five years anyhow—and longer, if things work out—the fields will be gaining, not losing.

And what about the brush? Well, I can't say I feel all that bad about the stuff that's got a foothold along the stream and the drainage ditches. Our place is a paradise for birds, and in the spring and summer my head spins trying to spot the veeries and warblers and yellowthroats and kingbirds and catbirds and white-throated sparrows that call for my attention. And then every once in a while a great blue heron will rise majestically out of that no-good, useless alder swamp behind the house, or we'll hear a bittern's pile-driving *un go-chunk, un go-chunk, un go-chunk* rise up out of it and echo around the valley at dusk.

And if the stream banks were clear of trees and brush and down elms, where would the trout find shaded pools to lie in and what would the beaver eat and make dams of and why would a moose bother to visit a farm that had no beaver bog to wallow in?

And the woods? What about those overmature oaks and that beech on the hill across the stream and those unpruned tangles of softwood? Well, I guess I feel that where woods are concerned no management is better than poor management, and if I can't get around to cutting the trees myself the way I want to cut, and if I can't find somebody who will cut to my admittedly cranky specs, then the woods can continue to tend to themselves.

Wendell Berry has said that every farm needs a sacred grove, a place where no work is ever done, a place within ten minutes walk of the back door where we can always go and see (or at least begin to imagine) what the world was like before we ever touched a hand to it. There is no mistaking the sacred grove on our place. The hillsides dropping down into the little glen are too steep for man, beast, or machine ever to work on them, and tossed out on the glen's floor like a handful of dice are glacial erratics bigger than skidders and bulldozers, some of them bigger than houses. Porcupines den in the caves in the winter and leave quills scattered on their verandahs. A tiny rivulet runs under the snow, slips down over mossy rocks in the summer, opens into a deadwater, then into a miniature lake surrounded by marshland.

I like the idea and the reality of a sacred grove, and I may well let sacredness spread on my woodlot, for much as it pains me to see farmland go back, it pains me just as much to see every bit of land "managed" to suit the needs of humankind. Do I contradict myself? I certainly do, and at this point in my life, I've given up on achieving single-minded clarity about anything. I feel good if I can just sort out the strands of my confusion into some surveyable order.

I want to see land used and managed and productive, and I want to see land left alone. I want to see farms, and I want to see wilderness. I want my own place to be both farm and wilderness, a place where the forward tasks and the slipping down are in some kind of equilibrium, where the domestic and the wild can live hand in hand, where the lamb can lie down with the lion, where I can put down the shovel and pick up the fly rod. And what I see from the ridgepole is just that: a semi-cultivated semiwilderness, scruffy around the edges but hospitable to all the creatures who live on it and from it, a scene pleasing not only to bitterns and beaver but also to gods and men.

# The Lawn

I use the term "lawn" advisedly, seizing on it only when I need to designate with a single word the mottled green vegetation that grows around our house, garden, and outbuildings, proof that this old farmstead is not abandoned, that someone lives here, seeing to it that this place, though somewhat scruffy, is not giving way to total seed and weed.

When Rita and I moved in here the house and grounds had been abandoned for three years, so one of the first things I did was clear the place with a brush scythe and a chain saw. Then I bought a walk-behind mower to keep this hodgepodge of vegetation trimmed down enough for us to get around on and not be wading through out-of-control timothy, meadowsweet, dogbane, and hawkweed.

Needless to say, the results in no way matched those velvety green suburban lawns I had mowed in my New Jersey boyhood to earn pocket money. Their owners had put those lawns there on purpose. They had cleansed their lawn plots of stumps, weeds, and witchgrass; they had hauled in truckloads of topsoil; they had raked and seeded and watered. Once their lawns were established, they tended them with loving care. They plucked out alien organisms like dandelions. Come a dry spell, they rolled out the hoses and sprinklers. They did not let their lawns turn dry, yellow, and sere.

The only care our Temple lawn continues to get now is regular enough mowing to maintain those brush-free spaces I cleared nearly half a century ago. If we were to pull out all the non-grass plants in our lawn, we wouldn't have much left. A hasty inventory I took recently turned up some twenty-five plants that would have no place in a real lawn: wood sorrel, ragweed, burdock, purslane, ground ivy, plantain, lamb's quarters. . . . Those aliens don't bother me at all. I'm actually quite fond of them. They make clear that our lawn is really a self-propagating garden with enough edible plants growing in it that I could turn myself out to pasture on it just about all spring, summer, and fall.

Dandelions, those arch enemies of real lawns, are welcome old friends at our place each spring, first for the salad greens their early leaves provide, then for the glow of their flowers. Along with the dandelion blossoms come scattered patches of tiny blue violets that I mow around for the pleasure of having them with us for as long as they last.

My son, Greg, who's been living with me here lately, is a knowledgeable and dedicated vegetable gardener but no greenskeeper. He thinks the modest patches of lawn I keep open are excessive. From an early age he has hated the noisy, fume-spewing rotary lawnmower, declaring it a health hazard and a waste of his own and anyone else's time. Given his druthers, he'd allow our wild plants pretty much free rein, junk the lawnmower, and use a scythe to carve out trails from house to raspberry patch, to clothesline, to compost pile, to wherever else we need to go time and again. But because Greg has proved himself a willing worker not only in the garden and on the woodpile but also on the myriad other chores around this place, I've spared him the lawn mowing, a concession I find it easy to make because I enjoy mowing grass myself. I can do the whole place in two hours, but I like stretching the mowing out in half-hour sessions at the end of summer days and working up a good sweat before heading for a swim.

I like trimming down, one row at a time, the shaggy mix of grass, clover, and whatever else grows on the gentle slope between our house and garden. I like maintaining our more or less orderly little plots of land in the midst of this teeming wildness all around them. I like knowing I'll have to come back again and again to this job of giving shape to the given, knowing the shagginess hasn't been done in. It's still there, growing again the second after I've trimmed it back. That's fine with me. I find figuring out how to live thoughtfully and respectfully in and between the wild and the domestic is one of life's most engaging tasks. Our dooryard dilemma—to mow or not to mow or how much to mow if we mow—is a small dilemma that's part and parcel of our much larger one that Barry Lopez neatly summed up: "[One] of the great dreams of man," he writes, "must be to find a place between the extremes of nature and civilization where it is possible to live without regret."

I have my share of regrets, but that doesn't prevent me—whether the issue is mowing the lawn or writing a management plan for our woodlot—from looking for that sweet spot between those two extremes where the flourishing of all animals, vegetables, and minerals is best served.

In any case, if somewhere on my search for that spot I should happen upon a knockout recipe for Joe Pye weed, I'll be sure to pass it on to you.

# The Table Manners of Birds

It is no doubt rash of me—if not downright foolhardy—to be commenting on the table manners of birds. My ornithological credentials are scant at best, though I suppose I can qualify as an amateur bird-watcher, but even back in the day when both my hearing and eyesight were at their best, I was still only a C-minus birder. Then too you might object that birds don't have tables and therefore have no need of manners at them anyway. Granted, none of our bird-feeding equipment here in Temple bears the slightest resemblance to a table. We have a suet cage hanging in our dooryard lilac bush, a tubular plastic feeder, and a 9-by-11-inch hopper that delivers black sunflower seeds to troughs on both of its sides and can accommodate several birds at once.

Though our feeders are not literal tables, they are figurative ones we've laid in a spirit of hospitality toward our avian friends, hoping to provide some nourishment for them in times of scarcity and, in times of plenty, to continue rejoicing in their company. Our most numerous and reliable year-round guests are chickadees. They usually come in small flocks at just about any time of day. From their perches in the lilac, they flit down to the feeders, fetch a seed, then fly back to the lilac where they expertly strip the seed of its husk, then fly repeated sorties for another and another. They don't linger at the feeders, and if by chance two chickadees should arrive at the same place at about the same time, both seem to yield to the other by unspoken agreement. Then they fetch their seeds and make way for the next two or three of their comrades.

Their manners—if I may anthropomorphize a bit—are impeccable, and their gathering, preparing, and consuming of their food neat, efficient, and not the least bit wasteful. Also, despite their tiny size, they don't shy away from creatures like me filling the feeders but will swoop in and out around my head and might even come to a handful of seeds, although I've never been patient enough to make that offer. No wonder the chickadee is Maine's state bird: thrifty, industrious, good humored, neighborly—in short, the model citizen we should all aspire to be.

When goldfinches arrive in numbers, the scene can turn a bit rowdy. If two or three birds are intent on settling in for lunch on a particular place at the hopper, there'll be flapping of wings and bumping of hips and shoulders in a contest of king of the feeder, though after enough familial juggling, they'll realize there's room and food enough for everybody. Interlopers, however, are another matter. I recently saw a goldfinch fly up in the face of an approaching tufted titmouse, who despite his—or possibly her—advantage in size and weight, decided he would do best to back off.

If it's sedate dining you're looking for, the cardinal pair who turn up in the fall and early winter at our place are the models for that, as are some other birds with those big bills that look like a cross between an anvil and a splitting maul and that can crack open a sunflower seed with one bite. In the spring these last several years, a pair of rose-breasted grosbeaks have not only graced our place with their song and their beauty but also made themselves welcome, placidly munching away among our regular guests. The same can't be said for purple finches who swarm the hopper feeder, shoulder everybody else aside, and then chow down voraciously, tossing seed hulls right and left.

So it would be mistaken to say that table behavior at our feeders is always a model of decorum, but if I consider the birds who live on our place year-round, plus all the warm-weather visitors as well—the robins and phoebes, the swallows and sparrows, the warblers and woodpeckers—their ordinarily amiable behavior can lull me into thinking that birds, by and large, have a built-in tolerance for their feathered cousins that we humans would be wise to adopt. But then I have to think again, because for a sharp-shinned hawk most of those birds at our feeders are potential meals, not dinner companions.

Cornell's Ornithology Lab tells me in *All About Birds* that 90 percent of the sharpie's diet is songbirds and that the nestlings and fledglings of those birds make up much of the food these hawks feed their own nestlings. I can't condemn sharp-shinned hawks for the meat-eating appetites they were hatched with, but I'm grateful they've been rare in our neighborhood where in all the years we've lived here I've witnessed only one sharpie's pursuit—unsuccessful—of a song sparrow. And I'm of course more grateful than I can say for the mostly small birds whose live-and-let-live manners have let them share the tables we've spread for them over those same years. We couldn't care less whether they've read Emily Post or whether they always know which fork to use. Nor do they ever need to worry about wearing a tie or not. Mealtime here is always pot luck and come as you are.

# Consolation Prizes

For the last six years, I've done most of my hunting with my friend Harry at his place. We see eye to eye on many things, Harry and I do, and when it comes to deer hunting, we could not agree more that the ultimate goal of the enterprise is meat. Harry's place has been good to us both. In four of those six seasons, I've packed deer meat into the freezer. Harry has brought home the venison in five out of six.

Intent as we are on food acquisition, we seize whatever advantages are within the law and our own sense of what constitutes decent behavior. We regularly apply for the any-deer permits the Maine Department of Inland Fisheries and Wildlife offers in limited numbers and assigns to hunters by lottery. Hunters far more skillful than I never bother applying for any-deer permits. Among them is my sometime hunting companion, Jerry, who has never once in the past thirty or thirty-five years applied for a permit but has nonetheless hardly ever failed to bring home a deer—always, of course, one carrying antlers. Not being in Jerry's league, I do not scorn any-deer permits. With one in hand, your chances of success improve by more than 50 percent because you don't have to hesitate when a deer comes within range. You don't have to use up crucial seconds peering through binoculars or a scope to determine whether a deer that at first glance could be either a doe or a spikehorn is in fact a male carrying spikes long enough (three inches) to qualify him as a legal buck. With an any-deer permit, you can shoot first and settle those questions later.

Another advantage I've allowed myself is a scope sight. I finally had to admit, after missing two shots several seasons ago, that my aging eyes were refusing to line up the open sights on my old Winchester 30/30 with the necessary degree of accuracy, so I upgraded to a scope mounted on a brand-new Marlin lever action, a rifle I realized I'd been secretly lusting after for years anyhow.

But then, despite the scope, the any-deer permit, and the superb habitat of Harry's land, there comes a season when all those factors seem to add up to naught.

As a barren hunting season progresses through the third week, then into the fourth and final one, and as my desire to bring home some meat intensifies even as the time left to satisfy that desire shrinks, I also start to wax philosophical, finding consolation in the pleasures these days have brought me.

High among those pleasures is companionship. Harry and I hatch plans. He'll take a stand up on the ridge where we know the deer head up over the hill, and I'll do a slow sweep through the little valley below him. If I'm careful enough, I may get a shot. Maybe, but far more likely not, because deer are much better at hearing than I am at moving quietly.

Or maybe I'll push a deer uphill to Harry. But again, most likely not, and when I meet him a couple of hours later, he's frozen through from hunkering motionless at his stand, so we head back to his house to warm up with hot coffee and some serious grumbling about no deer and the ineptitude of politicians in Augusta.

If it's Saturday, his wife, Debi, may be home and willing to make some pancakes. We all sit together and eat and talk and enjoy each other's company, which we rarely find the chance to do at other times of the year. Harry and Debi's place is just far enough away from mine that I don't see them often during most of the year. Hunting season is when we always look forward to getting together and having a chance to catch up.

And there are the moments of watching in solitude, that time at dawn when the sun creeps up over the hill in the east, poking its light through the treetops at first, then gradually climbing high enough in the sky to take the night's chill away. On a morning when the oak leaves have reached that point when strong enough puffs of wind can dislodge them, I listen to rustling flurries of falling leaves. Sitting on a downed log at one of my favorite stands, I see a red-backed vole scurry out from under the fallen trunk, run over my foot, and disappear under a tangle of roots. At dusk, I watch a flock of wild turkeys' comic but ultimately successful attempts to roost in some tall pines. The big birds land on branches too slight to carry their weight and tumble off into thin air, flapping wildly to get airborne before returning in search of firmer footing.

So if you ask this utilitarian-minded meat hunter at the end of an unsuccessful season how things went, I guess I'd say just fine. I went afield in good company and saw and heard at least some of the myriad small miracles there are out there to see and hear.

# Silent Nights

Winter is, most of the time, a quiet time; the deeper the acoustic blanket of snow gets, the quieter the world becomes. As the snowbanks grow higher and higher along the Intervale Road here in Temple, they muffle the sound of a passing car to a mere whisper. But the epitome of blissful silence comes with a snowfall of soft, fluffy flakes on a wind-still night. Rita curls up in her armchair; I settle in my favorite corner of the couch; we pick up our books. Clunker— our burly tiger cat who played tackle for the Green Bay Packers in his youth—joins me and rolls over on his back to have his belly scratched. We tuck the silence in around us. We hear nothing but Clunker purring, the turning of a page.

As a rule, however, we can't count on this reign of sweet silence continuing through the night. Often, after we climb the stairs and crawl in under our down comforter, we hear the creatures of the night just getting underway. We hear in the walls and ceiling gnawing and thumping so loud we wonder if beavers have moved in. We hear rustling and scuttling. We hear the patter of what seem to be dozens of little feet— maybe the latest litter of mice romping about? Red squirrels playing soccer with an acorn?

I've done my best, without success, to halt or at least stem the fall rodent invasion. This old farmhouse sits on a loose-rock foundation. Try as I will to stuff all those endless cracks and crevices with mortar, it isn't long after the first cool night or two that we hear our returning tenants whipping their nests into shape, putting up storm windows, and stocking the shelves for winter. Soon they're ready to begin the nocturnal parties and track meets they'll enjoy for the next few months.

But this past winter, for the first time we can remember, all that changed. Nobody took up quarters in the fall. We kept waiting for shoes to drop all November and December, but none did. And then not a sound for the rest of the winter. We reveled in the peace and quiet but couldn't help wondering to whom or what we owed this respite.

Then, on a sunny afternoon in May, I saw Clunker crouched in front of a bookcase whose lowest shelf was just a couple of inches off the floor. He was peering intently into that dark crevice and hissing occasionally. A flashlight showed me a handsome milk snake close to three feet long. I shut Clunker up in the next room, and thinking I was doing the snake a favor, I carried him outside into the sun and warmth of that spring day. But a little later I had second thoughts. Maybe we hadn't had any racket all winter because that milk snake, before he went into hibernation, had gobbled up rodents by the dozen and scared off any he hadn't eaten? Or maybe, in the relative warmth of our dirt-floored, rock-walled cellar, he hadn't hibernated at all but had just dozed, ready to leap into action the minute a mouse showed its face? In short, maybe I had been an idiot: instead of taking that snake outside, I should have given him our guest room on a permanent basis.

Realizing I'd been anthropomorphizing enough about rodents and snakes, I decided to talk with someone who could rescue me from my fantasies. Jonathan Mays, a snake expert in Maine's Department of Inland Fisheries and Wildlife, said, yes, February encounters with milk snakes do occur in cellars, but the snakes' feeding behavior doesn't extend beyond mid-September, and they remain inactive all winter, though they sometimes do start feeding again in the spring while there is still snow on the ground.

So, the answers are, no, our snake hadn't been knocking off mice as they made their way through our permeable foundation; and no, he hadn't interrupted his winter's rest to patrol the house for food. Jonathan speculated, but speculated only, that the presence of a milk snake or two might have discouraged the fall in-migration. And he allowed that the snake (or snakes) might have made a dent in the rodent population over the previous summer and so reduced the number available to rattle around in our house over the winter. Then, too, our winter's silence may have been the work of a weasel or of a cyclical downturn in the mice population.

So my lovely story about an altruistic milk snake who had decided to stay awake all winter so that we could get a good night's sleep? Well, that was just a fairy tale that hadn't come true. But I still regret having put that snake outside. I hope he realized how remorseful I was and how much pleasure I took at finding him under one of our bookcases. I hope, too, he found his way back into the house this past August and cleaned out any resident mice before he settled in for his long winter's nap.

# The Ripeness of Deadwood

I t takes about four cords of fitted stovewood to heat our place through the winter. You'd think it would take more, given where this house is located and given its age. We live on the Temple intervale, perched up on a little knoll that keeps us well above the frequent floods that wash over our bottomland fields. Old-timers picked their building sites well and oriented their houses to take advantage of whatever gleanings of heat the winter sun afforded. This house and its ell, stretched out east–west as they are, get maximum exposure to the winter sun as it makes its shallow arc across the southern sky. And Dana Hamlin, the farmer who lived here from 1901 until 1968, increased the passive-solar benefits of the location by replacing the original windows on the south side with much larger ones.

On the north side, he wisely kept the windows few and small because, sweet as the view up our little valley and onto Spruce Mountain and Potato Hill is, Temple Stream valley is a veritable wind tunnel. February gales play on our metal roof like a drummer in a rock band, and though we insulated and tightened this old place up when we moved into it thirty-five years ago, this was before the more recent building technology and materials that make new and newly remodeled houses considerably tighter than I made this old nineteenth-century one. And, of course, we did add some glass to the north side because we couldn't stand diminishment of the view from our kitchen table.

But for all that—our expanse of glass and our northern flank laid bare to boreal winds—we still use only about four cords each winter. Sometime around the middle of October, I bring the seasoned firewood into the wood room from our outdoor woodshed and from whatever stacks I've had drying here and there in the wind and sun with just a strip of old tarp to keep the worst of the rain off them. When I get it all inside, piled from one side of the wood room to the other and seven feet high, I look at it and invariably say, "Well, yes, it looks like enough, but to be on the safe side, I'd better get a bit more."

So where, at this time of year, can I locate some dependably dry and easily accessible firewood? I would much rather the world had done without Dutch elm disease, but since I had no say in the matter, the least I can do is make some good use of the carnage it has left behind. When we first moved in here, there were three huge dead elms of classic form near the house, great graceful fountains spraying their wind-and-rain-polished limbs and branches up and out against the sky. They weren't close enough to the house that I worried about them dropping their tonnage through the roof but were close enough to shed widow makers on unwitting husbands—not to mention wives, children, and dogs—wandering below. Beautiful as those skeletal trees were, I cut them. Safety took priority over aesthetic contemplation; convenience, too, for at that time I had no tractor, and it was a boon to be able to cut and split wood already dry on the stump and near enough to the house that I could haul it in garden cart loads straight into the wood room.

Now I do have a tractor, plus a trailer to hitch on behind it, and the big old monster elms are gone. Now, in October, I can drive down onto the hayfields and test the dead elms along the drainage ditches for their ripeness as firewood. If the bark on the trunk is split and, with a little effort, you can tear it off in good-sized sheets, the tree is probably just about right: still sound but plenty dry. Wait another year or two, though, and it will be going punky.

With these elms in the field—trees that disease cut off before they could grow to maturity and that time has seasoned after their death—I can saw most of the limbs into stove-length chunks that need no splitting, and any sections of the trunks that will not yield to maul or wedge (and elm is notoriously hard to split) take only three or four cuts with the chain saw to make into stove billets.

To speak of ripeness in dead trees may seem oxymoronic, if not a bit ghoulish. But "ripe" and "reap" come, after all, from the same root. "Ripe" means ready to reap, and for a man looking to top off his woodpile in October, a sound, standing dead elm is the image of ripeness.

# The Ice Cutter's Song

Until last winter, my only experience with an ice house was helping to empty it, not fill it. One of my summer chores at my father's sporting camp on Big Jim Pond was digging a couple of blocks out from their sawdust blanket in the camp ice house every few days to fill the ice compartment of the kitchen's big walk-in icebox. I was never there in the winter when Don Yeaton, the camp caretaker, would hire a friend to help him cut several hundred blocks and pack them away in the ice house.

But this past winter, I got a chance to catch up on what I had missed, all courtesy of our neighbor John—a man of many skills, whose first project on moving to Temple a few years ago was to build himself a compact, elegant house that he can heat with only two cords per year. Then, intent on meeting as many of his needs as possible with local resources that are carbon neutral and free for the taking, he decided to harvest ice, a reliable Maine crop that grows abundantly in Drury Pond, just a couple of hundred yards from John's dooryard.

So John kept an eye out at yard sales and antique shops for ice saws and tongs, and he built an ice house. It's much smaller than the one at Big Jim Pond because he doesn't need enough ice to cool a walk-in icebox. Then, too, his ice house is a lot tighter and better insulated, to boot.

Come a Friday night in late January, I get a call from my friend Chris. He and a few other neighbors will be helping John cut his ice, and would I care to join them? It's overcast and snowing lightly in the morning. By the time I get to the pond, Chris and John have cleared the snow off a patch of ice and scored a checkerboard of 12-by-16-inch rectangles onto it with a chain saw. Chris has already started the first cut, wielding the long ice saw with a slightly circular motion, pushing almost straight down then pulling back at an angle, forward and down, back and up, over and over. Lean, young, and tough, Chris saws away, steady and tireless as a pump on an Oklahoma oil field.

I grab the other saw and start a fresh cut. Once we have two parallel cuts the length of our checkerboard, we stab down into the scored crosswise lines with ice chisels; the blocks break off as cleanly as window glass along a scored line. Yesterday's heavy snowfall is pressing down on the ice, and the instant Chris and John punch through it to clear away the first block, water gushes up around their feet. As we yank block after block up and out, we haul more water up, making our work site wetter by the minute. So along with the slipperiness of the ice comes the lubrication of water on top of it, and yanking a hundred-pound block of ice out of the water without getting yanked back in yourself is no mean feat. I sink the tongs into the block, give it a push downward to take advantage of its buoyancy as it bounces back up to the surface, then use that momentum to slide the block up and over the lip of the ice.

By now, Luke, Steve, and Joe have arrived, filling out our crew: one of us can keep on sawing and two can pull the loose blocks out and slide them over to the trailer where another two—each using shorter tongs—team up to hoist the blocks onto the trailer for John to shove into place. When the trailer is full, John runs the load up to his yard, where he and whoever has gone along for the ride skid the blocks into the ice house on a chute, pile them up, and fill the gaps with sawdust.

At noon, we head into the house for Karen's chicken soup, homemade bread, cookies, and beer. The crew's wives and kids are all invited, too, so a crop of footgear sprouts up inside the door, jackets pile up in the stairway, and we feast amidst the voices of young and old and everyone in between.

Before we head back out to cut the last load, John regales us with his Ice Cutter's Song.

> So pull on your wool socks and union suit
> It's cold outside, but we don't give a hoot.
> Some people would say the weather ain't nice,
> but we like it best 'cause we're gonna cut ice.

The harvest for the day? One hundred and ten blocks of ice, 12-by-12-by-16 inches each, for a total of about five tons.

Lessons learned for the next ice cut: Wear knee-high rubber boots, maybe crampons, too.

# Three Tractors

I own three tractors, a number that seems excessive to me, particularly during those times when not one of them will run. They don't often strike on me all three at once, but when they do, I have to ask myself again why I don't sell the lot of them and buy a single new tractor versatile enough to meet all my rather modest needs.

A few years ago, clever friends of mine in the neighboring town of Wilton, Maine, did just that. They bought a new midsized four-wheel-drive that's big enough to plow up their sizable farmstand garden and cut a few acres of hay, but not so big that it's hard to maneuver in the woods where, as soon as the ground is frozen, they go with tire chains, a winch, and a snatch block to cut their firewood, as well as some pulpwood and sawlogs. When the snow gets too deep, they knock the logging off until the next fall and winter.

How rational! How sensible! One tractor competent in both field and forest and manufactured recently enough that it requires nothing but routine maintenance to keep running smoothly and starting on command year after year. So why don't I follow my friends' rational, sensible example?

For one thing, new tractors cost a lot of money. The purchase price on my 1940 Cletrac crawler was zero. Furthermore, it is not only an antique but also an heirloom—an inheritance from my father. I ran that tractor many a summer at his sporting camps at Big Jim Pond in northern Maine, cutting firewood; and when the camps closed in 1973, my father passed the Cletrac on to me. I've used it ever since in our woodlot here in Temple. It's the ideal tractor for my small-scale woods operations: only four feet wide and seven long, low-slung, maneuverable, and sure-footed, even in fairly heavy snow.

Unlike the Cletrac, my 1940 Ford 9N has not been part of my life for the past fifty-five years, but only a mere forty. I bought it from a neighbor soon after we moved to Temple: $1,200 for the tractor with a sickle-bar mower and a snowplow blade and harness thrown in. The 9N is a wheeled tractor, of course, but like the Cletrac its low center of gravity and small size make it stable, maneuverable, and agile. With a small trailer hitched on behind, the 9N is my tractor-for-all-chores: hauling lumber or hay bales around the place, picking up the driftwood the spring floods leave scattered over our bottomland fields. It, too, has a straight four-cylinder engine. Both the Ford and the Cletrac are simplicity and elegance incarnate. I understand four cylinders. I understand carburetors and distributors and magnetos and spark plugs. On these uncomplicated, easily accessible machines, a set of wrenches and a screwdriver are about all you need to make any repairs short of rebuilding the engine.

Only six years younger than I, my Cletrac and Ford 9N are almost my exact contemporaries. In this age, when cars and new tractors and—heaven help us—computers are way beyond my capacities to diagnose and repair, I'm grateful that my Cletrac and Ford 9N are not beyond me. We're brothers, born at the same point in technological evolution.

I have no such fraternal compliments to offer my larger, more powerful, more "modern" diesel 1980s vintage tractor, which I bought primarily for bushhogging my fields where the hardhack, tansy, goldenrod, Joe Pye weed, arrowwood, and alders were fast taking over. What I needed was a tractor with more horsepower than the Ford, as well as a transmission with a low range that would allow it to creep through the dense brush while the bush hog kept chewing away at 540 rpm. Most folks would probably think this tractor "old," too; but it's not old enough for me to cotton to, much less develop any affection for. Its wiring diagram is more complicated than the illustration of the human nervous system in *Gray's Anatomy*. Everything is so tightly packed into the engine compartment that even a small-boned contortionist couldn't get at the oil filler cap. In short, I keep the diesel on my tractor team not because I find it personally compatible, but simply because it does a job I otherwise couldn't do.

Not so with the Cletrac and 9N. They've been my faithful companions for most of my adult life, and apart from the gratitude I owe them for the help they have given me over these many years, I've just plain grown fond of them. I admire their simple, straightforward design, their ruggedness, their lack of pretension. They say to me, "Wow, I bet those guys who built me back in 1940 would be proud to know I'm still working away here in Maine in 2011."

I bet they would be, too.

# Larix Laricina

I'm not much of a collector of souvenirs, although I do have a soft spot in my heart for rocks. If I see a gorgeous specimen like the one I'm looking at here on my desk right now, I pick it up and bring it home. This one is light gray with thin blue striations running through it. I was smart enough when I got it to label it right away: "McPhayden River Trip, last camp, Aug. 16–18, 2005, Menihek Lakes, Labrador," a site memorable for the banging on pots and pans we did there to scare off a bear. But because I usually forget to label my rocks, I quickly forget where they came from, so any mnemonic, much less sentimental, value they might have had is lost.

The keepsakes I have the most of and treasure the most are photographs: a small, framed, full-face photo of my lovely Rita as a young woman, maybe in her mid- to late twenties; then, some thirty years later, she's sitting under a blossoming apple tree, a first touch of silver in her hair; our son, Greg—we have photos of him from cradle to tricycle to college to teaching English in Brazil. And of Lucy, too, our best dog ever.

But on the shelf above my desk there's room for some special items, such as the brown bear's tooth an old hunter in the Komi Republic in Russia gave us as a souvenir of our visit to his tiny village on the banks of the Vychegda River; also a Yoda figurine left over from the *Star Wars* set Greg had when he was a little guy (May the Force be with us).

On that same shelf is a small, wooden disk three to four inches in diameter, about an inch thick, and bearing this legend:

Larix Laricina
167 yrs. Approx.
55° 49'
64° 17'
July 26, 2001

Those map coordinates mark the home of this memento at the north end of a small, unnamed lake in northern Quebec where our canoe party camped en route from the Dumans River to the southern end of Mistinibi Lake. The date marks the next morning when we six paddlers woke at 5:30 a.m. to a stiff wind and a mix of rain and snow so thoroughly uninviting for canoe travel that we adjusted our rain tarps for maximum protection and hunkered down for a day of sipping hot tea and reading.

I don't recall anyone remarking how nearly impossible it was to count with the naked eye the number of growth rings packed so snugly together in the tamarack billets we gathered for firewood, but a few weeks after we had come home from our trip a padded envelope, with the return address: Hugh Stewart, Wakefield, Quebec, arrived in the mail. In it was this lovingly preserved cross-section of what was for us out there, under the lash of that wind-driven snow, just one more chunk of solid, dry, but otherwise unexceptional wood to feed our fire and keep us warm.

Hugh is a builder of classic wood-and-canvas Prospector canoes and has paddled those canoes on just about every major wilderness river in Canada from Labrador to British Columbia. In his skilled hands this little slab of wood had become more than the sum of its growth rings. He sanded both sides of it to silky smoothness, gave it three coats of varnish, then found a nearby artist who carefully lettered in the Latin name and Hugh's approximate tally of those growth rings. She painted the first layer of those letters in white paint, then went over them with black. Here and there, the white paint shows up around the edges of the letters and numbers, creating a sense of depth, light, and shade. Finally, Hugh added two more coats of glossy varnish that set the whole piece glowing and highlight those tightly packed rings that seem to orbit around a tiny pinpoint sun.

I treasure this little disk of tamarack as a memento not just of our weather-bound layover day but of our whole trip, starting on Lac Leif and ending about 290 miles later at Kangiqsualujjuaq on Ungava Bay. I treasure it not as a curio but as a blending of craft and nature, in which a long life is at once visible as a whole and, if you look closely, in considerable detail as well. It's a record of this small tree's mostly lean years in its early decades but then some expansive ones in its final years where the growth rings can be separated by as much as a thirty-second of an inch.

If it were not for Hugh's eye that was sharp enough to see and appreciate the miracle of this tree's life and if it were not for his art that enabled him to capture what he saw for the rest of us to see, the record of that one tamarack's 167 years would have gone up in smoke.

Stop, look, pay attention, this keepsake tells me, and, grateful for that gentle reminder, I mean to keep this keepsake close to hand.

# Survey

During our first couple of years here in Temple, I felt fairly confident that I knew what the property lines of this essentially rectangular old Maine farmstead were. On the west side, an intact stone wall ran along our entire boundary. To the east, remnants of a stone wall interspersed with shreds of rusty barbed wire marked the line, and Howard Mitchell's mature pine plantation to the north made clear where our hayfield ended and Howard's land began. On our south side, only short, scattered runs of stone wall remained, but they were still adequate to orient ourselves by.

Four years after we had settled in, however, when we bought an adjacent lot on our south side, the vagueness of the deed regarding the length or bearing of any of this lot's lines ("beginning at the south-easterly corner of land now or formerly of John Doe, thence northerly along said land of Doe to a point . . ."), and the lack of any obvious markers on the land, left me with only a foggy sense of where the new lot's south line might be.

The need to have exact knowledge of it emerged only thirty-five years later, when a logger planning to do a cut on our southerly neighbor's land asked me to walk the line with him. Unable to supply the clarity he and I needed at the moment and wanting that clarity for the sake of posterity as well, I called on my surveyor friend Creston Gaither and volunteered right away to be his gofer for the project.

I've always felt great admiration for the skills of surveyors, those men and women who can lay out where the next road cut should go or determine whether the Joneses' neighbors did in fact build their fence on the Joneses' property and will now be obliged to move it. I've also felt no little envy for the surveyors who got the job of scrambling over mountaintops and slogging through swamps to lay out the township

**110**

lines in Maine's great north woods, and who are still called upon to keep the blazes on those lines clear today.

Our project, I knew, would not be that adventuresome, but I was sure it would be instructive and eye-opening. I had originally thought I would have a go at producing the title flowcharts for our place, but just a few hours of work in the Franklin County Registry of Deeds quickly disabused me of that idea. Unraveling the tangled chain of previous sales and resales of fragments of our land in records that went back as far as the early 1800s was way over my head, and I handed that part of the job back to Creston, who needed some thirty hours to finish it.

Then, when we went out onto the land, I realized I had to look more sharply than ever before if I hoped to find clues to a property line now invisible to the casual eye. It's reported of the Zen master Ikkyu that when asked by a visitor to write down a distillation of the highest wisdom, Ikkyu wrote one word: Attention.

Not satisfied with the brevity of this reply, the visitor asked, "Is that all?"

Whereupon Ikkyu wrote down two words: Attention. Attention.

Doubled, if not tripled, attention was what we needed as we searched for ancient blazes not yet totally grown over and for tiny fragments of barbed wire sticking out of one tree here, another there. This kind of minute scrutiny, combined with determining lot line distances and bearings with Creston's GPS equipment, proved instructive and eye opening indeed. We discovered, first of all, that the southerly line of the lot Rita and I had bought those many years ago did not run west in a straight line from our new southeast corner down to Temple Stream, but made a right-angle turn to the south before it ended on a horseshoe bend in the stream, which meant that a few acres I had thought we owned belonged in fact to our neighbor. That was just the kind of clarification this whole exercise was meant to provide and therefore didn't strike me as an unwanted surprise at all.

Some ten years later now, I occasionally take down from the shelf the final plan Creston drew for us. I find it a joy to behold, not only for its precision in visual detail and in its explanatory notes but also because looking at it recalls for me an important insight that occurred to me during the surveying process: I realized—despite the endless exploring of our place I had done over the years—that I was still a gray-haired schoolboy just beginning to discover the treasures this patch of Maine woods and fields held. If I had learned that much by carefully tracing our land's actual boundaries, how much more might I learn by walking every last square inch of our place, alert to everything I may have seen before but not taken in, every rock, tree, and shrub, every leaf, blossom, and bird, each one deserving every bit of my attention.

# The One That Got Away

About twenty years ago, when my wife, Rita, and I were still renovating our Maine farmhouse, we did much of our refurbishing with materials scrounged from old buildings that were falling to the wrecker. So it is that our house is now clad in clapboards I carefully peeled off the doomed corn cannery in Farmington, and the door to our living room is a castoff from Grant's Kennebago Camps, which were undergoing some major remodeling at that time.

I confess to an infatuation with that door. That it came from Grant's—one of the oldest, most revered trout-fishing camps in the Rangeley Lakes region, in all of Maine, and indeed in the entire United States—was, of course, enough to give it the status of an icon in any fly fisherman's eyes. The door's outward aspect, though, could hardly stir the heart. The door was painted a dull gray and had stenciled on it in black paint, at about eye height, the number 8. Dull gray was not the color either Rita or I would have chosen for our living room door, but our tastes at the time ran to the funky, and it seemed sacrilegious to alter a relic from Grant's, an act as blasphemous, I thought, as using splinters of the True Cross for kindling.

Soon after the door was installed, the latch mechanism in it broke, leaving the knob to spin ineffectually in the hand and the door impossible to open unless we resorted to the thief's trick of inserting a putty knife (we didn't even own a credit card) to push back the bolt. I removed the latch and never replaced it. Two generations of dogs and cats have rejoiced in having one door in the house they could open with a nudge.

But after twenty years of noses, paws, and human hands, the gray of our door had progressed from solemn to downright dingy. Cleanliness now seemed preferable to funkiness, and with time feeling more precious to us than money, we delegated the refinishing of the door to our friend Carol.

She laid the door over two sawhorses in the woodshed and attacked the gray paint with Zip-Strip. I was outside, scything down the meadowsweet, dogbane, and raspberries that seemed determined every summer to reclaim our yard and garden, when Carol called out. "Bob, I think you'll be interested in this," she said. "Come see."

Carol's scraper had peeled away the chemical muck to reveal the muted, mellow grain of poplar, which at first glance was all I noticed. But on second glance I saw the pencil outline of a fish on the center rail of the door. The tail of the fish was square—a *brook trout*. The rail in the door measures twenty-one inches long by seven inches wide, and the outline of the fish filled it completely. What would a deep-bellied squaretail that long weigh? Five, six, eight pounds? Did it matter? Even in its bare outline it was beautiful. It was magnificent.

On the right-hand stile was more: a drawing of a man standing waist-deep in the water, fly rod in hand, the rod arched, the line taut. And under this drawing were some barely decipherable names and dates:

| | |
|---|---|
| *Thos. G. Sandland* | *William S. Barret* |
| *N. Auburn, Mass.* | *Aug. 17, 1879* |
| *May 1, 1879* | |
| *May 4, 1880* | |
| *J. A. Haskell* | *A. Atwood* |
| *Mrs. J. A. Haskell* | *June 7, 1878* |
| *July 18–25, '78* | |

I stood there marveling at this piece of history I'd been living with for the past twenty years but was seeing now for the first time. I realized that our nondescript gray door had to have seen service in the Kennebago Lake House, which was built in 1871 and didn't come under Ed Grant's management until 1904. I was looking at a pre–Ed Grant trout, a trout from a mythic past before the name "Grant's Kennebago Camps" even existed. I felt like Schliemann excavating Troy.

Who, if any, of the five people whose names I was reading had caught the fish? I was rooting for Mrs. J. A. Haskell, whom I fantasized as a lean, tough woman of about thirty-five with green eyes, good cheekbones, and a delicate touch with a fly rod.

I was also reveling in the prospect of having this treasure preserved in our living room under a fresh coat of varnish. This ghost from the past gave me more pleasure than any taxidermied monster mounted on a board ever could. But even in the few seconds it took for these thoughts to spin through my head, I noticed my specter fish becoming more spectral. The remaining Zip-Strip was eating away at him, at the angler with the tight line, at Mrs. J. A. Haskell.

"Oh, my God," I said to Carol. "We're losing him. Get the net. How do you stop this stuff?"

Carol mopped up what stripper she could with clean rags. I ran into the house for some water. We flushed the afflicted area. We wiped it clean. We flushed and wiped again and still again. In vain. The paint remover had penetrated too far to be reversed. It had done its work well. The fish was gone without a trace. So was Mrs. J. A. Haskell, the most ethereal crush of my entire crush-filled life.

\*\*\*

My Kennebago camp-door trout, for as long as it lasted, was a pentimento. Pentimenti are what art historians call the sketches that an artist paints over that resurface in an old oil painting if the covering pigments fade. El Greco's *Laocoon* in the National Gallery sports a disembodied head that the master painted over and put on a full-length figure farther to the left. Rembrandt's *Flora* in the Metropolitan wears a hat with two brims.

Scholars used to have to wait until time (or a restorer's overly zealous cleaning) brought these ghost imagews to light. Today, with X-radiography and infrared reflectography, they don't have to wait. With Superman's X-ray vision they can peer through a painting's surface and study the creative process from underdrawing to ground preparation to floating heads and duplicate hat brims.

On our art we had used Zip-Strip, a far cruder tool, which, in practically the same moment, let a wondrous beast rise into our present, then sink back into the depths of the past. In practically the same moment, we were exultant and downcast; we celebrated and mourned.

Now, whenever I sit in my living room and look at that poplar door, beautiful for its color and grain but minus its fish, I muse on images captured and lost. I delight in the photographs we have that recall what Rita, my only permanent crush, looked like twenty-five years ago—how she wore her hair, the big wool sweater she had then that is no more. I rejoice in the pictures of our son, Greg, when he was a week old, and a year, and five years, and ten, and twelve, and twenty. I ache for the pictures neither I nor anyone else took: Rita in her stunning black cocktail dress that also is no more; Greg at seven sliding down a steep, narrow road with all the unselfconscious skill and confidence of the invulnerable, invincible young. The pentimenti of memory rise to the surface, swirl there momentarily, and fade again. Even the images we think we have captured on film or in oil or watercolors are in fact not much more than a fading pencil outline of the living creature, the living moment. Carpe diem. Seize the day.

# The Weather

Talking about the weather is supposedly the height of dopiness, a display of intellectual poverty so extreme that it evokes neither pity nor contempt from those exposed to it, but only embarrassment and a desire to escape. If you can't think of anything better to talk about than the weather, the conventional wisdom says, then hold your peace. Just shut up.

I do not agree. I've always loved conversations about the weather—weather present, weather past, weather future. I'm particularly fond of our upcountry Maine weather, so I like to brag about it any chance I get, even though I can't take the least bit of credit for it.

What spectacular weather we had, for instance, on February 7, 2013, a brilliant, bracingly cool (12°F) but not bitterly cold winter day, with the sunlight booming down out of a sky as blue as a sky can be and fading to a lighter, paler cornflower blue around the horizon. A couple of fat gray squirrels reveled in the warmth of the sun as they lunched on sunflower seeds the birds had let fall from our feeder. In the Temple post office I found general agreement that this was a nippy day, but one whose nippiness in no way detracted from its beauty and the sense of well-being it inspired in humans and gray squirrels alike.

But then, Nemo, the Blizzard of 2013, moved in for the next two days, just as the meteorologists told us it would, giving us about seventy-two hours of more blowing than snowing. The official snowfall, measured right next door to us in Farmington, was a mere 9.2 inches. Given the wind, however, those 9.2 inches translated into only 4 in our driveway but 32 right outside our kitchen door. On Sunday, February 10, we went right back into another halcyon day as sunny, windstill, and sweet as the Thursday before.

Now I know that halcyon days—if you chase "halcyon" back to its origin in Greek mythology—can apply only to those days in midwinter when Aeolus, the god in charge of the winds, reins them in and calms the waves so that his daughter, Alcyone, whom the gods transformed into a kingfisher, can safely build her nest and lay her eggs on the shore. But what I find so remarkable about our local weather is its ability to produce halcyon days year round: sunny Indian summer days when the air is crisp and clean, spring days when the hills first start greening up, even midsummer days when the humidity lifts and you think you could reach up and touch the top of the sky. Halcyon days—whether they come winter or summer, spring, or fall—are days of calm; days when we may be busy but are unhurried, content and carefree; days when all feels right with the world.

None of this should come as a surprise. All of Maine is right in the middle of the northern temperate zone, but our little region is even more middling than the rest of the state. We're smack-dab on the forty-fifth parallel, midway between the North Pole and the equator. We're sixty miles from the Canadian border and sixty miles from the Atlantic coast. We do get occasional inklings of the Arctic in winter (-39°F) and the tropics in summer (101°F), but most of the time we're a model of moderation, as middle of the weather road as you can get.

Our location does not, of course, make us immune to weather disasters—witness the hurricane of 1938, the April Fools' Day flood of 1987 that swallowed houses and bridges in one gulp, and the ice storm of 1998 that may well hold the record for property damage statewide. Still, events that devastate coastal New England with hurricane-force winds and storm surges often just sideswipe us as they pass by. So it was with Nemo; so it was with Irene in 2011 and Sandy in 2012.

But getting off light is no cause for full-scale rejoicing if the homes of your friends only twenty or fifty or two hundred miles down the road are getting torn off their foundations. And when, in a span of two years, we've had two hurricanes, a record-setting blizzard, and a fluky warm winter visit our region, even the most sanguine weather observer has to sit up and take notice.

Then, too, the animals have more and more to say about our weather every year: the northward march of ticks, the squadrons of turkey vultures circling in our skies, the tufted titmice and the red-bellied woodpeckers at our bird feeders, the New Hampshire bears that have given up hibernating. As a Koyukon elder once said to anthropologist Richard Nelson, "Every animal knows way more than you do."

# Saint John Memories

Vladimir Nabokov wrote a book called *Speak, Memory*, and as I recall, his memory spoke of his childhood and youth in minute detail and with an authority that took my breath away.

If I ask my memory to speak, I sometimes get utter silence and sometimes vivid recollections that prove delusional when held up against indisputable facts or the memories of family or friends who have visited the same places or shared the same experiences. The portion of my aging brain dedicated to memory I picture as a filing cabinet filled with millions of overstuffed folders, many of them bearing unhelpful labels like "Miscellaneous Miscellany" or "Random Notes on Various Subjects."

But when I reached for my mental Saint John River folder, I felt as confident as Nabokov. After all, how many times had I paddled that river? Six? Seven? Eight? So when my canoe-tripping friends from Vermont suggested an excursion there this past spring, I was keen to go, and even though I hadn't been back for several years (at least ten—well, maybe more like twelve or fifteen), I could still see the river unfolding, mile by mile, before my mind's eye. The Saint John is not just imprinted on my brain, I thought; it's engraved there.

Our shuttle driver dropped us off at Baker Lake, the usual put-in point for the 105-mile run down to the takeout in Allagash Village. Under a bright noonday sun, we grabbed a quick lunch, loaded our gear into the boats, and were off, the six of us: Al and Wendy, Dave and Ann, all from Vermont; Jerry and me from Maine.

I was gratified at first to see the river behaving just the way my memory said it should: a few miles of easy rapids just below the outlet from Baker Lake, then—for the next ten miles or so, before we pulled ashore to camp at Morrison Depot—pretty much flatwater through low-lying land.

When we set off the next morning, about ten o'clock, having waited for a heavy early morning rain to let up into a less forbidding drizzle, we were soon in a winding, wriggling stretch of the river, and I told Jerry about three times that around the very next bend we would be at the confluence where the Southwest Branch of the Saint John meets the Baker Branch we were on. When that confluence failed to appear after the next bend and the next, I said to Dave, "It's taking us a lot longer to get to the Southwest Branch than I thought it would."

"We passed it about half an hour ago," he said.

And so it went for the rest of the trip. Major landmarks like the remaining abutments from the old Nine-Mile Bridge and the unmistakable Seven Islands archipelago I recognized, but most stretches of river in between I might as well have never seen at all. My most recent memory of the approach to the Southwest Branch confluence was of picking my way slowly and carefully down a shallow, riffly bend with barely enough water in it to float my boat. This time, I soared around that bend and on downstream so effortlessly I didn't even notice I'd been there. If ever there was a river that proves Heraclitus's pronouncement that you never step into—or never paddle—the same river twice, that river is the Saint John, notorious for its rapidly rising and falling water levels.

But once I'd realized the folly of trying to make my flawed memories of the Saint John match up with its reality, I could rejoice in the river in the here and now. At a log cabin at Ledge Rapids, a windstorm had blown down a huge white pine standing close to the camp. Miraculously, the falling tree had just nicked the camp roof, tearing off only a few shingles over the eaves. We spent a bitterly cold and windy day in the comfort of that camp watching mid-May snow flurries blow horizontally down the river, and we weren't the only travelers who'd found refuge there from the cold and snow. Looking through a side window, we saw just a few feet away from us a yellow-rumped, a Blackburnian, and a Canada warbler sheltering in the thickly needled branches of that downed pine.

Two days later, when all five of my companions decided they'd enjoy a little nap after we'd finished our lunch at the Ouellette Farm campsite, I wandered the riverbank where spring flooding had left immense snow and ice blocks piled up at least twice my height, and where sun, rain, and wind had continued to work them into shapes any sculptor would envy, both for their conception and their execution: fanciful yet solid, blending the massive and the delicate slabs of ice and snowpack alternating in layers reminiscent of stratified rock. In mid-May, they still seemed as enduring as the Pyramids, but in a couple of weeks they'd be gone, high art wiped away by the barbarous late-spring sun.

What a lark it was to see this old friend of a river with a fresh eye. Stop worrying about what you've forgotten, it told me, and seize this day. But then there was one memory that didn't fail me. I remembered that paddling with my friends Jerry, Al, Wendy, Dave, and Ann was just as much fun as it had always been every time before—I was spot on about that.

# Our Butterfly Net

J ust about any wild creature either injured or in danger rouses the Good Samaritan in me. The victim need not be furry or feathery, though birds and mammals in need of first aid or rescue do turn up, but then so do spiders, daddy longlegs, turtles, snakes, and salamanders. On rainy spring nights, droves of spotted salamanders risk their lives crossing roads on the way to their breeding pools. I seize any chance I get to carry as many as I can across those killing fields. Female turtles, also driven by reproductive urgings, will often cross roads in search of good nesting sites to lay their eggs, and those pilgrims, too, I pick up and deposit well out of harm's way on the side of the road they've been heading for.

It's not, of course, just the slow-footed turtles or the herds of salamanders that are endangered on our roads. Nor, among mammals, is it just the waddling porcupines and skunks that get hit. It's the agile and fleet of foot as well: the squirrels, both gray and red, that wind up flattened on the pavement, not to mention the white-tailed deer whose carcasses have become all too common a sight alongside our superhighways. I even had a saw-whet owl collide with my windshield.

Now that I think about it, the situations that move me to rescue injured or imperiled animals are not ones that occur in nature's normal course of things. If I were to see a red fox dive through the snow and come up with a vole, I wouldn't rush to the scene and try to persuade the fox to spare that innocent rodent and find something else for lunch. Foxes' eating small mammals is an arrangement finely tuned by millennia of evolution. It's when animals minding their own business get in trouble by tangling with the works of humankind, such as roads, that I feel compelled to step in.

123

Here's another example: I recently helped a dear friend and neighbor get rid of a gray squirrel that had climbed into the top of her Metalbestos chimney and—gravity being what it is—wound up on display behind the glass door of her heater stove. A squirrel at the bottom of a metal chimney is as helpless as a spider in a bathtub: both are held captive by walls too slippery to climb. Lacking an arm-length gauntlet impervious to squirrel teeth, I was reluctant to reach into the stove and grab our captive, who was in a rotten mood and as eager to be gone as we were eager to see him go. Unable to think of any better way to be rid of him, we opened all the downstairs doors that gave access to the outside then opened the stove door.

Our squirrel, trailing a plume of gray ash and leaving pawprints, went nearly everywhere: up and down two sets of curtains, through and around some potted plants, down on the floor, and up on the sofa with us closing in on him and trying to herd him toward the open front door. I have to give him credit: He took the hint and was out that door in a matter of minutes.

At my own place, most of my rescues have been of birds knocked out after colliding with our windows or the sides of the house. If these birds haven't broken their necks or sustained any major injury, there is always a chance they'll recover. I put them in a well-ventilated cardboard box and leave them alone in a quiet corner. When I check back after a few hours, I find, more often than not, a chickadee or sparrow ready to fly off from my hand. For birds that are injured, we're fortunate to have a bird rehabilitator in nearby Farmington.

Instead of running into buildings, wayward birds will sometimes fly inside them through open doors. We see this happen fairly often in the fall, when we're bringing our winter's firewood into the space in our ell that used to serve as a carriage house. Instead of turning around and going back out through the wide-open, barn-sized doors they used to come in, birds will fly from one window to another, growing more frantic with each failed attempt to escape.

This past fall, after trying several times to catch just such a panicked chickadee in my hands, I remembered the butterfly net we've had standing unused in our ell for years. Equipped with our net, I was able to catch that bird and release it outside in no time and with minimal distress to both it and me.

So even if you've never harbored ambitions as a lepidopterist, I can recommend a butterfly net for small-bird rescues. And a long-handled fisherman's net might be just the thing, too, for scooping up any gray squirrels you find running loose in your living room.

# A Legacy Maple

It's about three feet in diameter at breast height. At eighty feet tall or so, it towers above the standing-seam roof of our one-and-a-half story Cape. This is no sugarbush maple tucked in among its neighbors, standing straight and nearly limbless for much of its height. It's a yard maple that grew up with all the light and space in the world to spread out in. Its huge lower limbs reach out for a few feet, then swoop upward in graceful arcs, looking, in winter, like the arms of a huge asymmetrical candelabra. In the spring of good seed years, the abundance of yellow flowers makes the tree glow with its own soft light, an arboreal candelabra after all. And in October . . . well, no need to tell you how brilliantly it lights up then.

This maple is a thing of beauty, a blessing on our lives year round, and if that were all it was, it would be worth its keep many times over. But it has its utilitarian side as well. All the neighborhood chickadees perch on its branches to wait their turns at our nearby bird feeders. In the summer, its far-reaching limbs spread a green canopy over most of our roof, keeping the house blissfully cool without benefit of air conditioning.

For all the comfort and joy this tree has provided us we are probably indebted to Dana Hamlin, who lived and farmed on this place from 1902 to 1968. Probably, I say, because we have as yet been unable to find any written record of when this maple was planted and by whom, and though we were lucky enough to know Dana, who died in 1980, we never had wits enough to ask whether he had planted this tree or whether it was already in its infancy when he and his wife bought the farm from her parents. Going on the testimony of Dana's grandson, Don, who remembers it as still a young tree of perhaps fifteen or twenty years in the late 1930s, we give the nod to Dana both because the timing seems about right and, more importantly, because we loved Dana and want to believe this tree came to us from his hands.

As Keats famously told us, "A thing of beauty is a joy forever: / Its loveliness increases; it will never / Pass into nothingness . . ." I like to think that sentiment is, in some absolute sense, true, but at the same time I have to acknowledge that Dana's maple, however beautiful it may be, is as mortal as any other living thing. Because Dana lived to be a hundred, we're hopeful that some of his genes for longevity rubbed off on this maple, but even if they did, our tree is surely pushing a hundred itself, if not already past that mark. The piety due our elders is reason enough to lavish some loving care on it, but because this tree stands only seven feet away from the front of our house and extends the tonnage as well as the shade of its limbs over our roof, practicality and self-preservation call for preventive maintenance.

So every once in a while, my friend Alan comes over with his arborist's gear—a lightweight chain saw, hand saws, climbing harnesses, and an outsized slingshot we use to fire a light throw line into a treetop and then haul a heavier climbing rope after it. Soon we're swinging about like Tarzan, pruning away any deadwood we find, cleaning out crevices, poking and prodding for signs of decay or weakness.

So far, Dana's maple seems to be holding its own. But guardedly optimistic as I am about its being with us for several more years, I can't help but recall an article ("The Yard Maple") in the Winter 2007 issue of *Northern Woodlands* in which Stephen Morris described how maples "start breaking apart in chunks when they reach a certain age, how they die from the center out." Just this past December, we witnessed a vivid demonstration of Morris's point: A heavy windstorm ripped through the big maple that stands in front of the Temple Historical Society's little red schoolhouse headquarters half a mile up the road from us, tearing away the tree's crown and, with it, a huge slab of the inwardly decaying trunk.

That tree could be the twin of Dana's, so we'll be watching carefully for intimations of mortality, hoping they will not become so severe that we will have to bring this tall tree low. Against that day, we planted ten years ago a young maple that will eventually succeed Dana's. Our regret, of course, is that we didn't plant it thirty years ago, that we'll most likely be leaving to our successors a mere stripling of a tree, not another mature maple in all its glory. But then maybe Dana felt similar doubts. Planting a tree is an act of faith, and look how well Dana's act turned out, how much delight he must have taken in this maple, and how much he left to us in his legacy tree. We can only wish the same for ours.

# A Dog's Life

As a lifelong word watcher, I'm well aware that the sands of language are continually shifting under our feet, but I was surprised to learn a few days ago that what I thought to be a rock-solid idiom is undergoing just such a shift. From at least the sixteenth century on, "a dog's life" has meant a life of misery: subservience to abusive human masters, a wretched hovel that's boiling hot in the summer and blood-freezing cold in the winter, a diet of meager table scraps, curses, and kicks. But now—with supermarkets stocking quarter-mile-long aisles of canine gravies and kibbles and krunchies and with pooches sleeping on memory foam dog beds from L.L. Bean snugged up to the family hearth—more and more dogs are living higher on the hog than ever before.

I should have known this change in dogs' lives was going on because Rita and I have been doing our best for decades to spoil any dog who's come within our reach. We've done so without ulterior motive, but we have sometimes remarked that if we could offer nothing else to St. Peter to justify our admission at the pearly gates, we could at least say we've provided a good home for several stray dogs and cats, not to mention a few score sheep and chickens that also enjoyed blissful lives in the open air and sunshine of our home (before we killed them and ate them).

But we are pikers compared with my friend Wes, a Maine poet of no little distinction, and his wife, Diane. We have succored dogs who came to us; Wes and Diane have gone far afield in search of the homeless. Six years ago on a Saturday morning in December, they appeared at our house to introduce us to Gus, a young Australian shepherd and maybe black Lab or Newfoundland mix whom they found at a dog-rescue organization in Arkansas. A puppy on the verge of adolescence, Gus was long-haired and black but also with multi-shaded mottling, the incarnation of Hopkins's line "Glory be to God for dappled things." Gus licked our hands, offered his floppy ears for scratching, let us know he was more than ready to be our pal. We were smitten.

Then, when it became clear that Gus would lavish most of his love on Wes, Diane went back to the Arkansas rescue folks to get a dog that would be hers. She found Rosie, whose naturally bobbed tail also indicated partial Australian shepherd parentage but whose pointed ears and white, short-haired coat touched with a golden patina could imply anything from part-husky to part–golden retriever and anything else in between.

Gus has shed his mottling and grown into a burly, galumphing, pitch-black bear of a dog. He plays the charging linebacker to Rosie's broken-field runner as the two of them chase each other endlessly through the woods around Wes and Diane's summer camp on Drury Pond here in Temple. Though Gus and Rosie have never said as much, it's clear from their behavior that this camp and this pond are their idea of heaven on earth. Knowing this, Wes sees to it that they have as much time here as possible. As soon as the dirt road to the pond is open in the spring and the ice has gone out, he brings the dogs into camp and tosses sticks into the water as tirelessly as Gus and Rosie will dive in to fetch them. Later, when the water has warmed up and Wes and Diane are staying full-time at the camp, the dogs follow Wes on his daily swim, their three heads—one human, two canine—carving a long loop up along the east shore of the pond, then circling back to the dock.

Whenever Rita and I go to join them for a late afternoon swim and an occasional beer afterwards, Gus and Rosie race up the path barking wildly and go into full-body wagging once they meet up with us, Gus often adding his special howl—not a howl of pain or anger but a wolf song of greeting, "Owoooooooooo, we've got company!" Then they both run off in search of sticks for us to throw for them.

But idyllic as life at camp is, it is not twenty-four-hour fun and games. Everybody has to eat and sleep, do the dishes, sweep the floor, fix leaky faucets, reshingle the roof. Then, too, Wes has as many—if not more—commitments, both familial and professional, as the rest of us. Though high on his list of loves, his dogs are not the sole objects of his devotion. Every morning he heads up to his writing cabin in the woods a short way back from the shore of the pond. That's okay with Gus and Rosie. They don't begrudge him his writing time. They curl up on the rug near his desk and nap. They know that the generous kind of poems Wes writes and the generous kind of guy he is are the reasons why their lives are just the way a dog's life ought to be.

# Remote Ponds, Wild Trout

Maine's Land Use Regulation Commission—the agency responsible for overseeing the roughly ten million acres of timberland commonly referred to as Maine's wildlands—has classified as "Remote Ponds" 177 of the state's 1,104 lakes. Remoteness ranks high with me, so if I'm told a pond is remote, I perk up my ears and start planning when I can go take a look at said pond.

But before any of us get too excited about this venture, expecting an expedition into some wilderness paradise, we'd better keep in mind that this is Maine, not Alaska or Labrador or the Northwest Territories. Given that Maine's wildlands are laced through and through with about thirty thousand miles of logging roads, remoteness is a relative term here. To qualify as remote, a pond has to be only a half-mile away from access with a two-wheel-drive vehicle. Half a mile from where you can park your Ford Taurus does not strike me as particularly remote. Still, many remote ponds do more than meet the minimal distance requirement, and to get to them, you have to bushwhack for a lot more than half a mile.

But two other criteria also apply to remote ponds: they may not have more than one non-commercial camp on them, and they must support a cold-water fishery. In twenty-seven of the state's remote ponds, the Commission has rated those fisheries as "outstanding." When Judgment Day arrives, I do not want to have listed among my sins of omission that I had not wet a line in each of those twenty-seven ponds. So late this past August, realizing that the summer was fast slipping away and I had not yet this season made my way to a new remote pond, I picked one out from the magic twenty-seven and called my friend Steve.

"I know it's August," I said, "and I know neither of us has time for an overnight, so we'll miss the evening and early morning fishing . . . and I know the nearest woods road is well over a mile away from the pond and there's no trail on the map and it's all uphill . . . and I know it's highly unlikely we'll catch any fish in there at high noon. Doesn't it sound great? How can you possibly resist this invitation?"

"I can't," he said. "I'll pick you up about seven in the morning."

We drove to the end of the pavement and navigated our way through a labyrinth of woods roads to the torn-out bridge that had once crossed the outlet stream from our chosen pond. There we began our uphill thrash in and out of the stream gully, into and out of old cuttings and raspberry patches, on and off skid trails, until, topping the hill, we entered uncut woods and soon spotted the glint of water through the trees.

Even if just reaching this pond had been all we accomplished, the day would have been well spent. Fish or no fish, I love popping out of the woods onto the shores of these sweet little ten- or fifteen-acre ponds tucked into the hills, this one with the dome of a mountain covered with black growth rising up behind it into a blue summer sky. The breeze keeping fair-weather clouds on the move overhead was just barely riffling the surface of this sheltered pond.

Densely wooded as the shores of these ponds are, they make it next to impossible for a fly fisherman to make a cast unless he has some way to get out onto the water. We had a small pack canoe on the roof of Steve's four-wheel-drive but had decided to leave it there until we had found out how rough the portage in would be. Then, too, at a surprising number of remote ponds, there will be a battered but still seaworthy canoe or little john boat snugged away in the brush somewhere, courtesy of a fellow fisherman who had either carried it in or skidded it in over the snow in some winter past.

To our delight, we found a hogged but watertight fiberglass canoe and a couple of paddles just a third of the way around the pond from where we had first come onto its shore. It was eleven o'clock by now; but, undaunted, we set up our rods and were soon out on the pond, casting bucktails into some fishy-looking lies next to downed trees and overhangs along the shore.

I missed my first strike but not the second one, a scrappy ten-inch brookie, brilliant with jewel-like color in the midday sun. I released him, and within minutes, Steve caught and released another.

That was the end of the action but not of the joy of discovery this day had given us.

"You know," Steve said, as we settled down on the shore to eat our lunch, "what we have to do is come back here for an overnight in the spring."

"Amen," I said, already picturing the surface of this pond dimpled with trout rising in the fading light of a long June evening.

# Northern Jungle

Last summer was downright sodden here in western Maine. When it wasn't raining, it was hot—not dry hot but wet hot: humid, tropical, sticky, sweltering. Stuff grew and grew. Bottomland ostrich fern and tansy shot up tall as I am, not that I'm all that tall, but still. Joe Pye weed went way over my head. Branches of a young red maple that had been reaching out to grab our clothesline for the last couple of years finally got hold of it. Rita, for the first time in her life, hired some help to battle weeds in the garden. The water in Temple Stream never got low enough that I could take a tractor across the ford and bushhog our back field.

Indoors was nearly as wet as out. The white and green heads of strike-anywhere matches in our kitchen match holder got so mushy they turned into strike-nowhere matches. The humidity's all-present tongue licked the flap of every envelope we owned and left it glued shut. If I wanted to mail a letter, I had to pry an envelope open with my pocket knife (yes, I still send some letters by U.S. Mail) and then reseal it with transparent tape.

Hot, drenched summers like this last one often moved my father to call our forested corner of Maine "the northern jungle." Plants ranging from molds to mighty oaks thrive in that kind of weather. Something there is in the rain-and-sun-driven surge of summer vegetation that doesn't love the works of man. "Get the hell out of our way," it says. "We were here first. You want to grow your potatoes and carrots and peas in this 50×50-foot plot you've cleared? Fine. It will cost you eternal vigilance. You can weed and mulch and cover crop this patch of dirt all you like, but leave it alone for as little as a year, and you'll be lucky if you can find it again the spring after that."

How little time it takes for alders to close in on a neglected hayfield and shrink it out of existence, how little time for fir seedlings to grow in so thickly on an old woods road that it's easier to walk on either side of it than on it.

And buildings, wooden ones? They fare no better. Alternately soaked and baked, their paint blisters, flakes, and peels; their clapboards once spanking white are soon a weathered gray, soon shrinking and curling, soon hanging from a last rusty nail.

Subarctic winters inevitably follow these seemingly equatorial summers. Roofs left unshoveled—buried hip deep, waist deep in snow— cave in under one too many March storms. The upstairs then the downstairs floors rot; the walls fold in to the center. What once was a house is soon a tangle of splintered rafters, studs, shingles, and sheathing. In far less than a man or woman's short lifetime, nature can chew an abandoned building up, spit it out, and leave nothing but the rock foundation behind.

A year or two ago, I went to revisit a small two-bunk tar paper camp that my old friend and woods mentor, Don, had built decades ago as a layover shelter at the far end of his winter trapline up near the Canadian border. I didn't expect to find it in tiptop shape. It had not been built for the ages, and I hadn't been back to it for at least one of those decades. I did, though, expect to find it. But when I reached the northeast corner of the pond where I could have sworn the camp had been, it wasn't there. I'm old enough to know that memory is not always to be trusted, so I made a complete circuit of the pond but had no better luck.

Back where I had first thought the camp to have been, I drew a mental grid back from the shore of the pond; and feeling a bit like an amateur archaeologist, I started walking its lines, looking for a rusted-out bucket or stove lid, probing the ground with a stick for shards of wood or tar paper.

Halfway through my sixth or seventh traverse, the ground under my feet didn't feel quite like the forest floor. It sagged slightly under my weight and rebounded when I backed off. A little scraping with my stick revealed a span of tar paper and disintegrating boards, whether roof or wall I couldn't tell, nor did that matter. I was glad to have found the camp's remains, sad to know this fragile little structure where Don had found warmth and shelter on many a sub-zero winter night was no more.

So be it. This ravenous land with its crushing snows and jungle summers may be bent on taking down whatever we put up, but it's also those cycles of decay and lush new growth that give us our bumper crops of raspberries and keep the trees growing up toward the sky. Not such a bad trade-off after all.

# String Fever

If you want to get a seat at the Annual String Celebration presented by the music department of School Administrative District Number 9 in Farmington, Maine, you have to get to the Mount Blue High School gym early. Show time is 7:00 p.m., but by 6:30 the parking lot and the bleachers are already crowded. No, this is not a championship playoff game in Class B basketball. No, the Grateful Dead are not putting in an appearance. There isn't even any marching or drums or trumpets or trombones at this annual rite. This is a *string* concert. And if you think a school string concert has to be a rather sad event at which a few brave and dedicated kids scratch out a little Mozart to an auditorium empty of all but their brave and dedicated parents, think again.

For one evening every March, this place literally teems with music lovers—the gym floor with the students who play, the bleachers with the friends and relatives who come to hear them. About ten days before the event, string teachers Karen McCann and Monica Valentine send a memo home with their students that says, in part, "Mark the date of the celebration on your calendar and tell all relatives to come." To say that everybody and his grandmother attends the concert is to report a fact, not employ a figure of speech. This year, my neighbor Roy Darlington, who has a good eye for estimating crowds, estimated, "Twelve hundred at least, maybe more."

The musicians begin drifting in at about six o'clock. This year there were 370 of them—violinists, violists, cellists, bassists—ranging in age from five to sixty-two. The great majority of them are students, grades four through twelve, enrolled in the School Administrative District 9 string program. But this is also a regionwide community event that welcomes string students from neighboring districts as well as the ones too young or too old to be in any school program.

As performers arrive, parent volunteers route them into the caf-
eteria where they pick up and pin on ribbons representing their level
of achievement. The ribbons aren't "prizes" the students have won in
competition with one another. They simply reflect the degree of profi-
ciency that each student has reached, and the great genius of the string
celebration is that it has a place for all players wherever in their development they are. It would be hard to imagine a sweeter blend of art and
democracy.

The gym floor is filled with two banks of folding chairs set up facing each other across the center line. To the right are levels 1–5; to the
left, levels 6–10. Students wend their way among the chairs, finding
their proper sections, settling into their seats, tuning instruments, rosin-
ing bows.

Sitting over in level 6 this year, looking utterly at home in the company of his grade-school cohorts, was Bob James, a pulp-mill supervi-
sor at the S. D. Warren mill in Skowhegan. Bob, at sixty-two, was the
oldest player performing—and the only one with three grandchildren
also playing. "I've been studying with Amy LeBlanc for three years,"
Bob said, adding somewhat sheepishly, "but I don't practice as much
as I should."

Next to him was Lila Balch, mother of two and a psychologist with
a private practice. Lila, also a student of Amy's and also level 6, has been
taking lessons for only about a year. To what does she owe her rapid
progress? "I practice violin instead of doing the dishes," she said.

When I asked Molly Gawler, age six, over in level 1 how long
she has been playing, she said, "Oh, I don't know," implying that she
couldn't possibly remember *that* far back. Her mother, Ellen Gawler, a
string teacher from Belgrade Lakes, wasn't altogether sure, either.

"Well," she said, "let me think a minute. I bought her a violin when
she was two-and-a-half, but I don't think she actually started until she
was three."

\*\*\*

How, you may ask, can all this be? How can a rural region of Maine
that has been described in print as "west-central nowhere" fill a whole

gymnasium with string players and produce one of the liveliest and most successful school string programs in the state, one that supplied the year's All-State Orchestra with more than one-quarter of its string section and the Mid-Maine Youth Orchestra with thirty-three of its thirty-five string players? One reason is that folks up here in west-central nowhere love music and will make major sacrifices for their kids to learn it. Karen McCann remembers one mother who put off major dental work she needed so that she could afford to rent an instrument for her child.

Then, too, the last ten years have seen a staggering influx of high-powered string teachers into the area, several of whom, like Karen McCann, either are or have been members of the Portland Symphony Orchestra and play in any number of professional chamber-music ensembles. Farmington alone has four private string teachers, all of whom have as many students as they can handle. One of these teachers and McCann's predecessor in SAD 9, Nancy Beacham, was so successful and charismatic a teacher in the school program that about 10 percent of the third graders she introduced to strings when she started teaching in the schools are still playing in high school now. At the same time, the demand on her as a private teacher grew so rapidly that she left the school system to devote herself entirely to her private students.

"What we have now," says McCann, "is a mutually beneficial relationship between the schools and the private teachers. Students who catch fire in the school program go to the private teachers for lessons, and because those students make such rapid progress, that improves the level of orchestral work we can do in schools."

\*\*\*

By seven o'clock, the squirming, seething, bubbling, and roiling had ceased. Everyone was seated. Everyone was ready. Everyone was quiet. The program consisted of ten selections arranged in decreasing difficulty. Level 10 kicked things off with Haydn's *Perpetuo Mobile*, Opus 64, No. 5. Level 9 joined them on an excerpt from Vivaldi's Concerto in A Minor. Then level 8 stood up to swell the ranks even more for

Saint-Saëns' *The Swan*, which sounded so much the way a swan ought to that any real swan would have felt like a bum beside it.

And so on down through the rest of an eclectic program that included Lennon and McCartney's "Eleanor Rigby," some 1950s nostalgia with "Moon River," and even "Happy Birthday" for anyone lucky enough to have a birthday that month.

At about this point in the program, Hank Washburn, himself an accomplished fiddler, joined me where I was standing in back of levels 1–5. Hank had two daughters performing this year.

"This is such a gas," he said. "I can't believe how good they sound."

But of course he did believe it, and so did we all, because they did sound good. They sounded terrific. And when, at the end, the announcer asked level 1 to stand and all 370 players knocked out "Hot Cross Buns," those few simple notes filled the Mount Blue High gym with an all-enveloping sound guaranteed to convince even the most hard-bitten cynic that sweetness, harmony, and light will prevail in this world after all.

# Flummy

I know several men who are excellent cooks. I'm sorry to say I am not one of them. But let me be clear: my failure to achieve distinction in the kitchen is not rooted in disdain for the culinary arts. I have nothing but admiration for all those cooks, male or female, who are not just talented dilettantes who put on an occasional festive meal now and then but who—like my wife—perform at a high level over the long haul, day after day, year after year.

Cooking well calls not just for the craftsman-like virtues of discipline, persistence, attention to detail, but also for the artistic imagination to combine seemingly incompatible ingredients into a hitherto unknown taste treat, a kind of fresh gustatory metaphor. Faced with Rita's ability to work that kind of magic and conjure savory meals out of just about nothing, I realized early in our marriage that I stood little chance of ever catching up with her. So I decided to leave the cooking entirely in her hands; almost entirely, I should say, because there are a couple of staple items in our diet that she leaves to me. The most important of these is flummy, and if I haven't produced one for quite a while, Rita will remind me that it's high time I did.

Flummy (etymology uncertain) is the Labrador trapper's trail bread. I learned how to make it from Horace Goudie, the last of the Height of Landers, those amazingly skilled and rugged trappers who traveled each September two hundred miles upstream on the Grand River (designated on maps now as the Churchill River) to reach their hunting grounds on the Labrador plateau. On a canoe trip down that same Grand River undertaken in the fall of 1990 to celebrate Horace's retirement from guiding at age sixty-eight, we Yankees cajoled Horace into showing us, on a warm, sunny layover day, the fine points of flummy-making.

The ingredients: three cups flour, a rounded tablespoon of baking powder, a scant teaspoon of salt, a scant cup-and-a-half of water. The total absence of shortening is one thing that separates flummy from bannock or biscuit. But another thing Horace stressed is that success with flummies is "all in the mixing."

Okay, so you stir the dry ingredients together as you would for any old batch of biscuits. But then you dig a deep well into the center of the mix and pour the water in. With a spoon, you slowly peel the flour from the sides of the well into the water, stirring and peeling, until you can't stir anymore. Now you start folding the remaining flour in from the sides and working it down into the dough with your fingers, half folding, half kneading. Handle the dough only enough to round it into a ball you can pick up and flatten out into a round cake pan or frying pan, the bottom of which you have dusted with flour before you even started mixing the dry ingredients. The flour works like grease or oil to keep the flummy from sticking to the pan.

Next, you bore a hole into the middle of the dough with your trigger finger and set the pan over a low enough campfire that you don't burn your dough but not so low that the dough won't bake and rise. After fifteen minutes or so, or whenever the flummy is baked firm enough to hold its shape, you turn it over and jiggle the pan often so that the flip side won't burn. In the winter, when you're cooking on a tent stove, you control the baking temperature by sliding the pan around on the stove to find the exact amount of heat you need.

A little scorching on one side or the other can be tolerated, but the one cardinal flummy sin is soggy dough left in the middle. The Labrador adjective for this baleful condition is "dunse," etymology again uncertain. The "u" in this word is pronounced somewhere between the "u" in "dunce" and the "e" in "dense," which would suggest that anyone who produces a dunse flummy is a dense dunce.

Having an oven in our kitchen at home, I haven't hesitated to use it in pursuit of the perfect flummy, and I offer herewith my prize-winning recipe: two cups all-purpose white flour and two cups whole wheat, a heaping tablespoon of baking powder, a teaspoon of salt, and a tad under two cups of water. Bake for twenty-five minutes at 450 degrees, turn it over for ten more minutes at 350, and perfection is yours. Note, however, that a four-cup flummy is—in my experience—best reserved for oven baking at home because it takes a lot of time and attention to get it baked through over an open fire.

And remember: should you ever produce a failed flummy, keep Horace's admonition in mind next time and stick religiously to his mixing routine, complete with poking a hole in the middle of the dough before baking. The magic is all in the mixing.

# Dish-Fed Retainers

When we first settled in Maine in 1971, I dutifully read Scott and Helen Nearing's *Living the Good Life*, a book that enjoyed near-scriptural status in the back-to-the-land movement of those days. Scott and Helen were full of excellent advice on how to live a healthy, economically independent life that called for mornings of physically beneficial labor in the field and forest and left afternoons free to cultivate the arts and live the life of the mind.

I had not gotten too far into this book before I formed the impression that the Nearings were awfully sure of themselves. Scott, I thought, if some turn in his youth had not led him off the beaten path and onto the byways of leftist politics and rural life, might well have wound up as president of General Motors. He seemed to me to possess the single-mindedness, the drive, the self-righteousness, the obsessive devotion to mission that has made America both great and such a terrible mess.

What I found most irritating about the Nearings, however, was that they were often right, with that kind of schoolmasterly, ex cathedra rightness that inevitably evokes in me a perverse, schoolboyish desire to be as wrong as I possibly can. Actually, I didn't have far to go. The Nearings pointed out, for example, that it was imprudent to buy an old, wood-frame New England farmhouse and try to restore it. No matter how much money and energy you put into it, the building would always be leaky and drafty and in constant need of upkeep; you would be forced to live out your days putting up with all the original builder's design mistakes: the too-small kitchen, the overly large, space-wasting parlor, the upstairs ceilings that were oppressively low. If, on the other hand, you were to build a new stone house, you could design every last detail to suit yourself; the building would be warm in winter, cool in summer, and require only minimal maintenance on such trivia as trim and window frames.

A stone wall was recommended as a garden enclosure instead of some slipshod mess cobbled together out of cedar posts and chicken wire. Farm animals were dirty, expensive, an albatross around your neck, and of course eating either them or any of their by-products—eggs, milk—was bad for you. The wise homesteader would avoid such foods as conscientiously as he would addictive poisons like caffeine and alcohol.

But if there was anything or any creature upon which the Nearings heaped their most withering scorn, it was dogs and cats. Dogs scared away the wild animals; cats ate the birds; and both of them, the implication was, just ate and ate and dragged fleas and filth into your stone house and shed all over the place and gave you nothing—nothing, mind you—in return. Pets were "dish-fed retainers," a burden on the world's resources.

Now, as I was reading *Living the Good Life* and absorbing all this good advice, I was sitting in a leaky, drafty old New England farmhouse we were in the process of restoring. Evening was coming on, so I put the book down, drained the bourbon-on-the-rocks I'd been sipping as I read, put the kettle on for tea, eased the cat off my lap, and took some lamb chops out of the freezer. Then, as I headed out past the garden with its post-and-wire fence to feed and water the sheep and chickens, it finally dawned on me why I felt a nagging sense of incompleteness about our place: We had no dog, and I resolved to correct that deficiency first chance I got.

Since that evening, two dogs have entered and left our lives, and we are now living with Lucy, our third. I have loved all three, but to say merely that I love Lucy would be to say way too little. The love of man for dog and dog for man, as that love is usually understood, is much too platonic, much too companionable and chummy, to even begin to describe what our dog Lucy and I have going. The dog in the classic Lassie/Rin-Tin-Tin scenario is loyal, brave, clever, obedient, adoring. The man is strict but kind. With a firm but gentle hand he exacts well-deserved obedience and loyalty from his brave, clever, adoring companion and chum.

None of that Boy-Scout stuff for Lucy and me. Our relationship has been one of unabashed dithering devotion from the moment we laid eyes on each other. No sooner had the attendant at the Franklin

County Animal Shelter ushered Rita, Greg, and me into the kennels than I was smitten. In that godawful hubbub of yelping, yapping, yipping, barking, leaping, pacing mutts she caught my eye instantly. She had her front paws up against the kennel fence. She was all black. Her coat was just long enough to have a slight curl in it; she wore the fringed leggings of a setter or spaniel; her tail was a great black plume. She was deep-chested, slim in the loins. And her ears—she had perfect ears, a bit longer than a Lab's and black and silky but not those absurdly long cocker ears that the poor little hyper-bred beasts stumble over and drag in the mud.

Within three seconds, I was ready to sign on the dotted line, but to maintain at least a semblance of democratic process and to mask my hopeless crush behind a display of civilized behavior, I agreed to consider a few other candidates. To give us a little peace and let us get at least superficially acquainted with our possible choices, the attendant turned us and our few selected dogs out into a large, fenced-in yard.

Rita and Greg were both drawn to Lucy, too, but unlike me they had not been blinded by instant unquestioning love. Every leaning they expressed toward some other dog I tried to counter with a rational argument and a display of indifference I hoped would conceal my real intentions and so not evoke suspicion and resistance. The German-shepherd-and-something-else mutt that Rita had taken some fancy to was, I claimed, too big. His tail was high enough and heavy enough to wipe off the kitchen table with one wag. He would knock little old ladies down and break their bones; we would be sued; he was an obvious menace to our physical and economic well-being.

Greg, who was a savvy sixteen at the time, had his eye on a rough-haired, terrier-looking tyke, a thoroughly unglamourous little mongrel who was so homely he was endearing. Greg is not one to be taken in by fluff and frills and beauty that is only skin-deep. He is drawn instead to characters of real integrity who, though unprepossessing on the outside, remain doggedly true to themselves no matter what, gently defying brainless authority and making their way in the world on a combination of subversive intelligence, spunk, high spirits, and laughter.

"He's too small," I said. "We need a dog big enough to take on long hikes. And I bet he's a yapper. And did you see what he did the minute he got out in the yard? He raced around scarfing up every last bit of shit he could find."

"All dogs eat shit," Greg said.

"Maybe they do," I said, "but he could have been a little more discreet about it. He could have waited until we left."

"I like his honesty," Greg said. "I like how up front he is."

Lucy, meanwhile, had behaved admirably. She had welcomed our attentions but been neither coy nor pushy. She had not barked once. She had shown no interest in poop.

"Well," I said, after ten minutes or so, "I've by no means made up my mind, but that long-eared black female has some good points."

"She looks like a sophomore at Wellesley," Greg said.

"Exactly!" I leaped back. "Young, attractive, intelligent, interested in getting a good education, just the right size, not too big, not too small, looks like a strong swimmer, clearly has some retriever blood, athletic, lively, obviously affectionate, charming, beautiful . . ."

I realized, too late, that I had started to babble.

"I think," Rita said, "we should go home and sleep on it. She is a nice dog, but I like that shorthaired, part-dalmatian, too. He probably wouldn't shed much, and he seems sweet natured."

"I still like the poop eater," Greg said.

I was in agony. What if, ten minutes after we left to go home and sleep on it, somebody came in and adopted Lucy on the spot? First come, first served was the rule. You couldn't buy an option. You couldn't put money down. Maybe I could bribe the attendant? If I slipped her ten would she lie for me and say someone had already signed for Lucy?

No, no, no. I couldn't do that. Rural Maine is, by and large, still an honorable place. People don't lie and bribe and cheat here. The attendant would horsewhip me out the door. And even if she didn't, how would I—burdened with a Calvinist conscience the size of a woolly mammoth and still unable to forgive myself for the few white lies I've told in my half century plus—how would I ever be able to live with myself if I did something so scurrilous? That such a thought even occurred to me suggests the intensity of my infatuation.

I told myself it was late in the afternoon. Probably nobody else would come in to look at potential adoptees today, and if I called first thing in the morning, if I had that phone ringing at 8 a.m. tomorrow morning when the attendant walked in the door, then probably I'd be okay. Probably, probably, probably. Would I be able to survive sixteen hours of probability? And just as important, would I be able to convince Rita and Greg that Lucy was indeed the dog they too wanted?

Imagined obstacles loom mountainous; the real ones turn out to be mere bumps in the road. At our suppertime dog deliberations, Rita and Greg agreed that if we were going to bring home only one dog and not all the dogs in the shelter, or even the five we had taken a closer look at, then Lucy was the best choice. By 8:30 the next morning I'd signed the adoption papers and Lucy was on her way to the vet to be spayed. Three days later she was home with us.

She was still very young when we got her—around six months, the vet estimated. That makes her ten years old now, eleven next spring, mid-sixties, pushing seventy in human terms. Preparations for walks and swims still send her into whirling, wagging tizzies of delight, but she no longer has the staying power of youth. Even two years ago she would still be perky at the end of daylong bushwhacks in Maine's western mountains, still eager at day's end to race after still another red squirrel and bark up his tree. Now an hour's easygoing ramble is more her speed. Where she used to take long, looping forays into the woods ahead of me, always circling back to the dirt road or trail or just my line of travel to check up on me, she now tends to trot along placidly at my heels or, if I decide to jog for a quarter mile or so, even to fall behind. Molly, our neighbors' collie-beagle pup, would wrestle and cavort ceaselessly if Lucy would have it, but she won't. Ten or fifteen minutes of that are enough, and she calls a halt to the horseplay.

Her muzzle is gray; her eyebrows are gray; the fur inside her perfect ears is gray. Rumple those ears, and the silvery gray hair flashes into view. A few years ago, when the gray first started to show, it was the badge of her prime and the full flowering of her beauty, just as the first streaks of gray are in a woman's hair. Now the gray is more prominent; it isn't just an accent in her otherwise totally black coat. Her gray, like mine, is now the mark of late maturity, early dotage, call it what you will—not, I hope, the ultimate chapter in either of our lives but surely the penultimate. Like her people, our dog is eligible for Social Security.

Lucy is a glowing example of just what the Nearings deplored: a useless, mooching creature. She does no work and never did. She doesn't pull a sled, sniff out stashes of dope in airport lockers, or carry shots of brandy to travelers stranded in the snows of the Saint Bernard Pass. (Actually, Saint Bernards don't do that either.) She doesn't herd sheep or point at quail or partridge or retrieve ducks, all activities the Nearings would have deplored, too, examples of depraved humans dragging their already debased dish-fed retainers down a rung or two lower. Had I been keen on upland hunting when we got Lucy, she probably could have learned to be a good bird dog. She has the right genetic makeup. But my interests and focus were elsewhere at the time, and she has remained uneducated as a hunting dog. She eats, sleeps, plays, clowns, schmoozes. She is a pet, and though we may keep pets for companionship, we also keep pets for petting, for the physical warmth, affection, and contact they are almost constantly eager to give and receive. With animals we call pets, petting constitutes a major part of our interaction with them.

In addition to Lucy, we have a hulking tabby cat we call Clunker. I'd be ashamed to say how much of my time I invest in going over him with hands any masseur would envy. If he jumps up on the couch next to me while I'm reading, I start with a couple of strokes on his back, running my hand firmly down the length of him from his neck to the base of his tail, thumb and fingers straddling him, squeezing and pressing just enough to evoke an arching of his back and a look of witless glee on his face. If I scratch his cheeks, he'll lie down and roll over on his back, exposing his chin and throat, the stroking of which soon has him slack-jawed in supine surrender. I move from his throat down to his chest and furry belly. He writhes and opens his mouth in a soundless moan of delight. He stretches his front legs alternately, first left, then right, then left again. His paws spread out wide, and I stick the tip of my index finger into the little pocket that opens between the heel pad and the toe pads. His paw closes, capturing my fingertip in that warm, silken crevice. I cup my hand around the fullness of his belly. He rolls from side to side in flipflopping ecstasy. He is a shameless voluptuary and proud of it.

Lucy does not engage in such brazen displays. Her style has always been more modest; and now, at her advanced age, she is, if anything, more affectionate than ever but not the least bit importunate. Where our neighbors' young dog, Molly, plunks her head in my lap and gazes up at me with eyes desperate for love, Lucy quietly sits down next to my chair and leans her head against my leg. If I gently rumple those perfect ears of hers, she is happy; but she is happy to just sit there too, to just be in touch.

The touching makes us both happy. Petting my cat and dog gives them pleasure, and I take pleasure in petting them. Petting is a manifestation of love for the creature world, and it's one we ache to extend to creatures other than cats and dogs. Stories and legends that link us physically and, often, sexually to animals are legion in every culture. Native American mythologies tell endless stories of the "old time" when humans and animals were much closer than they are now, when people understood animal languages and could talk to all the creatures, when animals could turn into people and people, into animals. People mate with bears, rattlesnakes, owls, and, interestingly enough, even with dogs. These marriages are not trouble-free and endlessly blissful any more or less often than marriages between humans are, but they attest to a kinship in which human and animal cohabit in every sense of that word, sharing both hearth and bed, and they suggest to me how much we humans want to affiliate with the animal world, not just metaphorically but in the flesh. The "caribou man" of the Montagnais and Naskapi lives among the caribou, eats caribou moss, sires caribou, and yet is not a caribou. The animals allow him to kill some of their number and use their skins for his clothing; they sleep close to him at night to keep him warm. He is both of them and not of them, and it is he who dispenses caribou to the deserving among his human brethren, denying them to hunters who disobey the law by killing more than they need and wasting food.

If the human–dog bond originated in a hunting partnership, then it would seem that from some very early time in human history the dog has been involved in our primary economic activities. Predators ourselves, we joined forces with a fellow predator whose vastly better nose and ears and much faster legs made him a great help to us in the hunt. Then, by genetic engineering, we produced ever more specialized hunters: pointers, terriers, hounds, retrievers. When we became herdsmen instead of hunters, we started using dogs to guard our domestic animals rather than hunt wild ones; and here, too, we introduced specialization, breeding dogs that became primarily guard dogs or herding dogs. It is not surprising that over those centuries of working relationships bonds of affection and trust developed between humans and dogs. Bonds created by working together at basic life-sustaining tasks are among the strongest bonds there are.

But the most radical step in the human–dog relationship has been a by-product of industrialization and the industrialization of agriculture and animal husbandry. For anyone who sees humankind's evolution from hunter-gatherer to agro-industrialist as an unmitigated disaster for both humans and the natural world, the genetic engineering of the dog from wild canid to the many highly specialized breeds we have today is bound to appear as a parallel disaster. If the step from hunter to herdsman-plowman was the first great step in the process of alienation from nature and self, then surely the step from herdsman-plowman to city dweller, driver of combines, and feedlot engineer has all but completed that process. We still have hunting dogs, and we still have herding dogs, but we have vastly more companion dogs.

As we human beings have retreated more and more from the wild world ourselves, we have bred more and more wildness out of some dogs until they have been almost totally stripped of their animality. Lapdogs and toy breeds have been so drastically engineered away from their wild origins that about the only role they could assume in the wild would be as prey, not as predators. They haven't legs enough for either pursuit or flight. They haven't teeth or jaws enough to kill, scavenge, or defend themselves. Like pointers or border collies, lapdogs too have been bred for a special purpose: not to hunt or herd, however, but to be petted and coddled.

Over the past few decades the late Paul Shepard wrote about such matters, deploring the awful fix we human beings got ourselves and the rest of all creation into when we gave up the hunting and gathering life to raise crops and keep domestic animals. The degraded creature I see in the coddled toy, however, Shepard sees in any and every domestic animal—"the mindless drabs of the sheep flock, the udder-dragging, hypertrophied cow, the psychopathic racehorse, and the infantilized dog." For him, my amiable, easygoing mutt is every bit as much a neurotic "protoplasmic farrago of dismantled and reassembled life" as any lapdog:

> [Dogs'] relationship to us is not symbiotic, either, or mutual or parasitic. None of these biological terms is suitable to describe organic disintegration in a special vassalage among creatures whose heartwarming compliance and truly therapeutic presence mask the sink of their biological deformity and the urgency of our need for other life.
>
> Less than kindly euphemisms for "companion animals" come to mind—crutches in a crippled society, candy bars, substitutes for necessary and nurturant others of the earth, not simply simulations but overrefined, bereft of truly curative potency, peons in the miasma of domesticated ecosystems.

Well! I think, with no little indignation, Paul Shepard may be able to get away with saying nasty things like that about lapdogs, but he can't say them about *all* dogs. Lucy is no candy bar or peon. No lapdog this, no ludicrous little Chihuahua or Pekingese or shih tzu that a coyote could make one mouthful of. *My* dog is a sturdy, noble mutt who can run and swim for miles, chase red squirrels up trees and bark wildly and gleefully about her accomplishments, flop down in the shade and snooze and hang out with me contentedly, even if I'm doing all those dumb things people do that aren't any fun for dogs at all: splitting and piling wood, reading, writing, shingling roofs, weeding gardens.

But rejoice as I will that my dog is indeed a cheerful all-American and not an overbred freak, I still have to recognize that in many respects she can't measure up to her wild cousins. When I see coyotes whirling off across the snow like wisps of snow in the wind themselves or when I watch the precise, purposeful economy of the red fox's energy-saving trot and see the luxuriant magnificence of his red tail flowing behind him, I know I'm looking at beasts of a different order. The memory I have of a pack of wolves running along the bank of the Grand River in Labrador—those great, lean creatures striding out with a grace and power that seemed to practically lift them off the earth into skim-ming flight, how they materialized out of nowhere, leaped silently along beside our canoes for a few hundred yards, then disappeared again up over the bank—when I remember that, I gasp all over again with wonder, admiration, amazement at the glory of those animals. My dog, much as I love her and delight in her, cannot compare with them. When we are out rambling together and I see her trotting along with her tongue hanging out in her big grin, her head and tail up, the bounce and lilt of her gait as her black-fringed legs flip the miles out behind her, I grin too. She is fun; she is charming; but she lacks the high seriousness of the wolf. Her tracks in the snow belie her. Where the wild canid moves with care and intent, Lucy travels in extravagant, wasteful loops and sorties. Where she is sweet and clinging and a little clownish, the wolf is independent, self-contained. It has a kind of stat-ure no dog can match.

Konrad Lorenz gives lower marks to the spaniels and long-eared gun dogs than to the huskies, chows, and German shepherds, which are of wolf lineage. Lorenz allows that setters and other longhaired, long-eared breeds are affectionate but, for his taste, affectionate to a fault. Too "sentimental," he calls them, affectionate to the point of fawning. They lack the spunk, feistiness, and independence of the more wolf-like dogs. The drooping ears and short skull base that the setters and spaniels retain throughout life occur in wild canids only in their early development and disappear in the wild adult. But then all dogs, in their dependence on their human masters, remain "childlike" to a greater or lesser degree throughout their lives. "It is a remarkable fact," Lorenz writes, "that a dog, which fits into human society better than any other domestic animal, owes its major behavioral characteristic to neoteny . . . ; just like actively investigative openness to surroundings in human beings, fidelity to a master represents a persistent juvenile characteristic in the dog."

Lucy is clearly of long-eared, gun-dog lineage, and she is just as clearly sentimental and soulful. But then I'm soulful and sentimental myself. Maybe that's why we get on so well. I know she lacks the wild grandeur of a wolf, coyote, or fox, but then I lack the wild grandeur of a Masai or Apache hunter. In his sentence about neoteny, Lorenz is saying, in somewhat arcane language, that Lucy and I, each in our own distinctively canine and human ways, have just never quite grown up. Her fidelity to and dependence on me and my "actively investigative openness to surroundings" (read: childlike curiosity about the world and wide-eyed fascination with it) are persistent juvenile characteristics. Lucy's seemingly wasteful circling and sniffing is the image of the human mind actively investigating its surroundings, often randomly, often barking up the wrong tree. That both of us have the luxury of squandering our energy this way is, depending on how you look at it, either a benefit or a curse of domestication.

The idea underlying Paul Shepard's trenchant attack on our keeping and breeding of any and all domestic animals—indeed, the single informing idea in all his work—is that the development of human intelligence is inextricably linked to the separation of nature and culture and to the hunter's consequent attention to animals "not as stuff or friends but as resplendent, diverse beings, signs that integrity and beauty are inherent in the givenness of the world." Conversely, the blurring of the line between nature and culture, the consignment of some genetically engineered animals to our laps, the milking barn, and the slaughter-house, and the concomitant withdrawal of our attention from wild animals all bring about impoverishment in both our internal and external worlds. With "nothing but our own image to explain ourselves by" and our gods created in our own image, the only reference point that matters is the human one. We spin about in ever-diminishing circles of selfhood, as the bookstore shelves sagging with self-help so eloquently testify. In our narcissism, we try to squeeze all external reality inside those same little circles with us.

The force of Shepard's argument is compelling. As the human population grows and grows and as our destruction and domestication of wildlife habitat continues to drive increasing numbers of wild creatures into extinction, it is hard to resist the idea that our agro-urban world, with its overpopulations of humans and domestic animals, is destroying the integrity and beauty of the given world. When I go into my local supermarket and see an entire aisle taken up with pet foods, I too can see all those cans and boxes and bags as evidence that we are investing vast amounts of energy and resources in maintaining the "wrong" animals. But still, I leave the store with my twenty-five-pound bag of Dog Krunchies, and though I find the case Paul Shepard makes elegant and persuasive, the nature–culture division underlying it remains, as Shepard himself says, "merely methodological." His argument seems a bit like a small-scale planimetric map that provides the overview necessary for seeing where we are in the world and in relation to our ultimate destination. But for day-to-day travel, we need large-scale topo maps that show us the bogs and tiny brooks, the mountains, cliffs, and canyons.

What Shepard's map tells us is that we have stumbled so deep into settled, domesticated territory that we have lost touch almost completely with the wild world and so with the wellsprings of our own mental and physical health, and on his map we can see the direction we need to go to get out of that fix. But for today's journey, I need the large-scale map of my immediate surroundings, too; and on that map, the companionship of my dog, my affection for her, her affection for me, and the heavy petting I bestow on her all loom large.

If we have sinned by overindulgence in pets, then our sin—like so many of our sins—is one of degree, not kind. We are not sinners by virtue of our being tool makers. We are sinners only in having made too many tools that are too dangerous and destructive and in using them so recklessly. If we have bred physical and psychic flaws into dogs and if we have let their populations displace wild creatures, the sin is in our excesses. If farm animals are a link to the natural world, then dogs and cats are an even stronger one. They are—or at least can be—at once both "wilder" and "more domestic" than cattle; they range and forage, are capable of greater independence from us, but are the only animals that share our living quarters. Like us, they are creatures of both the hunt and the hearth. To say that there are too many of them and too many of us and that together we make excessive demands on our world's resources is not to say that either they or we are intrinsically evil. If only it were as easy to right the balance as it is to make that grand observation.

But whatever the big picture, the small picture of my life includes a bond with Lucy so strong I suppose it borders on lunacy. Even to my mind, which is not adept at logic, my affection for Lucy seems illogical. How can I insist on the grandeur and wonder of the wolf and still value, no, not just value but love, my dog, who is not as grand and wondrous? Have I no rigor, no standards?

A recently divorced friend of mine said of her ex-husband, "Oh, he's charming all right, but charm is not a cardinal virtue." Mary Oliver, in her wonderful diatribe against that revolting Disney vision that would make all of nature a petting zoo, writes, "Nothing in the forest is charming. . . . And nothing in the forest is cute." All things in the forest and we humans too are, again in her words, "wild, valorous, amazing."

"Humans or tigers, tigers or tiger lilies—note their differences and still how alike they are!" How different Lucy and the wolf are and still how alike. How different the old Naskapi hunter and I—yet still, I hope, at least a little bit alike. How impossible for Lucy and me to extract ourselves from the muddled past of our species and be anything but the part-wild, part-tame beasts we are. No wonder I love her. She is both of me and not of me. She partakes of my confusions. She is a messenger from the world of fur and fang I can not only reach out and touch but also live with and hold close. Her eye may never have harbored the "fierce green light" Aldo Leopold saw die in the eyes of the she-wolf he shot in Arizona, but in her youth Lucy was a beautiful creature, capable of great grace, of bounding valorous leaps; and even though that beauty and valor are muted now in her declining years, she still charges out into the world with an animal vitality that has its origins much further back than any human interference with her genetic makeup. Her being is not exhausted in her domesticity and charm. She may be "my" dog; I may, officially, have the power of life and death over her. But beyond all officialdom she is her own self, and when she snuffles and pounces in the tall grass in pursuit of rodents or rolls on her back in the snow, squirming in sensuous abandon, what she's telling me is this: "I may love you, man, and you may love me, and we may both like the hearth rug, but out here is where the real action is. Don't you forget it."

And because I love her dearly, I take to heart everything she says.

# November Epiphany

I t's the Sunday after Thanksgiving. The long ridge of Spruce Mountain we see out our kitchen windows is dusted with white, but down here, a thousand feet lower on the Temple intervale, what little snow fell this past week has melted away. If I choose to ignore that light frosting up there in the hills, I could kid myself into thinking the long, warm fall we've enjoyed this year is going to go on forever. But I read that snow on the hill for what it is: a wakeup call. "Get cracking," it says, "on the chores you still haven't completed." I've spent the morning cleaning up odds and ends: taking down the bean poles and tomato stakes and storing them away in the garden shed, picking up the last scrap ends of lumber and shingles from repairing the garden shed itself, draining the lawnmower oil, emptying the gas tank, stowing the mower away for the winter.

I come in for lunch, my mind already working up my list of chores for the afternoon: crank up the tractor and move the bush hog into the open-fronted shed, put away those old storm windows we thought we would use to make a cold frame this year but didn't. (Well, maybe next spring.) On the subject of storm windows, it's high time I got the storms on our bedroom windows upstairs, so get the ladder out, get the windows out, clean the windows, put the windows up; put weather-stripping around that leaky west window here in the kitchen.

When I'm halfway through my peanut butter sandwich, the phone rings. It's my neighbor Ben.

"Got any plans for this afternoon?" he asks.

"Sure I've got plans," I say, "more plans than I care to think about. But I bet you're going to suggest I forget about them and go for a hike instead, right?"

"Right," he says. "It's a gorgeous afternoon. We should grab it while we can."

I hesitate for a few seconds, thinking what a god-awful pain it will be to have to do this afternoon's chores if we should happen to get a foot of snow. But then good sense takes over, and I say, "You're a wise man, Ben. Let me catch my lunch, and we'll be off."

We take the trail the local snowmobile club cleared over Derby Mountain this past summer, a steep trail that has us puffing and, at the same time, admiring the engineering skills of the guys who brought an excavator in here to even out the trail and build bridges over a few brooks. Ben's Springer spaniel, Scout, splashes through the puddles left in the excavator tracks, then proudly displays for us his dripping, mud-caked legs and belly. Ben's wife, Ann, allowed Scout to join us only on the condition that Ben would give him a bath after our hike.

Higher up, a few inches of snow underfoot make for some slippery going as we push on to the crest of the ridge, top it, and start down through the open cuttings on the north slope. From here, we can see off to the northeast, where Day Mountain marks the far end of Temple Stream's valley. The sun has already dropped below the mountains to the west; but even though Day Mountain is now in shadow, its flanks still seem to hold some remnant of light, glowing gun-metal blue against the darkening northern sky. As we move on down the hillside, the trees cut off our view, but that image of Day Mountain sticks in my mind.

This whole afternoon ramble has been a joy: talking local politics and not-so-local politics with Ben, soaking up the last of autumn's sun on our backs as we made our way uphill and into the first of winter's snows. All that has been reward enough for stripping off my uniform of duty and taking Ben up on his invitation, but it's that brief view of Day Mountain that has been the special and unexpected gift of this afternoon, one of those moments on this good earth when light and shadow created by the turning of the planet in its diurnal and annual rounds conspires with the contours of the land and the tapestry of trees to make Day Mountain not just a Maine hill in late November but a vision, a moment when the mountain speaks to you with its voice of silence and says, "Behold, you lucky duck, the glory of this world. Aren't you glad you didn't spend the afternoon messing around with storm windows?"

"Oh, yes, yes," I say back to the mountain. "And how glad I am that Ben called me on the spur of the moment and that I had sense enough to heed his call."

When we part, Ben says, "Thanks so much for coming along."

And I say, "All thanks go to you, Ben, for seizing this day."

# A Raspberry Diary

I n the winter, this not-so-young man's fancy sometimes turns to thoughts of raspberries, often right around Christmastime. Maybe it's all those red ribbons on packages and the red stockings hung by the chimney with care that inspire my raspberry reveries. In a well-ordered universe, raspberries at the peak of their ripeness should be available, I think, in all climes and latitudes the year round. Since a universe so well-ordered is not the one we inhabit, I have—where raspberries are concerned—made my peace with the universe as it is. I've accepted that our little raspberry patch consisting of two twenty-foot rows of canes has its seasons and that we humans have to be constantly on the alert to nurture it and defend it against drought, disease, and competitors for its fruit.

This past summer, I had assured some dear friends that I would be able to supply enough raspberries, plus whipped cream, to make dessert for a small mid-July dinner party at their camp. Early in the month, with berries just starting to ripen, my son, Greg, and I spread netting over the canes to keep the birds from beating us to them.

Come the appointed day of July 19, we headed out to the berry patch with quart berry boxes in hand. Greg and I are finicky types, both of us set in our own finicky ways. Greg believes that no raspberry should be picked unless it has turned unmistakably red and will slip off its white conical receptacle at the lightest touch of the hand. In theory, I agree with him, but when I want to be sure I'll have enough berries for an evening dinner party, I'll sometimes fall for ones that are only a deep pink and may need more than just a gentle tug to unseat them.

"Those berries aren't ripe yet," Greg says. "You're picking them too soon."

"Well, they probably could use another day or so," I admit. "But they're close, very close, right on the brink."

In my heart of hearts, of course, I know Greg holds the high ground in this ongoing struggle against his father's ignorance and stubbornness. Though half my age in years, he has at least twice my gardening skills and experience, and he picks roughly twice as fast as I do. When we combine our pickings, Greg's truly ripe berries in his every two quarts easily outnumber and compensate for the failings of the 10 or 20 percent in my one quart that are only borderline-ripe. This discrepancy in favor of the genuinely ripe accounts for why the raspberries we serve our friends have always disappeared as if by magic and never drawn a word of complaint from anyone.

Then, too, as the season moves on, the number of ripe berries continues to grow day by day, making questionable berries scarcer and any quibbles about them superfluous. We eat raspberries with our granola at breakfast; we eat raspberries and yogurt for dessert in the evening. We scoop them up from the kitchen counter during the day. We eat them while we're picking them.

In the last week of July and the first few days of August, the canes really start playing full-court press. It's all we can do to keep up. Greg and I both pick in the late afternoon right before supper and each come in with a couple of quarts. Reaching for a clump of perfect berries, we may knock one off its receptacle, and because we can't stand to let a perfect berry lie on the ground and rot, we dive into the tangle of canes headfirst to rescue the lost one.

We could make jam; we could put some of our crop in the freezer; but we don't do either. We like to get the beauty of these berries hot, so we double our allowable intake while we pick, assuring ourselves once again that they really do taste best right off the cane.

But then the tide starts to go out as quickly as it came in:

**August 4:** Torrential rain all day. No picking.
**August 5:** Hot, dry day. Yield: only about half a quart apiece.
**August 6:** Screaming-hot day. Our shirts drenched with sweat, we pick tiny berries, many now overripe, that we would have left before. Yield: barely a third of a quart apiece.
**August 7:** Muggy, overcast, late afternoon rain. No picking.
**August 8:** Slim pickings.

**August 9:** Slimmer still.

**August 10, 11, 12, 13:** The leaves on the canes are starting to yellow. Some small berries are still unripe; others are rotten. We find barely enough edible berries to make a quarter of a box between us.

**August 14:** I go down to the patch alone, pick nineteen berries, and declare our raspberry season over.

But all is not lost. There are consolations: The crop of highbush blueberries on our friends' farm nearby is one of the best ever. And if winter solstice comes, can raspberry time be all that far behind? Not such a badly ordered universe after all.

# A Tale of Tall Snows

A mere two years ago, in this very "Upcountry" column, I was singing the praises of old-fashioned winters, the kind with deep snow and deep cold, the kind that start full-bore in December—maybe even with a heavy, fluke storm in November—and don't let go again until May. Winters of that stature, I opined, are a blessing and not, as some folks seem to think, a curse. In a deep-snow, deep-cold winter you can cross-country ski for weeks at a time on silky powder, and the silence of a wind-still, full-moon night is so profound that you can almost hear the moonlight flowing over the snow underfoot, the crackling of the stars overhead.

Implicit in all my enthusiasm for no-nonsense winters, of course, is the wish that we will experience such winters, that the snows will indeed fall in abundance, that the mercury will settle down around zero and stay there from Christmas to mid-February.

An old adage says to be careful what you wish for because you may get it. This past winter, we got it, one storm on the heels of another, a foot of new snow, then a foot and a half, then another foot. Our neighbor Rick, who plows our driveway, had to plow twelve times between December 1 and March 5, an average of once a week. Along about mid-January, I had to start dumping the piles back out of his way with the bucket loader so he'd have room enough to plow the next time.

I lost track of how many times I shoveled off the roofs of our outbuildings. In early March, my friend Wes and I cleared four feet of snow off our camp roofs at the pond. High time we did, too. Later that same week, the roof on Leon and Cynthia's garage in Wilton caved in. Ditto with Bill's garden shed, just down the road from our place.

Dennis Pike, who has been manning the National Weather Service's official meteorological station in Farmington since 1966, recorded a total snowfall of 139.6 inches last winter, quite a respectable tally, but still far short of the 200-plus inches that fell in northern Franklin County in 1968–1969, when I was wintering with my old mentor, Don Yeaton, at my father's camps on Big Jim Pond. Don's major winter responsibility as caretaker was to shovel off the camp roofs well before the snow load reached the cave-in stage. In an average winter, he cleared the roofs twice, once sometime in January and then again in early March, before the thaw and any spring rains could soak the snowpack and make it dangerously heavy.

But by mid-February of 1969, we had shoveled the roofs of the main lodge, the eight guest camps, and the ice house three times. The snow on either side of the path from the back door of our camp out to the woodshed was shoulder high. Then, when we woke up after the crown storm in early March, the woodshed was completely buried; only the peaks of the roofs of some of the camps were visible. If we had wanted to get in the kitchen door of the main lodge, we'd have had to dig our way down to it. The snow on the level in the camp yard was higher than the roof of the cab on the old Chevy truck we used to haul firewood, which is to say, the snow on the ground was at least seven to eight feet deep.

Each year come spring, I am amazed anew at how quickly the suns of April and May vaporizes those mountains of snow. No sooner are they gone than we forget just how deep the snow was not all that many weeks ago. How thoroughly Don and I forgot we learned in July, when we wanted to swamp out a new section of trail we had marked that winter. We thought we had blazed that trail more than adequately, but search as we would, we couldn't find a single blaze. Not, that is, until we realized we had to look for our spots not at eye level but about twelve feet up in the trees, for when we cut them, we'd been a good seven feet above the ground.

Far from convincing me, however, that my affection for deep snow and cold is wrongheaded, this past winter just reminded me of what those blazes way up in the trees had taught me back in 1969: the easiest, most enjoyable way to get around in a good old-fashioned winter isn't by pushing and heaving the snow out of your way but by getting up on top of it and letting it carry you on its back.

# Firewood from the Sky

When I realized several years ago that the twigs on a limb of the big sugar maple next to our house were beginning to scratch the metal roofing in heavy winds, that was reason enough to call in an arborist. More disquieting, this monster limb—heavy enough and long enough to be a fair-sized tree all by itself—was right over our son Greg's bedroom. When I asked a forester friend whom I should get to deal with this hazard, the prompt answer was Dale Gilmour in Kingfield.

A few days after we spoke on the phone, Dale and his assistant turned up in Dale's bucket truck, and in a matter of minutes of talking with this lively, engaging man, I was convinced he was a kindred soul. He was here not to deal with just one worrisome limb but to assess the overall health of the tree as well. I was grateful for that reassurance because this tree is one of the most beautiful things on our place, and in the summer when it spreads its green, cooling canopy over the house for much of the day, it makes air conditioning superfluous.

After Dale took the offending limb down piece by piece, he did a wellness check of this precious tree, then installed a heavy elastic brace around a fork high up in its trunk to keep it from splitting.

Recently, Dale has been back to cut out of our roadside trees all the dead limbs, large and small, hanging threateningly over the roadway below. After he'd stopped by to scope out the job, he came back the next morning hauling a good-sized flatbed trailer behind his bucket truck. Because much of the smaller wood he would be pruning out of our trees was dead and bone dry, all Greg and I would need to do to make firewood of it was cut it to stove length. Some of the heavier stuff we'd have to split as well, but picking up the wood Dale dropped to us out of the sky meant that for at least some of our firewood I would not have to buy it—or cut it and haul it in from our woodlot myself.

While Dale moved his truck or was piloting his bucket into position for his next cuts, Greg and I could safely load onto the trailer what he had just dropped. When it was time for lunch, we settled into the rocking chairs on our porch for food and conversation, which soon turned to Wendell Berry, an author Dale and I both respect for his lifelong spirited and spiritual advocacy for loving care of our home turf—fields and forests alike.

Then, because Dale and I are not as young as we used to be, we agreed that another couple of hours after lunch was enough. At quitting time, he backed his loaded trailer into our yard and parked it where Greg and I could saw up the day's haul and empty the trailer. Dale would come back a couple of days later to finish the job and leave a second trailer load of wood for us to work up.

Only after Dale had made a last special trip to pick up his emptied trailer did it dawn on me how generous he had been to leave his trailer with us twice and then make still another trip to pick it up when we were done with it, not to mention the pleasure of his company, his ready wit, and how much fun we had working with him.

Just as he was about to leave our place, the name of his business on the side of his truck caught my eye again: "Skyline Tree Service of Maine." Those words had always evoked for me an image of Dale swinging about in the treetops on his ropes and taking in the Maine mountain skylines he could see from his various high perches, a man who was his own boss and doing outdoor work that brought him every day a little bit closer to heaven than most of us ever get.

While that understanding of "skyline" supported my appreciation of Dale's chosen life's work and of the joy he finds in it, I found on visiting his website that in arborists' professional parlance a skyline is a steel cable used to transport heavy logs across sensitive properties like lawns, gardens, greenhouses, and rooftops. In any case, whether Dale is shuttling huge logs from work site to log truck with a cable and carriage or treating trees with insect infestations, what he's always doing is maintaining the health and safety of the trees in our yards and in the landscapes we frequent every day. A noble calling, I think.

# Footwear

The entrance to our house—like the entrances to many rural Maine houses—is not the front door, as the knee-high weeds sprouting in front of our front door testify. So if you plan on visiting us, just keep on moving past the front door until you reach the ell where you climb three well-worn wooden steps onto an unenclosed porch. If you continue on through the door into the combination mudroom/storage room inside, you may think you've entered a store specializing in second-hand shoes. Or that centipedes, not human beings, live here.

Prominent in this flood of footwear lined up against the east wall is the Bean boot, listed in the L.L. Bean catalog as the Maine Hunting Shoe. Other manufacturers have tried to muscle into the leather-top-rubber market, but you won't find any knockoffs in our ell. Rita has one pair of Bean boots in our shoe lineup; I have three. The newest ones, fully intact and well oiled, are reserved for serious duty, like hunting, of course, and canoe trips and extended hikes and explorations spring, summer, and fall, which almost always involve some over-the-ankle (if not over-the-boot-top) swamps and sloughs.

Cracks all the way through the leather of the next older ones disqualify them for dunking in water, but they're still fine for working around our place in wet grass and brush and even for sloshing through an occasional shallow puddle. They may not be in their prime, but there's still plenty of chore mileage left in them.

For those five-minute trips to dump the compost bucket or grab an armful of firewood from the drying shed, I have no-lace, step-in Bean boots, which you will not find in the catalog. These are just the rubber bottoms left over from an ancient pair whose tattered, nine-inch leather tops I lopped off with scissors.

What else is in my collection? A pair of ankle-high work boots, hiking boots, heavy-duty cross-country ski boots (not those funny little

Oxford-style ones), rubber knee boots for standing around in water and muck all day long, cushioned running shoes that save wear and tear on my aging knees, a pair of old running shoes so full of holes they function as sandals I wear to go swimming, felt-lined moosehide Steger mukluks for snowshoe trekking in northern Quebec and Labrador at twenty and thirty below zero.

Rita's mainstays are four pairs of those walking and running shoes with light fabric tops but soles solid enough to stand up to real work. The two older, dirtier pairs are for gardening, and when they finally succumb to several seasons of mud and hard use, the next generation of newer, cleaner ones will step into their shoes, as it were, only to be replaced themselves with shiny new ones that will double for her morning walks and for formal occasions like getting her hair cut or catching a movie in Farmington. Her cross-country ski boots, no longer in use now, keep company with three obsolescent pairs we keep around in case house guests would like to ski and have feet to match the sizes of these boots. In the step-in line, Rita has Birkenstocks for summer heat, rubber-topped clogs for wet-weather trips to yank a few carrots in the garden, felted wool clogs for cold weather indoors and, briefly, out.

Conspicuously absent from our ell lineup are dress shoes, and what few pairs have survived from our earlier lives languish now in a corner of our clothes closet. Even on the eight or nine occasions over the past forty years when I have worn a necktie, I still haven't felt that work or hiking boots, brushed clean, would be inappropriate on my feet. What's crucial for the feet after all is not to be dressy but to be well dressed for the prevailing weather and terrain.

Of course our mudroom would look neater if we tucked the winter boots away in the summer and the summer shoes away in the winter, but because northern New England weather is famously changeable, I may well need my ski boots in May and Rita her Birkenstocks in November. And because a Bean boot is as close to all-weather footwear as you can get, I'm sure to want all three pairs of mine handy year-round. So why store any of them away in some clever place I'll forget and then have to spend a frantic afternoon searching for them when I need them?

No, a country dweller's footwear should always be in plain sight. Some people in our neighborhood, realizing that if summer comes, winter will be here next week, never take the banking down around their foundations. Time isn't passing quite that fast for me yet, but the one gesture I do make to the fickleness of Maine weather and to the increasingly rapid pace with which one season gives way to the next is to keep all my footwear close to hand.

# Winning the Ice Out Prize

Unless you live right on the shore of a pond or lake, you've got to be on your toes to catch ice out, and even then you may get fooled. The retreat of ice proceeds by fits and starts, by melting and refreezing, by dawdling along in a cold snap and rushing ahead under a pounding spring sun. It all begins with a narrow little strip of water appearing around the shoreline. Then the snowpack starts turning to mush and water wicks up in ski and snowshoe tracks. Before too long you're looking at a black, waterlogged honeycomb, and if you turn your back on it today, you may find open water when you look again tomorrow.

The closest pond to us here in Temple, Maine, is Drury Pond, just a little under a mile from our house. I ski to it and on it nearly every day in the winter, but come spring, when the snow on my ski trail gives way to mud, my visits there become rare, and ice out is likely to sneak by on me. If I and my neighbors fail to note the passing of the ice on this little pond—not even half a mile long and less than a quarter wide—no one is likely to care, much less to chide us for our inattention.

But on Maine's big lakes like Moosehead and Rangeley, folks don't turn their backs on the lake for a minute. In Greenville and in Rangeley village, ice out is a major event; from early April on, everyone watches longingly for the telltale signs of it. Rangeley's twice-monthly newspaper, *The Rangeley Highlander*, publishes in its early April edition an invitation to take part in the annual Ice Out Contest: "Tell us when you think ICE OUT will be declared!!" You can submit your guess on the date and time of day to the *Highlander* either by U.S. Mail or by email.

Because anglers starved for the sight of open water are itching to get out there and start trolling streamers for landlocked salmon, determining just when the ice has, in fact, gone out is serious business and therefore delegated to the local game warden. Reggie Hammond has been

Rangeley's ice out judge for the last twenty years, a job he inherited from the wardens before him. "Everyone wants to fish ice out," Reggie says, "so my phone starts ringing constantly."

The traditionally accepted criterion for declaring ice out in Rangeley is whether you can travel by boat the roughly eight miles from Oquossoc village at the west end of the lake to the tip of Greenvale Cove at the east end. "Most times," Reggie says, "I jump in a boat to check it out, but not always. I keep a pretty close eye on the lake, and I have some pilot buddies who watch also."

Reggie is the first to admit that determining ice out is not a precise science. "I'm certainly not down there the exact second, minute, or even hour the ice goes out," he says. People understand that a game warden has plenty of other business to attend to, so no one has ever dreamed of quibbling with Reggie's judgment. This is, after all, a contest conducted in a spirit of fun and good will. The folks taking part in it aren't competing for glory or a megabucks-style prize, and though there are prizes—first, second, and third—awarded to the winners whose guesses come closest to Reggie's call, there are no real losers in this contest. Whether your guess was a mile wide of the mark or you didn't even bother to enter one, you still win the biggest prize of all, which is ice out itself. Of course, we may get another solid snowstorm or two, and of course, we may not be frost free for another month or more. But for all that, it's ice out that tips the balance from winter to spring more dramatically than anything else.

That holds as true on our little neighborhood pond here in Temple as it does on Rangeley or Moosehead Lake, and though I may miss seeing the ice actually go out most years, every once in a while luck is with me. I'll be at the pond at that magical moment when the honeycomb starts warping and undulating under a brisk breeze and breaking up into countless chimes of candle ice. If there's a canoe handy, I and anyone lucky enough to be with me can launch that boat; and as we paddle from one end of Drury Pond to the other, our paddles play on those chimes our serenade to the warmth of the sun on our backs, to the redwings calling in the outlet bog, to this first full-blown day of spring.

# Squirrel Brains

I recently learned in the course of my wide-ranging, catch-as-catch-can reading that the average adult human brain weighs between 1,300 and 1,400 grams. A squirrel's brain, this same source told me, weighs 7.6 grams. You'd think if you pitted a human being against a squirrel in any kind of intellectual contest, the human would win hands down, heavyweight versus featherweight.

That's what I thought anyway, so I went up against gray squirrels without much doubt that I would emerge victorious. So confident was I that when Rita and I needed to replace our battered bird feeders late last fall I didn't bother to research the many feeders the human mind has devised to keep squirrels from gobbling up our black oil sunflower seeds. Rita, however, is a sensible person who will always choose the most straightforward solution to any problem. She did her homework and bought a clever feeder that allows birds, who weigh only a few ounces, access to the seeds but blocks off that access when the weight of a squirrel pulls a metal cage down over the feeding ports.

All well and good, I thought, but that feeder doesn't give the squirrels a sporting chance. Furthermore, if I can manage to transform an otherwise simple project into a complex and challenging one, I will. So I bought a feeder that would hold a couple of quarts of sunflower seeds and gave the birds access to them through a flexible metal mesh reminiscent of the chain mail the Crusaders wore and fine enough, I thought, to exclude the teeth of hungry squirrels.

Our bird-feeding station consists of a peeled cedar pole with a crossbar bolted to it about seven feet off the ground. On one end of that bar we hung Rita's spring-loaded feeder; on the other end, my Crusader's feeder.

The next morning, when Rita looked out the window, she said, "Squirrel on your feeder."

173

"I'll show him," I thought, and I clad the cedar pole with some light metal sheeting.

"Let's see him climb that," I said to Rita, only to watch, an hour or so later, as our uninvited guest scampered up that armor-plated pole as if it were one of nature's own cedars, unadorned.

So I installed a cone-shaped aluminum baffle above the metal sheath on the pole.

On his next visit, this squirrel contemplated the baffle from different angles for a few minutes, then jumped up onto Rita's lower-hanging feeder, using it as a ladder to make his way onto the crossbar and thence over to my feeder, where he again settled in for an ample breakfast.

This squirrel was so round and well fed that even his tail looked chubby, so we nicknamed him Fat Tail, thinking he might take enough offense at that to just quietly go away. I also took Rita's feeder off the crossbar and hung it from a maple limb far enough away from my setup that not even a squirrel who had taken Olympic gold in the broad jump could hope to leap across that gap.

I had failed to notice, though our squirrel had not, how close a few branches of our dooryard lilac were to my feeder. So I trimmed the lilac back to close that route off.

In the meantime, Fat Tail had been jumping down on top of the baffle after every meal and, aided by some heavy winds, had managed to reduce it to a hunk of easily navigable rubble. Quite apart from that, we were now in late winter, and the snow dumped off our roof plus the snow already on the ground was deep enough that Fat Tail could almost walk up onto the feeder anyway.

By now it was dawning on me that a gray squirrel is no pushover, even for an adversary whose gray matter alone outweighs the whole squirrel by at least two to one. But what I was also beginning to appreciate much more than I ever had before is that the "brains" of this animal aren't contained in its few ounces of neural tissue but in the amazing combination of attributes evolution has given it: those powerful haunches for leaping, those dexterous front paws and nails for picking seeds out of my feeder, those rotating hind feet that let squirrels descend trees head first and eat hanging upside down, that tail that helps them keep their balance while performing their aerial acrobatics.

Nature has equipped gray squirrels with just the right physique and the seemingly endless energy and agility they need to thrive in the tree-tops and perfect the art of bird-feeder robbery. Confronted with that perfection, I'm moved to grudging admiration and even to a feeling verging on affection. Any animal that can be as pesky as a gray squirrel yet still manage to soft-soap me clearly has all the brain he needs. I'm glad his isn't any larger than it is.

# A Visit Down Country

John and I met in kindergarten and went through school together. We've been friends for seventy years, though not always in close touch. Our lives have taken us to places as far apart as Italy and Iowa, Germany and California, but whenever we've been within reach, we do what we've always done: go fishing, fool around in the woods. Two kids with white hair and gray beards.

John has a place in the Catskills now, an eight-hour drive from my home in Maine. I go down for a few days in May. Just the week before, John told me, he'd taken three nice browns in one of his favorite stretches of the Neversink. Prospects, he said, were good.

The morning after I arrive, we head for the river. John's dog, Chloe, a collie-German shepherd mix, comes with us. Chloe is thirteen. Her bark is hoarse and windy. Sometimes when she gets up, her legs collapse under her, but she totters to her feet again. John feeds her special geriatric dog food, microwaves chicken breasts for her. We take her for a mini-walk; then John helps her up into the backseat of the car and settles her on a rug. She'll sleep peacefully until we come back. "Chloe gets thousand-dollar-a-day, 'round-the-clock assisted living," John said.

Down at the river, our prospects don't look so good after all. It's been raining for much of the past week, and the Neversink is swollen and roily, the water up above our waists before we've waded in more than a few feet. A gentle rain sets in. The morning passes without so much as a strike. Then the sky opens up for real. Huge raindrops rattle on the surface like double-O buckshot. We retreat to a little streamside picnic shelter.

"This'll blow over soon," John said.

We sit there, talking, laughing, reveling in the thunder rolling long and loud around the hills and the rain pelting down so hard and fast it bounces back up off the river.

176

After forty-five minutes with no letup, we head back to the car and drive to the Rock Hill Diner for a lunch of mushroom soup and fried haddock. When fishing, always eat fish, even if you haven't caught any yourself.

An afternoon drive upstream looking for wadable and fishable water proves futile, and the deluge we see roaring over the spillway at the Neversink Reservoir tells us things are not likely to change in that river for the next few days.

So the next morning we head for the Beaverkill, where the river is clear and not brimming up in its banks. The sky is still overcast; we get occasional brief showers, but then the sun breaks through. Some may-flies come off the water. John catches a plump, fourteen-inch rainbow and lets it go.

We sit on the river bank in the sun and watch the show the birds are putting on. In full flight, the tree swallows pick mayflies out of the air and off the water. Going full blast, they twist, they dive, they climb, each maneuver quick as light. Bank, turn, swoop. Now you see the white belly, now the blue back, then belly, then back and belly again.

Fumbling around among these aerial acrobats are some grackles, their greenish iridescent heads gleaming in the sunlight. But what clods they are compared with the swallows. They fly out over the water and hover there like big, galumphing Huey helicopters, wings flapping, feet and tail practically in the water, bills reaching down to pluck spent flies off the surface. Then they chug aloft and head for shore to rest up for the next sortie.

A few kingbirds get into the act, but next to the swallows, even these flycatchers look like the Podunk High basketball team up against the Harlem Globetrotters. Sure, the swallows are out for a meal, too, but they can clown and play on the job, they can twirl the ball on their fingertips, roll it down their backs, and kick it off their heels to a team-mate. They hunt mayflies with such extravagant exuberance, such unity of mind, nerve, and muscle, genius on the wing.

On the way back home we hit a cloudburst so heavy the windshield wipers going at full speed can't keep up, so we pull off onto the shoul-der and wait it out. Another stop to pick up food for dinner: chicken breasts for us and one for Chloe, of course, potatoes, salad makings.

We light a small fire in the wood stove to cut the dampness and slight chill. We open a bottle of red wine, cook, eat, remember reading *Silas Marner* in Miss Kerr's ninth-grade English class, fishing for bass and pickerel in Birchwood Lake. John remembers things I don't; I remember what he doesn't. We fill in each other's blanks.

These last few days have been among the sweetest days of slow fishing I can remember: Chloe living out her last days in John's care; the swallows diving, swooping, soaring; time with a good friend of seventy years.

# A Mean Winter

L et me say straight off that I'm not ordinarily given to bad-mouthing winter. On the contrary, I love winter, most winters anyway. In the pages of this very book and elsewhere I've sung the praises of winter: the joys, for instance, of exploring previously unvisited corners of your forested neighborhood on powder snow and perfectly waxed wooden cross-country skis, of winter camping in a heated wall tent, a shelter unequaled for warmth both human and wood-fire generated. What can equal the comfort of peeling off your mukluks in the glow of your trail stove and settling back with a tot of bourbon and the company of folks who can't think of any other place they'd rather be than in this toasty, flimsy home with twenty below zero outside? Sound nuts? Believe me, it's not; it's lovely.

Let me also say that the data I've gathered in building my case against this past winter are drawn largely from my own observations and from many complaints and grumblings expressed directly to me or overheard in the post office. While the numbers in the official meteorological record might suggest that this past winter was not all that far off the averages of past years, those figures do not reflect the pain-in-the-neck factors of our 2018–2019 winter, first and foremost among them being that this past winter started a month too early and lasted a month too late.

Most years I can squeeze into November at least a few of the projects I meant to do in the summer or early fall but didn't. Most years we have just dustings of snow on the ground or only a few inches even as late as Thanksgiving, stuff neither deep enough nor heavy enough that I can't shove it out of the way with my manually operated, people-powered snow scoop. But there was no getting away that lightly this last November. Our neighbor Rick had to plow us out twice before the month was over.

Then, although we didn't have anywhere near a record snowfall, our snow was largely low-grade stuff. More often than not, our snowstorms were followed by rain then by a hard freeze that turned into armor plate what might have started out as acceptable snow for cross-country skiing. Snowmobile traffic on trails that skiers and snowmobilers share transformed those sheets of ice into fine crushed ice, marginally skiable but a far cry from the sweet, powdery stuff cross-country buffs love to see. Then, too, that same combination of snow, rain, and freeze-up turned driveways into poor quality skating rinks and made Yaktrax all but mandatory for safe trips from back door to car door.

Our road commissioner said he'd never had such difficult conditions to deal with. By midwinter the snow his crews had been winging back from earlier storms was nearly as high and thick as the Great Wall of China and nearly as impervious. Whatever snow the plow wings pushed up and back on their next runs would slide back down and freeze in place, narrowing the roads with an icy rim. Despite all that packed snow and ice stacked against them, the plow drivers still did a great job keeping our roads open.

Then, as if the winter weren't inflicting pain enough, we began losing birds from the feeders at our house along about mid-December, first the cardinal pair, who have been regulars at our place for the last few years, then the juncos, gold finches, white-breasted nuthatches, the occasional hairy and downy woodpeckers. Even the blue jays disappeared, leaving only our loyal and stalwart chickadees. Nothing like a miserable winter to show you who your real avian friends are.

I wish I could say the snowpack in the woods lasted well into May as evidence of this past winter's ridiculously long duration, but fact is there were only small, scattered patches of it for the first few days of the month. However, what did last through the end of April and on into May was a weather hangover, both in a meteorological and a physiopsychological sense. It was cool and gray and rainy enough that many of us in these parts were building quick morning fires most days just to take the chill off.

As for the psychic hangover, I have it from a medical friend that depression was a complaint that turned up in local practices more often than usual this past winter. I have no medical statistics to draw on, but the impression I have both from people I know well and from more casual acquaintances is that this winter has indeed left its mark on their souls. During a run of three rainy, gloomy days in May, I ran into one of my favorite people in these parts, a friend I've known from his boyhood on up and now a sunny, even-tempered, soft-spoken man in his fifties.

"Do you think this winter will ever end?" he asked.

"No," I said. "I don't believe it ever will."

We both laughed. But I'm still worried about the birds.

# Sightseeing

I imagine most folks who live in places like New York City or San Francisco would find Temple, Maine—or just about all of western Maine—sorely lacking in sights to see. No Empire State Building here, no Statue of Liberty. If it's urban action and hot spots you're keen on, then you'd best cross upcountry Maine off your list.

If, on the other hand, your tastes run to hills, mountains, trees, ponds, rivers, and bogs; if coming across a pale corydalis on an afternoon's ramble is your idea of a high old time; and if the whole twelve miles of the Bigelow Range seen up close from a canoe on Flagstaff Lake seems far more monumental to your eye than any monuments human hands have raised, then our neck of the woods is just the right place for you.

Local patriot that I am, I love to play tour guide and show company our sights, starting with some on our own place, then branching out afield. On our thirty-acre woodlot across the road from our house, we can admire some handsome trees: a tall, straight-boled red oak, a white pine it takes two of us to get our arms around. And if luck is with us on just the right May morning, we may walk into a tidal wave of warblers there: northern parula, Blackburnian, black-throated blue, black-throated green, black-and-white.

Sometimes the sights are on the wing; sometimes they're at our feet, like the patch of trailing arbutus Rita found on one of her walks farther up the valley a couple of years ago. Or that great mat of spring beauties I found higher up on the hill behind John Hodgkins's sugarbush. Or the little clump of twinflowers on the shores of Ballard Pond.

If our visitors will be with us for a few days, we can take the time to drive some fifty miles north to Big Jim Pond, where my parents took over the sporting camps in 1955 and where I first fell hopelessly head-over-heels in love with western Maine mountain country. When new landowners bought all of Jim Pond Township in 1973, they terminated my parents' lease because they didn't want a commercial camp in the township any longer. Everything movable—boats, motors, tools, furniture—my father sold. Friends dismantled several of the camps log by log and rebuilt them on their own lands. The few remaining buildings were burned.

I had often sung the praises of Big Jim to our friend Susan, so when she was here on a recent October visit, we strapped the canoe onto the car's roof rack and set out on an overcast afternoon to introduce her to the place. Fifty miles farther north and several hundred feet higher in elevation add up to a significant difference in climate. Snow comes two or three weeks earlier up there near the Canadian border, and in the spring, you can still be on snowshoes at Big Jim Pond when the grass is green down in Farmington and Temple.

By the time we turned off Route 27 onto the CCC (Civilian Conservation Corps) road that goes by the east end of Big Jim Pond, the sky was spitting scattered snowflakes at us on a stiff breeze out of the northwest. To reach the main body of the pond from this end, you have to paddle west through a narrow channel that was funneling the wind smack into our faces. Thinking we were doing Susan a favor, Rita and I set her up as passenger with a boat cushion and backrest, but by the time we'd paddled the mile and a half up through the channel to the site where the camps had stood, she was nearly blue from the cold, wind, and inactivity. A walk around the old camp yard warmed her enough that she could take genuine pleasure in the glories of the place—Farm Hill and Antler Hill and Shallow Pond Mountain rising up around the pond, the views off the water of Bigelow to the southeast and Snow Mountain to the west, the little sand beaches tucked into coves, the point we called Norway Point because of its stand of Norway pine and its Norway-like shape, even the bleak, metallic beauty of the water under that sunless sky.

Granted, a more thoughtful tour guide might have waited for a milder season to take a guest to Big Jim for the first time, but the bone-chilling cold of this gray, raw October afternoon didn't get in Susan's way at all. She had no trouble taking in the sights that matter. She could see why this place has a hold on my heart.

# Porcupine Stew
# and Asparagus

L ucy's sharp, yipping bark means she has come upon another creature, whether chickadee, red squirrel, chipmunk, or moose. I look
up from filing the chain saw on the back porch to see her dancing
wildly around a slow, waddling beast heading unperturbed toward our
abandoned sheep shed. Grateful that I'm on hand to intervene, I call
the dog off. She will be spared a nose- and mouthful of quills; I will be
spared the expense and inconvenience of another trip to the vet's office,
where a porcupine encounter sent us only two days ago.

I pick up my .22 and go down to the sheep shed, which now serves
as a catchall for lumber, fence posts, a johnboat. The porcupine has
sought refuge in a corner behind a roll of snow fencing, and when I pull
the roll away, the animal assumes its defensive posture, head tucked
into the corner, rear end toward me, quills fanned out like a peacock's
tail feathers. I shoot it in the back of the head; it slumps to the floor,
killed instantly; not a muscle or a nerve so much as twitches. But just to
make sure, I check with a stick from the lumber pile. I don't want quills
in my hands and arms any more than I want them in Lucy's nose. The
animal does not stir as the soft pine stick gathers a pompom of quills
from its back.

When I pick the porcupine up by its left hind foot, the long guard
hairs of its lower leg are soft in my hand. I carry the animal outside and
lay it belly-up on the grass under a lilac bush. A dead porcupine on its
back is a vastly different prospect than a live one on its feet, quills erect
and tail thrashing. If ever there was a soft underbelly, a porcupine's is it,
a vulnerable expanse of paunch, this one covered now after the spring
molt with only gray, wispy hair that barely veils the skin underneath.

The first cut I attempt tells me my pocketknife is dull, and I go up
to the house to hone it. Surely, I think as I work with the whetstone,

I had two legitimate reasons for shooting this porcupine. Preventing a dog–porcupine face-off may have been my first consideration, but then porcupine enjoys a well-deserved reputation as a bush delicacy. It has been compared with lamb, but that comparison is ridiculous. The glory of all wild meat is that it does not taste like any domestic meat. Young porcupine is sweet, tender, delicate, and tastes like young porcupine, like nothing else. And if all the children, myself included, who grew up detesting liver for the tough, stringy, leathery, murky-tasting stuff that store-bought liver usually is had ever tasted porcupine liver, they would detest no more.

So I can justify my action on two counts: protection of my domestic animal and hence of my economic interests (an agriculturalist's reason) and the acquisition of food (a hunter's reason). But will either of those arguments stand up to even a cursory moral critique, or am I just rationalizing what was at bottom the needless killing of a fellow creature?

My wife would argue later that I should have let the porcupine get away. Lucy's run-in with a porcupine two days ago did not make another inevitable. "If he'd stayed around," Rita said, "we could have taught Lucy to leave him alone. There he was, minding his own business, just trying to make an honest living, and look what it got him."

However skeptical I may feel about teaching a dog to leave a porcupine alone, I had to admit that I had sacrificed a wild animal to save myself possible expense and inconvenience. I've always proclaimed the priority of the wild animal over the domestic and condemned the destruction of wolves, cougars, and prairie dogs to make way for sheep and cattle. Consistency would seem to require that I shoot the dog, not the porcupine. My dog is a pet, a luxury; she contributes nothing tangible to human welfare. The stockman can at least argue that the loss of even one beef animal means not only economic loss for him but also the loss of food for others. I had killed a wild animal on the mere possibility, not the certainty, that it might cause my dog some pain and me some minor expense.

Well, all right. Chalk that one up against me. But surely the food argument is incontrovertible. If I kill an animal and eat it, I'm not dealing in maybes or possibilities. Meat on the table is meat on the table.

Killing for food is not killing to protect any questionable economic interests that probably would have gotten along quite nicely without protection anyhow.

Razor-sharp knife in hand, I head back to my skinning job. I cut around wrists and ankles, slit down the insides of the legs to the midline of the belly, cut down the midline from throat to anus. As I start to peel the hide back from legs and belly, Rita, who has been shopping in town, returns home and comes to see what I'm doing. That she will disapprove is a given, but there will be no harsh words. We are each too acutely aware of our own confusions, inconsistencies, and irrationalities to come down too hard on the other.

"Poor baby," she says, "look at the little hands and feet."

Her remark is not sentimental. She is not out to add Porky the Porcupine to the Disney pantheon of Bambi the Deer and Thumper the Rabbit. She is just acknowledging a kinship that the appearance of the animal's limbs instantly suggests. Despite the long claws and the pebbly skin, the feet with their five toes and naked soles look remarkably human, and even though the hands, which the porcupine does in fact use in handlike fashion for food gathering, have only four digits, their similarity to our hands is striking.

Decry this as blatant, unscientific anthropomorphizing if you will, but the human impulse to see ourselves in animals and animals in us, to talk with them, cohabit with them, be suckled and reared by them—all this from Leda and the swan to Romulus and Remus to Mowgli—testifies to a dream citizenship in a world where no sharp lines are drawn between gods, men, and animals. For hunting cultures, kinship with animals is a fact reflected in their totemism and mythology.

In the cosmology of the Koyukon people in Alaska, it was the Great Raven who created the earth, its plants and animals, and its human beings. In the Distant Time, animals and humans were the same. They shared a common language, and animals can still understand human speech today. The Koyukon may address an animal directly, pleading for its blessing and protection, and they are careful not to say things or behave in ways that will offend the animal. For them, not to anthropomorphize (and not to recognize that animals zoomorphize) would be a sign of colossal ignorance, willful denial of our common ancestry and shared life in the present. When Rita kneels next to a dead porcupine and says, "Poor baby," she is acknowledging that clanship, our common origins in the same mix of clay and breath.

The Cartesian proscription against anthropomorphizing has always seemed to me both obtuse and arrogant, a kind of professional prissiness some scientists adopt to set themselves apart from the ignorant masses who, on seeing a dog bounce up and down wagging his tail, venture to say the dog is "happy." But for the observer or scientist who recognizes a kinship with animals, the prohibition on anthropomorphizing is rooted in a humility that acknowledges the creature's otherness, all those ways in which human and porcupine are not alike and that constitute, perhaps even more than its kinship with us, the animal's mystery and sacredness. If we see only ourselves in animals, we will never see *them*. To anthropomorphize in that way is to sentimentalize and invent for white-tailed deer a domestic life that any 1950s family in Greenwich, Connecticut, would have been proud of.

Rita goes up to the house to put away the groceries; I finish dressing out the porcupine. I cut the tail free, put my foot on it, and lift the animal by its hind feet, peeling the skin away right up to the back of the skull, where I cut the head off. I open the body cavity, pull out a loop of lower intestine near the anus, cut it, and strip out the feces. I cut the esophagus free where it comes through the diaphragm and pull out the liver, kidneys, intestines. You don't have to have vast experience in comparative anatomy to realize that evolution has allotted most of the space inside a porcupine to its digestive system, which makes up one-quarter of the animal's body weight. A porcupine is a kind of mammalian pear or crookneck squash, its lower bulge filled with its long, labyrinthian guts, its proportionately tiny heart and lungs tucked in as an afterthought way up inside the neck.

Because the porcupine is not a long-distance runner, pulmonary and cardiovascular capacity is not a high priority. Far more important is the ability to convert bark and leaves into energy. Because those mainstays of the porcupine's diet number among nature's more intractable foodstuffs, evolution has seen to it that the porcupine has a physical plant that can break them down. In the caecum, a sac about the size of the stomach but located where the small and large intestines meet,

188 LOST BUT FOUND

bacterial enzymes accomplish what mammalian digestive enzymes cannot. But because the enzymes work slowly, the digestive process is also slow and the digestive tract long to allow for absorption of nutrients.

I am acutely aware of the genius of this animal as I dismember him, handling the pearly, undulating beauty of his guts, the red glow of his muscle, the still-present heat of this life I have ended. Even our most intricate human inventions seem clumsy and lumbering compared with the perfection of this modest beast, a perfection of mind and spirit as well as of body. In his many years of studying porcupines in the Catskills, Uldis Roze found that the animal was

> *a hunter of leaves. Unlike the grazing ruminants of the plains that crop a field of grass and find any number of species acceptable fodder, the porcupine must hunt its food by discovering the rare trees in the forest that will best sustain it. Out of a thousand forest trees in the Catskills, one or two are acceptable lindens and one is a bigtooth aspen. To locate and return to those trees, the porcupine uses all the skills of the hunter: memory, attention to landmark and local detail, persistence. That explains why the American psychologist L. W. Sackett (1913) found that the North American porcupine has an extraordinary ability to learn complex mazes and to remember them as much as a hundred days afterward.*

Would Descartes have said, "The porcupine thinks; therefore it is"? I doubt it, but I would hardly call Uldis Roze less a scientist because he uses words like *memory* and *attention, learn* and *remember*, to describe the porcupine's capabilities and behavior. I take at face value the remark a Koyukon elder made repeatedly to anthropologist Richard Nelson: "Every animal knows way more than you do."

The porcupine is skinned and dressed out now. No edible scrap of him will go to waste. At the outdoor faucet I rinse off the body, the heart, liver, kidneys. The skin, quills, feet, intestines, and bladder I will give an honorable burial. A pre-industrial hunter might have dyed the quills and decorated belts, clothing, moccasins, and pouches with them. Dried and mounted on a wooden handle, Uldis Roze says, the bristly underside of the tail that aids the porcupine in climbing trees makes an excellent comb. The long, curved claws that let the porcupine cling to fissures in rough bark I could make into a necklace or bracelet, but I will make neither. I live, after all, in a different economy, and I ask my porcupine's forgiveness for my yielding to other imperatives and for my failure of piety.

As I cut the animal up into stew-sized pieces in our well-stocked kitchen, I have to concede, too, that in the context of that same economy, my hunter's justification for this kill may not stand up either. We do not *need* this animal for food. We have plenty else to live on. We have storage tins full of rice and beans; we have little plastic tubs full of tofu in the fridge; we have dried bananas from Nicaragua and dried apricots from Turkey.

Given the ready availability of vegetable foods, one could easily argue that I killed this porcupine simply for a taste treat, merely to satisfy a trivial whim. One could argue that society's ability to grow adequate amounts of nourishing vegetarian fare makes the killing of any animal for food unnecessary. And if we add to that the darker side of growing vegetable crops by modern large-scale agricultural methods, a prohibition on killing animals would seem all the more urgent. Just consider how many animal deaths each cupful of granola represents. How many nesting trees were felled to clear the fields to grow the oats, peanuts, and sunflower seeds? How many buffalo died to make way for the wheat and cornfields of Kansas and Nebraska? How many raccoons, rabbits, squirrels, skunks, and porcupines have the trucks that cart the oats, peanuts, and sunflower seeds pulverized on our highways and byways? How many square miles of Alaskan wildlife habitat have been and will be destroyed to drill the oil wells that will keep our trucks and tractors rolling? With so many surrogate killers doing in animals to keep me in innocent, bloodless food, how dare I take the life of one more creature? The global network of industrial agriculture tells me I dare not. Hunting, the whole inexorable drift of our world tells me, is obsolete, passé. Hunting is nostalgic playacting.

If I pursue this line of thought much further, I'll soon be utterly depressed and dispirited. So I don't. "Lighten up, man," I tell myself. "Give yourself a break. Nobody's expecting categorical imperatives from you. Make a little sense of your life on your own turf and you'll be doing just fine."

In the course of the following week, during which our porcupine provides us with four superb evening meals—liver one night, porcupine stew for the other three, all with fresh asparagus from the garden on the side—I do lighten up considerably.

So does Rita. As we are sopping up the last of the gravy and sucking the last of the bones clean, she says to me, "You know, if porcupine were a vegetable, I'd grow it."

"And if asparagus were an animal," I say, "I'd shoot it."

# Our Drought

I call it "our drought" to stress its local nature and to distinguish it from widespread, long-lasting droughts in other parts of the country and world that make last summer's few weeks of sparse precipitation here in western Maine seem a mere drop in the drought bucket, as it were. Californians, who have watched drought-fueled wildfires rage in their state, would surely be justified in dismissing our drought as an inconsequential dry spell. But because we northern New Englanders often get more precipitation than we want rather than too little, it's not surprising that a nearly rainless July and August with temperatures consistently in the mid- to high eighties evoke some notes of discomfort, if not downright alarm.

Our drought this past summer was apparently serious enough that newspapers felt obliged to write about it. The *Bangor Daily News* ran an article headlined "Severe drought hits state for first time in more than a decade" and informed readers that "Severe Drought" was not a reporter's impressionistic assessment of how dry we were but instead a classification from the National Drought Mitigation Center. Severe Drought, on the Center's scale, ranks above Abnormally Dry and Moderate Drought but below Extreme Drought and Exceptional Drought.

But measuring by what I could see around me here in Temple valley, I would have given our drought a higher mark than just middle-of-the-scale Severe. Granted, I wasn't using any scientifically certified instruments to measure the moisture content of the soil, nor was I recording streamflow all over Maine and comparing it to historical records. Granted, too, my memory is not what it used to be, but from what I could recall, I hadn't seen a dry spell worse than this for many a year.

I could, for instance, walk across Temple Stream at a few places behind our house and barely get the soles of my work boots wet. When

192 LOST BUT FOUND

I poked a shovel down as far as it could go in our usually rich, damp garden soil and turned it over, what I got was stuff that looked and felt like brown talcum powder. Only by constant watering—we had a well drilled years ago to back up our dug well—could we keep our patch of lettuce and parsley and chard and carrots, our tomatoes and basil and leeks thriving. Deb, who has a vegetable stand at the outdoor market in Farmington every Friday, fared a lot worse than we did. She lives on higher land than ours and has a dug well that could just barely keep supplying her and her garden with enough water to get by.

We didn't lack sunny days for haying, but some first-cut yields in our area were down 20 to 40 percent, and several farmers decided the sparse, dried-up stuff left in their fields wouldn't make a second cut worth the trouble. The folks at the U.S. Geological Survey's Maine Water Science Center who monitor groundwater levels in wells found the lowest levels for July and August the Center had ever seen in the thirty years it has been keeping records.

All these dismaying figures cannot, however, be laid only at the feet of a hot summer with below-average rainfall. Last winter's measly snowpack was the real beginning of our drought. My gauge for snow-fall is how many times between December 1 and May 1 our neighbor Ricky plows our driveway. Last winter he had to come only twice, not his usual five or six times.

Finding silver linings in droughts is tougher than finding them in clouds, but I suppose the number of mornings Ricky could sleep a bit later last winter compensated him somewhat—though I suspect not nearly enough—for his loss of snowplowing income. Similarly, our drought spared me the almost-weekly summer chore of mowing the lawn. By the end of July, most of our scruffy carpet of grass and dande-lions had shriveled to a brown, bone-dry stubble, and in the few patches where it was able to find enough moisture to keep itself greenish, it grew so slowly the lawnmower and I had our most idle summer ever. Still, that relief from lawn-mowing duty was a benefit that came at too high a price. I'd gladly have given it up for the sight of lush green grass and flourishing squash plants.

But chary as nature's gods were in bringing us rain, they were more than generous in drenching us with beauty. I suspect there would be no way to prove a connection between our drought and what seemed to me last summer's especially rich evening displays of sun-tinged clouds and the play of low light and shadow working their art on the sky and on this little valley, but as I sat looking out our kitchen windows at suppertime, I took what I saw as a good omen anyway—a sign of a first autumn rain that might well come on a mid-September night, which it did. Clouds lined with silver after all.

Really, though, when it comes to droughts, about the only thing I feel I can be reasonably sure of is that Californians and lots of other people in this world would be delighted to trade their droughts for ours.

# Late-Summer Fishing

t's late August, about noon on a bright, sunny day. I'm gathering my fly rod, waders, vest, my elegant wading staff—a spruce stick with a hunk of clothesline tied to it—and packing them into the back of the car for an afternoon and evening's fishing with my niece's husband, Jon.

The prospect gladdens the heart for many reasons. For one, I like Jon. Because Kathy is not my daughter, I suppose I'm not entitled to the paternal pleasure a father must feel at seeing his daughter marry a smart, able, good-hearted, big-hearted man. But Kathy's choice of a husband has allowed me the perhaps lesser but nonetheless real pleasure of avuncular approval. Jon is a chemist who cleans up some of the toxic messes our industries have visited upon the world. He is also a skilled handyman who has renovated the family's New Jersey home from top to bottom. His values are impeccable: when Kathy and Jon and their son, Little Jon, who is now no longer little, turn up in our neighborhood for a couple of weeks' summer vacation, Jon may bring us a bottle of his superb applejack or a packet of smoked trout. He understands that, in the thick of life's duties and obligations, there is always time for really important things like food and fishing.

Several years back, Jon and I drove the hour or so from Temple to Fairfield and fished the stretch of the Kennebec just below Shawmut Dam. Jon took a special liking to the place—the broad sweep of the Kennebec there, the handsome farm on the hill across the river, the shaded trails on the west bank. And then, if the trout proved as uncooperative as they often do in late summer, he could always forget about them, pick up his spinning rod, and catch some smallmouth bass in the quick water right below the dam.

On this particular afternoon, we stop in Fairfield at the tackle shop appropriately called "Fly Fishing Only" and spend 15 or 20 minutes ogling and caressing the classy, expensive fly rods lined up on one wall and consulting with the owner on what, if any, flies might induce a trout to strike. He allows as things are slow on the river. Heavy rains have brought the water up. Fishing, we are given to understand, is not tiptop.

This news does not discourage us. We are here for whatever the day and evening will bring. We drive the few miles north to the access road to the dam site, head on down to the river, set up our rods.

The river is ridiculously high. Water is boiling down the tailrace at the dam, and as I wade in a few hundred yards farther downstream, I'm soon in above my middle and all too aware that just one misstep will let the force of the water knock me off my feet and send me tumbling head over heels. And with this heavy, racing water extending from bank to bank, how, if a fish ever should rise, will I ever manage to put a fly in front of that fish's nose?

Jon, with only hip boots, can't do much more than get in a few feet from shore where he has no room for a backcast and no access to any fishable water anyway. I soon see him climb out of the river and head back to the car, where he'll trade in for his spinning rod and head out after smallmouths.

I pick my way carefully to shore and walk farther downstream than I have fished before. There, around a gentle bend, I find some marshy little islands and slower water where wading is not life threatening, where no fish are rising, and where I fish nymphs until dusk, all to no avail.

It's always nice to catch fish; but luckily for the likes of me, catching is not absolutely essential to fishing. Puddling around in the water with a fly rod in my hand is its own reward.

Then there's the occasional last-minute surprise. While a big beaver swims a long loop around me on his way home, I tie on a bucktail and toss it out into some slack water. I get a solid hit, and after a few minutes, I've brought a chunky smallmouth bass to hand and released it. A few more casts and I have another and another.

Well, okay. No trout today, but catching these scrappy smallmouths has been an unexpected treat, and I'm betting Jon must have caught several up at the dam, too.

I head back upstream and find Jon still casting into the water just below the tailrace.

"What luck?" I ask.

"Zero," he says.

"The river's got everything backwards today," I say. "You're skunked, and I caught your smallmouths about a mile downstream."

"No problem," he says. "I'm happy just being out here."

A man after my own heart. So we head for home, two equally contented fishermen driving through the summer night.

# A Chance at the
# Mythical Buck

J ust about every fall for the last several years, in the first week after
deer season closes here in Maine, I have found the tracks of a big
buck on our thirty-acre woodlot on the hill across the road from
our house. I've never gotten so much as a glimpse of this animal, either
in hunting season or out. He must, I am sure, get his copy of the state's
*Hunting and Trapping Laws and Rules* in good time each year. He knows
just when to make himself scarce each fall and when it is safe for him to
come out of hiding again to prance around on my woodlot and drive
me crazy with those tracks of his.

For years this routine has gone on, had gone on, I should say,
because this past fall I finally did get a glimpse of him and then some.

I had just come back from a few days of hunting in northern Maine
with some friends. We take a wall tent and stove on these excursions;
we take canoes and paddle ourselves into some out-of-the-way corner
where we have a big chunk of woods to ourselves. We hunt hard all day,
come back to the tent in the evening, light the candles, crank up the
stove, sip on some bourbon, cook supper, yak. We have a wonderful
time and almost never get any deer.

I got home and had my stuff out of the car by four o'clock on that
Saturday afternoon. Legal hunting hours ended at 4:47 that day. So I
had about forty-five minutes of hunting left, barely half an hour by the
time I could get to a stand up on the hill. Dumb idea. Waste of time.
What did I think I'd see in this tiny sliver of time before it would be too
dark to see anyway?

But my first commandment of hunting is: yield not unto pessi-
mism, so I headed up onto the hill and took a stand alongside my
twitch road.

Expecting nothing, I had given in to a half-dozing reverie from which the appearance of a huge deer with a huge rack woke me. He had materialized out of nowhere; he was, I swear, close enough that I could have whacked him with a hockey stick. Well, maybe not quite that close. But close anyway.

The instant I saw him, he saw me, whirled, bolted out of sight. I didn't have time to even think about getting the rifle up. Gone.

I didn't move. I hadn't heard him pounding away through the trees, hadn't seen his flag flying.

I glanced at my watch. Only five minutes of legal shooting time left, and legal shooting time or no, darkness was settling in on this overcast afternoon.

After what seemed like half an hour of studying every inch of the woods in front of me, I could see him, just a piece of him, just his head, a miniscule target, peering at me out of a dense patch of young fir. Was he looking at me straight away, or was his body broadside or quartered to me on the right? Or the left? I didn't want to guess where his chest might be and risk wounding him. There wasn't time to wait for him to move into an opening, and where he was, there wasn't any opening anyhow. And I couldn't wait. Both the law and the fading light said now or never. I would either drop him with a shot between the eyes, or I would miss.

I missed.

So now I could get started on self-flagellation and all the what-ifs. What if I hadn't been standing there like a dummy, half-asleep? I could have seen him in plenty of time to get an easy shot. What if, after I'd spotted his head, I'd had wits enough to shoot a bit lower? I might have dropped him with a neck shot. What if I'd just gone in the house and poured myself a drink instead of coming out here to blow a chance at one of the biggest deer I'd ever seen? I'd have spared myself endless mental replays of this fiasco, endless speculations about what I could and should have done differently.

What surprised me most about this incident, though, even shocked me, was how much I had lusted after a trophy animal without realizing it. I've always claimed that hunting, for me, was only about that good lean deer meat and the joy of the days afield. But now that I'd bungled a chance at a buck that probably would have dressed out over 200 pounds, I couldn't honestly lay claim to that kind of subsistence-hunter purity. I've never yearned for a stuffed head on the wall, but I would like to have enrolled myself in my own one-man Big Buck Club.

Maybe someday I'll come to the philosophical view that still having a mythical buck in the bush is worth none in the hand. But I'm not quite there yet.

# Awesome—A Local Hero

In 1991, shortly after Steve Muise (pronounced "muse") arrived in Farmington, Maine, to take a job as a string teacher in School Administrative District 9's music program, my neighbor Sandy Gregor suggested to him that he expand the district's music curriculum to include some fiddle music.

Sandy's suggestion was—I think it's fair to say—music to Steve's ears. Steve had grown up in a musical family. His mother played piano, and his father, who emigrated from Nova Scotia to Massachusetts in 1952, brought with him both a guitar and a repertoire of French-Canadian tunes that Steve began learning to play by ear on the violin at age nine. The whole family—mother, father, Steve, his two brothers, and two sisters—often gathered to play their respective instruments and sing together. From Steve's infancy on, music was always present in his life, music homemade by people he lived with and loved, music everyone could take part in, dance to, laugh to, maybe sometimes cry to. But the schoolboy Steve could never have anticipated that this music he soaked up at home, music played in North Woods logging camps and at barn dances throughout New England, would prove to be such a strong card in his deck. And it would be nearly impossible to overstate the importance that learning that music by ear had in Steve's own development as a musician.

"When you learn to play by ear," he says, "you don't just learn to play a piece of music; you also learn to feel that music."

So for Steve, playing by ear is where his teaching begins. "For me, it's the first step in becoming a musician. The next one is dancing, that whole-body immersion in the music, moving with it and finding yourself at one with it. The final step is learning to play from a score, feeling your way from the page into the composer's intent. These stages in learning aren't necessarily sequential. You can be developing them all at the same time, and once you've integrated them, you can follow your musical path wherever it takes you."

Sandy surely had an altruistic motive when she encouraged Steve to have his students play fiddle music, but she also had a personal one: her son, Matty Goodman, was a member of a junior high string quartet that Steve was coaching. That small group would quickly grow into a full-scale, multi-stylistic string band, the Franklin County Fiddlers, and become one of the most popular activities for Mount Blue High School musicians to take part in. Its performances would also become one of the most popular events for mothers and fathers, aunts and uncles, brothers and sisters to attend.

"Some high school kids," Matty says now, looking back on his time with Steve some twenty-five years later, "may have thought fiddling was kind of old fashioned and geeky, but Steve's energy and love for it were irresistible. He made fiddling one of the coolest things a kid in Farmington could do. And of course it wasn't just fiddling he knew and loved. He'd gone to the Berklee College of Music in Boston and come out versed in everything from Bach, Beethoven, and Brahms to the Beatles, the blues, rock, and bluegrass. He was young and hip and about as knowledgeable a musician as Franklin County had ever seen, and he was brimming over with good stuff we kids all wanted to learn."

Today, the Franklin County Fiddlers are about twenty strong. Most of them play fiddle but there are a few cellos, a bass viol, a piano, and—because Steve is both inclusive and eclectic—he has also welcomed not only guitar and banjo players but a bagpiper and a flutist, as well. Occasionally, some members of the audience may not be able to resist dancing. When the fiddlers struck up a waltz at a concert in the University of Maine at Farmington's Nordica Hall a few years ago, a boy I guessed for a sophomore sitting in the front row got up, sought out his partner among the fiddlers, and the couple proceeded to dance. When the waltz ended and the dancers had returned to their seats, Steve—far from chastising the young man for luring away one of his fiddlers—had nothing but praise for him.

"What I always tell my students," he said, "is: Don't ever be afraid to be awesome."

That's exactly what Steve does himself every day of his life, and in exemplifying what it means to be awesome—to throw yourself joyfully and wholeheartedly into what you do—he inspires his students to do the same. To see him playing his fiddle among his young protégés is to see a man who has found his calling in the world and is loving every minute of it. Steve and the Franklin County Fiddlers light up any auditorium or grange hall they play in, and I'll wager the adults in their audiences are every bit as inspired by Steve's energy and joie de vivre as his students are. I'll wager, too, that if you ask any music lovers—young, middle-aged, or old—in these parts what they think of Steve Muise, the answer you'll get every time will be: "He's awesome."

# Unexpected Gifts

When Rita and I moved into our gutted handyman's special in the summer of 1971, what the place needed was a total overhaul, a full-scale renovation in the literal sense of that word: a "making new" from top to bottom. But all we could do then—and all we have been able to do ever since—is just make do, not make new. So what we have worked at over these past forty-five years, by fits and starts, is not renovation but periodic home improvements, making one thing then another better as time, energy, and bank account have allowed.

I began right away by replacing the rotten 7×7-inch sills on the north wall and making a crude (but insulated) studio apartment out of the spacious kitchen where we could live while we fixed up one room, then another and another in the following months.

These initial home improvements brought us the gains in safety and comfort we had hoped they would, but they brought us some unexpected gifts, as well. As we tore out the old walls in the post-and-beam half of the house, we found newspapers from the 1840s still pasted over the cracks between the sheathing boards. This attempt at blocking air infiltration was largely ineffectual, but a welcome historical marker suggesting that this house may have been built during those years. And just about every major project we've undertaken since then—converting half of the unfinished second floor of the ell into a bedroom, replacing our rattly old single-pane windows with double glazed ones—has turned up an item or two that Dana Hamlin, who lived here from 1905 to 1968, had left behind: shards of a bean pot, a tea saucer, half-a-dozen teeth for the cutter bar of a mowing machine.

But just this past summer when I asked Luke, our genius of a young carpenter here in Temple, to replace our ancient, cracked soffits and insulate the dead-air space behind them, we found a treasure trove of stuff. How or why these items wound up in such an unlikely place I leave to greater minds than mine. The first thing to fall out when Luke started prying off soffit boards was a rusted thirty-six-inch grass blade for a scythe. Next, in the utilitarian category, came a rusty horseshoe with four shoeing nails still stuck in it. Then five spools of varying sizes, only one of which had a legible label stamped into the wood: "Belding Bros.& Co., A, 100 yds.," accompanied by a pincushion measuring about four inches in diameter and two inches thick. Once white with decorative blue ribbons sewn across it, it was now—after a century tucked in under Dana's eaves—a uniform dirty gray.

How do I know that pincushion had been there for a century? Because not far from it we found a small pocket notebook that recorded, day by day, in pencil, wages at $3 per day that a fellow named Jack earned in the months of January and February in 1918. The front cover of this notebook was gone, but the text on its back cover makes clear what kind of product the long-lost front cover advertised: "The trouble with a great many of you who suffer continually with the stomach and bowels is simply this: your bowels are DIRTY. . . . You must CLEAN OUT . . . the bowels. And once you get the bowels clean, KEEP them clean."

But life in 1918 wasn't all about work and purging one's innards. We found several items meant for pure enjoyment, too: a brier tobacco pipe and three of white clay, which I thought had gone out with the Founding Fathers. And for the kids, a tiny tattered American flag much like the ones children still wave today at Fourth of July parades. The prize item in the toy department, though, was a miniature banjo only eleven inches long. The main body looks like a tuna-fish can; the neck is a half-inch dowel, the fingerboard a piece of tin bent up at the pegboard end and with slots cut there for the strings. The tuning pegs look like slightly hefty golf tees. I strung this mini banjo with Dacron fly-reel backing, and the thing actually gave off real, live notes. I could imagine a little kid—maybe Dana's son—happily plucking away on it for hours.

The final thing we found was a copy of the Somerset Farmers' Cooperative Telephone Company's directory, which lists subscribers from Waterville to Bingham to Stratton and Rangeley and back, including, of course, our little town of Temple. I count sixty-seven listings. Most of them have "residence" printed next to them, but a few note professions or businesses. J. A. Brooks was the town's stage driver; C. E. Gould, the paper hanger; and our own Dana Hamlin, the cream collector. I was tempted to pick up the phone and ask the operator to connect me with Dana's number: 1-25. I wanted to ask him if that pincushion and that toy banjo were Christmas or birthday gifts, homemade, as I imagined, fashioned by a loving hand from materials at hand. What better unexpected gifts could there be?

# Of Wind, Water, and the Best of Friends

At our place here on the Temple intervale, we often get winds that gust to gale force—and then some. Most of them come out of the northwest, where Spruce Mountain closes off the end of our valley. Once good, solid breezes make it over that ridge, they seem to think this little town is a great place to see just how fast they can get going. So by the time they reach our address, about four miles down the road, they're hitting at least thirty-two to thirty-eight miles per hour—High Winds, on the Beaufort scale—and have picked up momentum enough to set our old standing-seam metal roof banging and clanging, to tear heavy branches out of our trees, and occasionally, to topple a whole tree.

We all know how dangerous wind can be to life, limb, and property. Sometimes, when I wake in the middle of the night to the roar of the wind battering our old house, I wonder if this will be the night the wind peels our roof off like the top of a sardine can. But nerve-wracking as that can be, I'm still on solid ground and not, as I sometimes have been, caught out in a canoe on a huge lake or saltwater bay with a squall blowing up.

Twenty years ago, I joined five friends on a canoe trip of about 460 miles from Kuujjuarapik, on the east shore of Hudson Bay, to the village of Tasiujaq on Ungava Bay. Our route took us 180 miles north on Hudson Bay, until we turned inland to pond-hop and portage our way east to the westernmost shore of Lake Minto, the hundred-mile headwater lake of the Leaf River, which in turn flows northeasterly to debouch into Ungava Bay.

The six of us—Al and Wendy, Dave and Ann, Dick and I—were veterans of extended canoe trips in the North Country and accustomed to encountering plenty of wind, but after being windbound on a peninsula jutting out into Lake Minto for nearly three full days, we realized we'd been completely or partially windbound for ten of the thirty days we had been underway. We'd already used up three weeks to travel a little less than halfway to Tasiujaq. That left us with only two weeks to do about 245 miles if we were to catch the plane that would take us on the first leg of our journey home. About eighty of those miles were still on windy Lake Minto, but once we hit the river, the current helped us average around twenty miles a day and brought us within an easy morning's paddle of Tasiujaq with a day or two to spare.

When we started out on what we thought would be the last day of our trip, the sky was overcast, the water mill-pond smooth. Confident that the weather would hold, we chose to paddle six miles of open water across Baie Rouge rather than take the far longer, but more cautious, route hugging the shoreline. But when we were halfway across, a horrendous storm blew up within five minutes. We headed for the nearest shore, paddling through canoe-gobbling waves and heavy rain and fog that made it all but impossible to tell how far off shore we still were. Once on land, and relieved to find we were all accounted for, we settled in as best we could in a wind so strong we had to constantly lean into it to stay upright.

A few days earlier, Wendy had remarked that if any newcomers to canoe trips had been along on this one, they probably would never have wanted to take another. Granted, the weather gods had been unkind to us for the whole trip and then topped it off with this last-minute, life-threatening warning shot across our bows: "Never take a wind-still morning for granted."

Chastened we were, but not then or ever after did any of us say we wished we hadn't gone on this trip. We had, after all, camped on meadows abloom with beach pea, harebell, goldenrod, and many more flowers I didn't know—botanical displays both lush and delicate. We'd seen belugas breaching in Hudson Bay, had a big black bear walk along the river with us for a good fifty yards, had herds of caribou graze like cows next to our camps then plunge into Lake Minto to swim across vast expanses of water. Wherever they were going in this world of rock, sky, and water, only they knew. We travel to these still-wild places to get a sense of what our world was like in the beginning, and because we can't record it all in our journals or retain it in our heads, we have to keep going back.

The bush is no place for hubris; the wind taught us that once again, but it also taught us that it isn't an insurmountable obstacle, either—especially if you travel with friends like Dave, Ann, Wendy, Al, and Dick, some of the most competent trippers and just plain terrific people I've ever known. Warm in my bed when a winter storm is hammering on my roof, I often think of them with great respect and affection and wish them always-fair winds at their backs.

# Griff's Camp

The first time I saw Griff—his last name was Griffin—he was perched about seven feet off the ground in a red maple tree, sawing off a couple of limbs that extended out over an expanse of granite ledge below. As I was walking past, headed for our house a short piece farther down the road, he hailed me.

"You got a steak ready for me?" he asked. "I been working up quite an appetite."

"No," I said, "I don't, but why are you sawing limbs off a tree only a few steps back from the road and on top of a rock ledge?"

"I'm gonna put a school bus on this rock," he said. "Make me a nice little camp away from the village, out here where it's quiet and peaceful."

This exchange took place just a couple of weeks after we'd moved from frenetic Greater Boston to tranquil Temple and, as I've said, just a stone's throw away from our house.

Great, I thought, terrific. In the winter, with no leaves on the trees, we'll be able to admire a derelict school bus from our kitchen windows. We've arrived just in time to have the village eccentric—if not the village lunatic—move in on top of us. Who, in his right mind, would want to squat in a roadside school bus when he had, as Griff did, for his principal residence a perfectly livable trailer less than a mile away? But eccentric or not, he knew how to make things happen. Not many more days had passed before a school bus, minus its wheels, chassis, and engine, was perched on that rock.

My knowledge of Griff's personal history is scanty. I heard tell that he was a retired electrician from California. The electrician part was accurate because, within another few days, he had put an electrical entrance into the bus himself. He was no slouch at carpentry either. Once he'd made the interior of the bus livable, he set about beautification of the exterior, encasing it in wood, painting it canary yellow to maintain the bus's original color scheme, I guess, and setting off each of those porthole-like school bus windows with its own frame, lovingly fitted and painted robin's-egg blue.

But that was not the end of home improvement. A school bus was pretty cramped quarters for Griff and his wife, Hilma, so over the years one addition followed another: first, a bedroom and a closet-sized room for a chemical toilet built on behind the bus; next, a spacious sitting room; and, finally, a storage shed tacked on in back of it all. At some point in this series of projects, I assumed the trailer in the village had been sold or rented because Hilma and Griff were at the camp full time.

Along with the changes Griff worked on his camp, he and Hilma worked changes in me. We were neighbors after all. If I saw him working around the place I'd say hello, or if he was out for a stroll he might stop in and tell us excitedly about the latest rare coin he'd picked up for his collection. Then, when I first caught on that our dog Brandy was paying Griff and Hilma regular visits, I went over to ask if she was bothering them.

"Oh, no," Hilma said, "we love to have her come over."

Love my dog, and I'll love you. But I probably would have loved Hilma anyway, dog or no. She was one of the most charming women I've ever met, and because she never gave a thought to making herself charming, she was all the more charming for that. Her voice had a melodic Yankee lilt that made the simplest words sound like some old, gentle song.

Griff had fallen for that voice and its owner, too, and when I asked him once what had moved him to settle in Temple, he said with a big grin on his face, "I came to Temple to hunt for a buck, but what I got was a dear."

Hilma and Griff are both gone now, Griff first in 1987. The home he'd built out of a school bus needed his energy to keep it up, and when Hilma said she wished she could move into a nice new trailer she wouldn't have to fuss with, Rita and I bought the camp and helped her do that.

Griff's camp is now serving as a storage building for construction materials, many of them recycled, that a local church's housing ministry uses to help people renovate their homes. I think Griff would be pleased to know his place is helping folks do what he did: build a home from the materials at hand.

Was Griff an eccentric? Sure, but a good-hearted one. And aren't we all eccentrics, one way or another? It's often benign eccentricity—along with love—that makes the world go round.

# Of Skis, Moose, and Climate Change

Come late August or early September when the swamp maples start showing red, fall is on its way with winter not far behind, and I start fretting about what kind of skiing we'll get this time around. For most of the forty-nine years I've lived here on the Temple intervale I've been able on winter afternoons to leave my desk work around 3:30, step into my cross-country ski bindings, and use the final hour or so of daylight to clear my head with a ski run to Drury Pond about a mile away. I cross the ice on Temple Stream right behind our house, cross the big hayfield on the other side, and ski to the pond through my own and my neighbors' woodlots.

I can't recall exactly when I began these late-afternoon solo runs to Drury Pond, but I do know that once begun—sometime in the 1980s—they became something I did every day for years, not as a daily chore but more like checking in with a friend. Once at the pond, I'd take the half-mile run up to its north end, then the trail back home—sometimes in a snow flurry, sometimes by moonlight—back across the white expanse of our hayfield, the peak of our house visible above the trees on the far side of the stream, the welcome prospect of supper with Rita and our son, Greg, our curling up in the evening with our respective books or catching a movie on the VCR.

But over the past decade, our winters of deep cold and powder snow have given way to the recurring pattern of snowstorms followed by rain that makes for perpetually icy driveways, crummy cross-country skiing, an unreliable ice bridge across Temple Stream, and, this past winter, Temple Stream never freezing over at all. I know my loss is trivial compared with losses other people, lands, and creatures are already facing from climate change, but it's a loss of a pleasure, a ritual, that I've come to rely on.

In the final paragraphs of his article "Heritage Tested" in the Summer 2019 issue of *Northern Woodlands*, David Dobbs points out that the permanent protection the Champion deal has afforded the Kingdom Heritage Lands doesn't guarantee them immunity to the changes global warming is inflicting across northern New England. In Maine, where I live at about the same latitude as Vermont's northern border, moose calves are being decimated just as they are in Vermont by the ticks that they pick up by the tens of thousands in warmer winters. Taming global warming, which threatens to push the moose back north along with other flora and fauna we think of as integral to our forests, is a decades-long global project and not something we humans are likely to accomplish quickly enough to prevent those losses.

"It now seems near certain," Dobbs writes, "that some of this place's greatest distinctions—iconic species like moose, lynx, marten, brook trout . . . may disappear. . . . Can a culture that rose from such a particular habitat persist if that habitat and its iconic denizens essentially move out of reach? Does the land's very identity change? Does ours?"

Complex questions, and knowing full well that I'm rushing in where people far more knowledgeable in natural and social sciences than I am would fear to tread, I'm going to risk an optimistic answer: Yes, that culture can persist, albeit in a modified and modifying form, because of its own resilience and because of its resilient citizens. As a lifelong fisherman, I'd surely mourn the disappearance of brook trout, but I can't imagine even that loss could cut the invisible bonds that tie me to this western Maine hill country and its people.

Here in Temple, this past spring brought heavy, wet snow and winds that bent and broke our lilacs, flattened a good-sized white birch, and pulled down half of our old Red Astrachan apple tree. The loop trail in our small woodlot across the road was littered with everything from endless twigs to large branches torn out of our pines. Altogether, it was still another unwelcome visit from the weather gods to our little patch of the world, but one I could make peace with several days later by delimbing and sawing up the downed trees, hauling off the brush, and splitting the birch and a few hunks of the apple tree for firewood.

Then, the next morning, we found our sluggish spring had erupted into beauty overnight. The trees in our dooryard and on the hillsides up and down the valley had burst into fresh, brilliant green. Our shadbush blossomed. Our neighbor Jo called up to say her three apple trees had all blossomed, and a Baltimore oriole and a rose-breasted grosbeak were singing in the oldest one.

Coincidence perhaps, but I chose to take it all as a sign that for a moment—or for that morning anyway—all was right with our world.

# Clunker

cquiring cats is not difficult. Rita and I have never had to make the slightest effort to get a cat. Cats have come to us unbidden, like gentle rain or, more accurately, on those little cat feet Carl Sandburg attributed to incoming harbor fog.

Just as nature abhors a vacuum, so nature sees to it that a household welcoming to cats does not remain catless for long. Some of ours have come as gifts from friends or neighbors; others have just appeared on our back porch and made it clear they would like to stay. Notable among these was a burly gray-striped tiger who showed up about ten years ago on a bitter-cold January morning. Impressed by his mass and bulk, we called him Clunker.

When our queries around the neighborhood didn't turn up any missing cats, we took him to the vet for a checkup and immunizations, a step that made him our cat from that day forward. He quickly became fond of Rita and me, cozying up to us often for an ear scratch or a belly rub, which he usually acknowledged with purring gratitude, though he would sometimes haul off and whack us just to remind us that he had a wild, tough streak and we shouldn't take his amiability for granted.

Other human beings he wanted nothing to do with. A visitor had once caught him in an unguarded moment and managed to take his picture with a flash camera. That blast of blinding light left him permanently shy of strangers, and the mere sight of a camera would send him running like a movie star pursued by paparazzi.

His wild streak eventually proved his undoing. He insisted on heading out for a hunt every night despite our warnings about animals out there bigger and tougher than even the toughest house cats, and after one raw, rainy night in November, he did not show up for breakfast. We notified the Farmington Animal Shelter and our neighbors that he was missing, but after December and January had gone by, we had to accept the likelihood that this hunter had become the hunted himself.

Then, in May, our friend David phoned one morning to say a gray-striped tiger cat had appeared in his barn. He had called the shelter and was told we had lost just such a cat back in November.

"David," I said, "that can't possibly be our cat. He vanished six months ago."

"Well, I know it sounds unlikely," David said. "But stranger things have happened, and if it's not your cat, there's no way I can keep it because I'm allergic to cats. I'll have to get the animal control officer to come get it."

With that, David had both planted a seed of hope and appealed to our sense of loyalty. If, by some fluke, that cat really was Clunker, we couldn't disavow him and condemn him to an uncertain and most likely hazardous future.

"Okay," I said, "we'll swing by and have a look."

By the time we stepped into David's barn, we were primed to find Clunker there. We probably would have convinced ourselves that a coal-black Siamese was Clunker, but we didn't have to. When Rita saw that cat and blurted out, "Clunky!" he came racing over to her and rubbed up against her legs. He was Clunker, from the first whisker on his face to the last stripe on his tail. And hadn't he recognized us, for goodness' sake? He just had to be Clunker, but of course he wasn't.

We needed several days at home with him before we began to catch on. He didn't love just us; he loved everybody. There wasn't a human lap in the world he wouldn't curl up in. He'd pose for pictures all day. He loved watching movies on the VCR. Go out at night? You've got to be kidding. There wasn't a trace of the wild in him. A lackadaisical hunter at best, he wouldn't tackle anything bigger than a vole or a mouse, and he much preferred baby mice to adults. When the first snowfall came, he didn't like the feel of it. He shook one paw, then another, came back in the house, and never went out again until the grass was green. He's a big furry cream puff, 100 percent domesticated and loving every minute of it.

So, no, he isn't Clunker the First. He's a pretender to the throne, but because he's such a winning pretender, such a great conversationalist, such an affectionate and loyal pal who may bat you with a soft paw in play but hardly ever scratch, we don't hold that pretense against him. We rejoice instead in the company of Clunker the Second, clearly the world's handsomest, smartest, most perfect cat. Long live the king.

# A Navigational Muddle

Mainers like to brag about our lakes and ponds and rivers and streams, and with good reason. We have lots of all of them, and I haven't met any I didn't like. Granted, some of our waters are bigger, cleaner, wilder, fishier, more remote, or more attractive than others, but even the least of them, even those little bog holes tucked away in the middle of impenetrable swampy thrashes, are, like the beauty of the rhodora that flourishes around them, their own excuse for being.

I'm willing to go in search of any little pond for no good reason at all. The pleasures of the search itself are enticement enough: the studying of maps, the reading of compasses, the sweating, the swatting of black flies, the clambering over blowdowns, and, eventually—eureka!—striking water. Isn't that happiness enough for any summer day?

But then if you add to those pleasures the prospect of maybe catching a fish or two and doing a friend a favor, the lure of seeking out a pond not often visited by rational people becomes even more appealing. My friend Mike called. He needed, he said, for a series of short pieces he was writing on outdoor pursuits in Maine, to go trout fishing not in just any obvious place that you could drive to but in some out-of-the-way, hike-in pond.

"You've come to the right man," I said. "I specialize in out-of-the-way, hike-in ponds, and I've been eyeing one lately that meets your requirements to a T."

"Have you ever been there?" Mike asked. "Is the fishing any good?"

"No, and I don't know," I said. "But our mutual friend Steve has a map he found on the internet that shows a pretty direct trail to it."

"Pretty direct?" Mike said.

A few days later, the three of us left Steve's Toyota 4Runner on the side of a woods road many miles from any pavement and set off on the trail to what I will call Well Hidden Pond. I use this pseudonym because this pond's real name would only reveal what inept navigators we were that day and ruin our reputations as grizzled old woodsmen.

The trailhead had been easy enough to find, but after we had rock-hopped across a couple of shallow brooks, picked our way across a beaver dam, and then started up a progressively steep and ever steeper hill where the trail had been eroded away into a rocky, ankle-twisting gully, all the while carrying not just our daypacks and rod cases but also taking turns portaging a pack canoe we expected we'd need to get out on the pond to fish—after all this, the trail turned left and started following around the contour of the hill. We stopped for a breather, a drink of water, and a look at Steve's internet map. It showed the trail dropping quickly downhill to where it skirted Mud Pond, then swung northwest to Well Hidden Pond.

From previous rambles in this neck of the woods, Steve and I knew the only Mud Pond on this township had to be at least a mile or mile and a half south-southwest from where we thought we were. So we assumed this trail we were on was traveling a far more circuitous path than necessary and that we had better figure out a more direct route.

Just a few hundred yards back, we had seen a side trail heading up the hill, one shown on the map as the mountain trail to Well Hidden Pond. So we headed back to the junction, tucked the canoe away in the brush, and headed up and over the ridge, picking our way carefully along a trail that had seen next to no use in recent years and was heavily overgrown with brush for long stretches. But eventually it took us to our pond. Mike, a model of tact throughout this mismanaged morning, had never once said, "Pretty direct, huh?"

After a few hours of fishless fishing from a leaky scow we were lucky enough to find on the shore, we decided it was time to cut our losses. And we were curious to see where the trail that came in at the southeast corner of the pond went—out, we were willing to bet, but just how?

What we found, after less than a mile's travel, was the pond mislabeled Mud Pond on Steve's map, not the "real" Mud Pond but just a no-name puddle some internet cartographer must have thought would be shallow and muddy enough to join the company of Maine's sixty-seven other Mud Ponds. If we had taken the time in the morning to look closely at the scale on this map and calculate distances accordingly, we would have recognized this mislabeling for what it was and reached Well Hidden Pond a couple of hours earlier than we did.

A few weeks later, Mike, without any help from Steve and me, found his way to another out-of-the-way pond, caught a few trout, and wrote his article.

# Buying a New Fridge
# at Sixty-Five

When the guys from the appliance store rolled it into the kitchen on their hand truck, I thought, "Geez, this damn thing will probably outlive me." If it has anything like the longevity of our old one, the odds in its favor are good. Rita and I bought our old fridge secondhand in Haverhill thirty years ago just before we moved from Cambridge to Maine. Thirty years it lasted, after serving its first owners we don't know how many years. Both Rita and I are tightwads and conservation-minded. We don't go out buying new stuff recklessly and sloughing off the old on our overcrowded landfills. But, finally, one steamy summer morning, she said: "I will not ever again defrost that refrigerator." So we bought a new one, an energy-efficient, self-defrosting model. The light inside goes on reliably. This fridge has the look of permanence about it. I'm afraid it will be making ice and cooling beer long after I have shuffled off the stage.

That doesn't seem quite fair. The fridge has its uses, but it is not me. It lacks my human qualities. It is not, as I am, fond of dogs and children. It does not find tears filling its eyes when all the people at the Martin Luther King Day service stand in a big circle around the church pews and sing "We Shall Overcome." It does not struggle to speak in words so clear and limpid that the words disappear and heart speaks straight to heart. It does not vote a straight Democratic ticket every time. Whatever my failings—and they are many, many!—I still think, on balance, I'm more important than our new refrigerator.

The tombs of ancient Egypt are crammed with all the stuff the pharaohs thought they would need in the afterlife, and I've thought of that possibility. It's not that I begrudge the use of the fridge to others, but in a world overburdened with clutter it would be helpful if we could all take our stuff with us and make it disappear. But there's the rub. As early-twenty-first-century, middle-class Americans go, Rita and I live quite modestly, but even so we would need tombs that would rival the Great Pyramid if we were to take all our trappings with us: a couple of aging cars, a Ford 9N tractor, a rototiller, the Kenmore Two-Speed, Four-Cycle washing machine (also over thirty years old), the cherry dining table, our extremely comfortable Simmons mattress, our favorite reading chairs, and the books—good Lord, all those books.

Another option is to load me and all the stuff together on a boat, set the skiff on fire, and shove it out to sea in an offshore breeze. I vaguely remember reading somewhere about a band of old Norse warriors doing that with one of their dead, but all the guy had along was a couple of spears and a shield. I'd need at least one City of New York garbage barge, and if the idea caught on, the traffic in flaming funereal barges would turn the Atlantic into a sea of fire.

Like the airlines, we have to impose a size limit for carry-on luggage. So what would I like to take into eternity with me? In the rock cairns the Inuit raised over their dead, they put a lance, some fishing line, some hooks, things that would enable their dead comrade to feed himself on the other side. I've earned my keep by writing and translating. I could take my computer along, except that it's too bulky. I suppose I could manage my old Hermes Baby portable typewriter or certainly a pad and pencil.

But I want to do more than earn my keep. I want to have some fun. I need at least one canoe, a fly rod, my library card. I find I want just about everything but the kitchen sink. And then I realize I want the kitchen sink, too: the rusty S.O.S. pad, the ancient vegetable brush minus its handle, the mildewed latex caulking in the joint between the countertop and the splashboard. Oh, yes, give me the kitchen sink with its compost bowl reeking of discarded cabbage leaves, its drain basket clogged with old oatmeal and carrot scrapings, its cavernous cupboards underneath where the mice chew on the Ivory soap and where a few last inches of gin wait for hot, sticky summer afternoons when they too, like all the inches of gin before them, will be united with tonic in holy matrimony, a marriage blessed with a dash of lime juice, of course, and a few ice cubes from the new fridge.

What I really want when I die is not to. I want life, the whole nine yards, not heaven but earth. To hell with heaven. I want the smell of mud baking in the spring sun; I want to curse and carry on when the cellar floods or the pipes freeze. I want to put Rita to sleep reading to her in bed at night. I want to laugh myself into hysterical tears at some dumb joke that only my son Greg and I find funny. I want to meet my neighbor Arthur Mitchell hunting up on the hill and agree with him that climbing it was easier thirty years ago.

A Presbyterian minister (now deceased) in our shiretown of Farmington, Maine, was fond of quoting Corinthians whenever he officiated at a funeral: "O death, where is thy sting? O grave, where is thy victory?" I'll tell you where they are, you poor dopey preacher. They're right here in my aging, craven heart, in my uncomprehending brain. Death wins. Isn't that pretty clear?

We also had a Baptist minister who said at every funeral, "Our brother [ENTER NAME HERE] will no longer know care or pain or fear." Big deal. He'll no longer know vanilla milkshakes either, or making love to his lady fair on a picnic blanket on a warm September afternoon or seeing *Casablanca* again for maybe the tenth or twelfth or fifteenth time.

"Play it again, Sam." That's what I say. Who can ever see Bogart and Bergman and Claude Rains too often? Who can ever get enough love, catch enough trout, dance enough waltzes and polkas, eat enough pesto spaghetti or cherrystone clams on the half shell?

While one's body and brain are still in working order, there's no joy in thinking we'll have to say goodbye to all that. But I know the flesh is weak; I know that even the toughest and most resilient of it will yield to the tooth of time. I know this packet of bone, muscle, blood, nerve, and gray matter that is not me but without which there is no me, this inseparable stew of spirit and flesh that is so much one that even to speak of it as two is an insult to it, I know it will finally fail. Perhaps it will give me a moment to wave farewell; perhaps not. Maybe I'll be ready, maybe more than ready; and then again maybe not at all.

Many years ago, a man a couple of decades my senior who had recently lost his wife said to me, "Once the people close to you are on the other side, crossing over yourself looks a lot easier."

When the priest at a Christian mass of burial a few weeks ago told us we would all one day be reunited with our sister in Jesus Christ, I thought to myself, "Shame on you, you old charlatan, fobbing off fairy tales like that on your friends and neighbors." But then, of course, I had to eat a little crow, maybe the crow's tail feathers anyway, because the good father had it at least partially right. We will all one day go over to the other side, wherever and whatever that is. I'm not expecting to take the fridge along or to find Bergman and Bogart there to greet me. But if the other side is good enough for them, if it's good enough for Plato and Walt Whitman and Ella Fitzgerald and for Ben Staples, who used to deliver the mail here in Temple, and for my old buddy Don Yeaton, who could build beautiful log camps with just an axe, a hammer, and a crosscut saw and went on occasional herculean binges, if it's good enough for my dogs Tex and Tippy and Brandy and Lucy and for that big fir tree that snapped off in the wind yesterday just like that, if the other side is good enough for them, then, by the Jesus, as Don was wont to say, I guess it's good enough for me.

# No Bugs

I don't recall exactly when it was last spring that I began to feel something was wrong, late May maybe. No, more like early June. Or maybe I should have begun feeling something was wrong as early as late February, when the weather turned Marchish, if not downright Aprily, and the sap began to run by the bucketful.

Well, weather is weather. We've all seen early sap runs before and never been the worse for it. But when day after day went by—June fourth, fifth, and sixth, June tenth, eleventh, and twelfth—and I hadn't seen a single black fly, I started to get concerned. Instead of giving in to full-fledged worry, though, I took refuge in denial.

Nothing was really wrong, I told myself. You'd have thought that with a mild winter and early spring, the bugs would have been out in force in April, but maybe black fly larvae are cagier than we give them credit for. Maybe they were thinking to themselves, "Aha! It's warm way too early. I bet what comes next is a serious cold snap in late May. The weather gods are out to kill us off en masse. We'd better lie low and wait until July to swarm out in our usual numbers." So I decided to calm down and wait for the bugs to appear when they felt like it, not when I thought they ought to. I waited patiently through the rest of June, but no bugs came.

Out of long-established habit, Rita had put on her Bug Baffler and headed out for her first days of gardening with her head, arms, and torso completely enclosed in bugproof mesh. When she realized, after another few days, that there were no flies zinging around her head, she unzipped the hood and pushed it back. A few days later still, she hung the Bug Baffler up on its peg in the ell and never wore it again the rest of the summer. I could spend an afternoon and evening fishing in the little mountain trout streams of northern Franklin County—the kind of cold, pristine waters black flies just love to breed in—and swat scarcely a fly. Almost forty years we've lived here in Temple and never before have we had a spring with no bugs.

And so it went through July and August. Not until I encountered a fairly respectable swarm of flies up on the Penobscot in September could I relax a bit and begin to think maybe 2010 would not be the year the black fly disappeared from Maine never to return again.

This past November, when all hope of sighting any more flies was long gone, I finally thought to consult with Charlene Donahue, a Maine Forest Service entomologist and president of the Maine Entomological Society, to see if there were reports of missing black flies from elsewhere in the state and, if so, whether this past fly-less year was just a fluke or signaled some catastrophic decline in our fly populations.

There had been word of fewer flies than usual in some locales, she told me, but that probably suggested no danger to the long-term health of our bugs. Even entomologists, however, know precious little about black fly population dynamics. They speculate—but speculate only—that dry springs with little flooding may mean fewer flies because some fly species lay their eggs in leaf litter on stream banks where, in normal years, the eggs are then washed into the water by spring freshets. The task of sorting out all the variables that could affect fly populations is daunting to the point of impossibility and, let's face it, not really worth the trouble.

In any case, what Charlene Donahue told me was comforting. Flooding was a bit below normal in 2010, so it would appear our beloved black fly may not be in danger of extinction after all.

"Beloved black fly? You've got to be kidding." But no, perverse as that may seem, I'm not kidding. We northern forest folk don't love the black fly only because its larvae are a crucial food source for trout. We love the flies because they're an equally crucial part of our emotional landscape. If a bright, breezy afternoon keeps them temporarily at bay, we are grateful for the relief, but if they swarm around us and crawl into our ears and eyes and noses and up our sleeves and pant legs and down our necks and socks, then we're grateful, too, for a chance to brag once again about how bad the bugs were.

What else but love could have inspired those bug enthusiasts over in Machias to found the Maine Black Fly Breeders Association, a great tongue-in-cheek organization that does not really breed black flies but does write songs and limericks in their praise, sell T-shirts that read, "Black Flies, Defenders of the Wilderness," and support worthy causes in the community? I'm going to join on the hunch that a little appreciation from us humans may well be all the flies need to keep their morale and numbers up.

# Leaf-Peeping Season

Fall—as all we northern woodlanders know—is leaf-peeping time. If the hills ablaze with red and yellow were not evidence enough, there are other signs to alert us: the tour buses, for instance, tall, sleek ones with windows you can see out of from inside but not into from outside. It's not unusual come October to find these landlocked cruise ships parked in downtown Farmington while their passengers debark for lunch before heading north to take in the peak foliage on Maine's western mountains.

The charter bus companies are not alone in recognizing the value of this autumnal resource. Maine's Department of Agriculture, Conservation, and Forestry even has an official website (www.mainefoliage.com) where you can sign up for weekly reports on current foliage conditions in the state's seven different foliage zones. John Bott of the department tells me the foliage website got 574,000 hits last year. Or for up-to-the-minute reports anytime during the season, you can call Gale Ross, the department's fall foliage coordinator, at (207) 287-5153. All this is as it should be. What better use for buses than taking people out to see the splendor of Maine's forests. What better fun for Gale Ross than telling folks just when and where to see one of nature's greatest shows on earth.

The ideal vantage point for day-tripping leaf peepers—whether they get to it by bus or on foot—is a high elevation with a 360-degree view, or at least a 180-degree one. The desired effect is a panorama filled with the nearly infinite variety of color combinations visible from that kind of perch. Most years I'll take time off on peak-color days and climb one or two of our nearby mountains that reward the hiker with just that kind of macrocosmic view. And on days when I need to work close to home, I can indulge in backyard leaf peeping, watching the first tinges of red and yellow seep into individual trees and then infuse them wholly with color.

The next step in this more microcosmic approach is to focus on individual leaves. In *A Year in the Maine Woods*, Bernd Heinrich recorded the colors he found in fallen red maple leaves he picked up on a short walk. In his sampling of twenty-seven leaves, he found an amazing variety, ranging from "yellow with small purple blotches" to "bright vermilion red with yellow veins," from "uniform orange" to "greenish yellow with one bright red corner." So I find myself wondering whether each red maple leaf produces its own unique coloration, something like snowflakes retaining their six-pointed form while producing endless variations on it.

Granted, the fall show is spectacular, whether you're looking at one leaf or untold millions, but it's far from the only show our leaves put on. Where fall rushes in with fanfare and dazzles us, spring tiptoes in, clothing the hillsides with poplars' soft, gauzy green and red maples' crimson haze. And along with those delicate colors that must drive painters wild with envy come the emergent leaves. The trees and shrubs around our dooryard—the maples, ash, black cherry, chokecherry, shadbush, to name just a few—make it easy for me to watch the quite rapid day-by-day growth of their leaves to adulthood, a process lovely to behold. It's like being in a nursery school on fast forward where toddlers might shoot up to adolescence in a matter of a few weeks.

When I'm out on a ramble in the woods and find an infant leaf I haven't seen grow to maturity before, I cut off a twig and put it in a water-filled Mason jar on the kitchen table to see what its leaves will develop into. This past spring I brought home a cutting with seven tiny green canoes on it, each about an inch and a half long and with radical tumblehome curling the gunwales in so far they nearly met the inside of the hull. After a few weeks they grew up into adult hobblebush leaves.

For my eye, spring, with its flowering and leafing out, is every bit as beautiful as fall, if not more so, but then why quibble? Leaves never disappoint. In mid-summer's days of ubiquitous green, the different shapes and shades of leaves give each tree and hillside its distinctive tones and contours, and on a breezy day a tall gray birch just fifty yards from our back door will turn up the silvery bottoms of its leaves and put on a show of fluttering and flashing that would put a sequined ball dress to shame. Even in winter, when the branches of most deciduous trees are bare, beech leaves—ribbed, papery, and translucent as Chinese lanterns—are still holding on. Somewhere in the forest you can always find a leaf: a reminder that the snow will melt, the sap will run, the leaves will burst out once again; a reminder, too, that there's never a dull moment among trees and no such thing as a closed season on leaf peeping.

# A Swiss Canoe Trip

First, a few clarifications. This trip took place neither in Switzerland nor in a Swiss canoe. What made it Swiss was the presence here in Maine of our Swiss relatives, Vreni and Ueli.

Before they came for their first visit nearly twenty years ago, I was afraid they—or at least Ueli—would find our northern Appalachians a bit tame. They live in the spectacular Bernese Alps with the most storied of those mountains, the Eiger, Mönch, and Jungfrau, at their doorstep. Ueli is a tall, lean, rugged man in his fifties who spends much of his free time hiking, climbing, or skiing in the mountains or hang-gliding off four-thousand-foot "hills" that are almost as high as our highest peaks here in western Maine.

But my worries were groundless. Vreni and Ueli didn't come to Maine looking for another Switzerland. They came looking for Maine, and they liked what they found. They liked climbing our modest mountains and seeing unbroken forest stretching out in every direction. They liked strapping the canoe onto the car roof and heading up to Rangeley where they could picnic on the islands of Upper Richardson Lake and explore miles of undeveloped shoreline.

But ever since I showed them some pictures from more ambitious canoeing ventures I've been on in Quebec and Labrador, they had a yen to take not just a day's outing in the canoe but an extended trip. A month in the Canadian north was longer than their time with us would allow, but a week's trip in Maine would suit them just fine.

The classic West Branch Penobscot trip seemed the ideal choice. About forty miles altogether, the trip begins on Lobster Lake and ends on twenty-mile-long Chesuncook Lake with Katahdin in full view. I had no trouble enlisting my friend Steve and his son, Ethan, to join us, providing both additional muscle power and the pleasure of their good company. This would be, I thought, a comfortable, leisurely, and scenically rewarding trip just right for our guests, and also one I had not taken myself for over fifteen years and was eager to revisit.

My memory was that the twenty miles or so on the river were pleasant enough but that the lakes at either end were the high points of this trip. When we paddled into Lobster Lake about two o'clock on a warm, sunny, late-September afternoon, I realized that my memory was correct, except that the lake was, in reality, even more beautiful than any memory of it could ever be. Katahdin rose up about thirty miles away on the horizon to the east, and to the south, the great green loaf of Big Spencer Mountain seemed almost close enough to touch.

We pulled into a campsite on Ogden Point and set about enjoying the first idyllic afternoon of a short canoe trip on which the gods would smile from beginning to end. We set up the tents, gathered some dry-ki for firewood, brewed a four-o'clock coffee, went for a swim, and lounged like seals on the sun-baked ledges next to our private beach. While Steve stayed in camp to cook up supper, Ethan and I took off in one canoe to see if we could find the trail that goes up Lobster Mountain from Jackson Cove. Vreni and Ueli took another to explore the western shore of the lake's major island.

That evening, when Vreni and I were sitting by the coals of the fire just before bedtime, she said, "Thanks so much for putting this trip together for us, Bob. After just this one day, it already feels like a dream come true."

"Well," I said, "I'm betting the whole trip is going to feel that way."

If anybody had taken me up on that bet, I would have won it. The weather held. Total rainfall was about three drops as we were paddling the last couple of miles on the river, and then the next day heading south on Chesuncook, where ferocious winds can pin canoeists down for days, we had a brisk tailwind helping us on our way, cloudless blue skies overhead, and Katahdin visible all day.

We camped that evening five miles short of the takeout, expecting to paddle an hour or so and be on our way home by noon the next day. But during the night, a gale blew in from the northwest and refused to let up. We grumbled a little and settled in for a windbound day, walked the shore, read in the tent. Ueli, ever inventive, built a huge, stork-like statue out of dry-ki.

The next morning, we saw that the gods had done us a favor after all. The sun coming up in the east backlit Katahdin, setting the clouds around the peak ablaze; and once it topped the mountain, it filled the mist hanging over the wind-still surface of the lake with light. Hard to imagine a more glorious finale to our Swiss canoe trip than this. Vreni had it right: a dream come true.

# Rita's Memorial

My lovely and beloved wife, Rita, who has figured prominently in many of these "Upcountry" columns I've been writing for the past ten years, died suddenly and unexpectedly this past December of a ruptured aortic aneurysm, a medical catastrophe rarely known to give quarter. She died quickly, as she had always wished to. No lingering, debilitating illness, no waning of mind or spirit. I find some comfort—though not nearly enough—in that knowledge, and surely I can rejoice that the successful kidney transplant she received thirty-seven years ago, after four years on home dialysis, made a rich and active life possible for her until her death just short of her eighty-second birthday.

Rita was born on January 6, the Feast of the Epiphany. It's hard to imagine a more appropriate birthday for her, since just about every day brought her some kind of revelation. Beneath her quiet demeanor, she was always seeing, listening, feeling—always engaged. She had a low tolerance for phoniness and careless thinking but an unfailing instinct for the genuine, the essential, and the true, whether in books or in the life of her family and community and world. She was both hardheaded and big-hearted, practical and generous. Those three wise men who followed the star to Bethlehem had nothing on Rita when it came to seeing the light. I've often wondered what the visit of the Magi would have been like if she had been along to give those three kings a little coaching in the needs of a young family forced to take shelter in a stable.

"Look," she might have said, "gifts of gold, frankincense, and myrrh are all well and good, but what these people need right now is a warm blanket for their newborn baby and a pot of thick pea soup for themselves."

She was quick to see and think and act. I'm usually a much slower study, but when I met Rita forty-six years ago, I had wits enough to know right away that the brightest star in my life had just come over the horizon. That same bright light drew the nearly two hundred people who came to her memorial service on a late January afternoon.

Because Farmington's small Quaker meeting—of which Rita was a dedicated member—has no space that can accommodate large gatherings, the parishioners of Trinity United Methodist Church in Farmington welcomed us with their sanctuary's movable chairs arranged into three large concentric circles. Like most Quaker meetings for worship, this one, too, was a silent one, but anyone moved to speak out of the silence was invited to do so. And many were so moved.

Suzy, who shared an apartment with Rita in Cambridge, Massachusetts in the mid-1960s and has been her loyal friend ever since, spoke of Rita's "unquenchable optimism and her faith that the steady, relentless assertion of what appears to be right will ultimately make a difference."

Rita acted through that optimism and faith on many fronts. For the last fourteen years, she stood outside the Farmington post office every Friday at noon in a vigil for peace. With her friend Beverly, she visited juvenile offenders in Maine's Long Creek Development Center once a month. In these last few years she worked tirelessly to establish—and raise money to support—a homeless shelter in Farmington. To all her causes, she brought her soft-spoken gusto, a kind of gentle, persuasive ferocity that made clear that she knew where she stood and that she meant business.

Our friend Susan, who lives on the Maine coast, reflected on the kind of community spirit that Rita took part in and that is alive and well in her small town and in ours. "Our communities are far apart," Susan said, "but they are motivated, I believe, by similar impulses: we work to make our neighborhoods better, fairer, happier, smarter places, whether it's a shelter for homeless people, learning about Native American issues or prison issues, standing against war. We show up. We do the work. Rita was a firm believer in this sort of participation, and so, I believe, are you, and so am I. And in this way, in this kind of work, her energy continues with us."

A few days later, this note from our friend Janet came to me: "I was so impressed with the memorial for Rita. From my vantage point, I could feel so much love in the room that it felt like millions of raindrops dropping gently on all the people and the same drops of love rising from us back up to her. . . . Somehow it was easy to feel Rita's presence. And it was easy to love the many wonderful individuals gathered to celebrate her life. I felt so proud of our community and its abundant compassion."

I, too, was proud of our community and grateful to be a member of it there, in the hospitality of that church, among so many friends who had come to speak their love for Rita and to honor her spirit. Rita and I have lived our life together in this community and in these hills of western Maine. This is our home. This is where our ashes will lie, Rita's and mine.

# Asparagus

In the summer of 1971, when Rita and I were just beginning our life here in Temple, Maine, the first thing we planted, after rototilling and forking up and weeding our prospective garden plot as best we could, was asparagus. You'd think we would have chosen something that would come up fast and start feeding us in a matter of weeks, and we did get around to some lettuce and radishes fairly soon. But as life-long asparagus addicts, we felt we had to get our asparagus crowns into the ground straightaway. Conventional gardening wisdom told us we should not cut any shoots for the first two years after planting so that all the crowns' energy could go into putting down deep, strong roots. The possibility that we might have to wait that long to harvest our first asparagus only added to our frenzy to get it planted.

But conventional wisdom also told us that if the first year's growth was vigorous, an impatient gardener could risk defying that two-year prohibition and sample at least a few spears the following spring. That possibility fueled our frenzy all the more. Other pressing chores were put on hold: insulation in the one big multipurpose room where we would eat, sleep, read, and write in the coming winter; new porch steps; new shingles on the chicken coop roof. All that could wait.

The 50×50-foot plot we chose for our garden was far from any shade trees and received the full benefit of the sun all day long, an ideal place for asparagus. Also, because this plot was near a recently demolished barn and had received decades' worth of cow manure, the soil was rich to begin with. Still, once we had dug the one-foot-deep-by-one-foot-wide ditches prescribed for an asparagus bed, we added more rotted manure and some compost for good measure.

Given the superb soil of our garden plot and the abundant sunshine that fell on it, plus our careful preparation, we thought we might well be able to allow ourselves at least a taste of our own garden-fresh asparagus the next spring; but even if that failed to be the case, we were confident we had laid the groundwork for an asparagus-rich future.

If we had come upon Ruth Stout's *No-Work Garden Book* before we had dug our ditches, we might have spared ourselves all that work and instead done just as she did, defying all expert opinion and just laying some crowns on the ground and piling mulch hay over them.

In the book, Stout also recounts how "in a dozen or more places— in the meadow, by the woodshed, and around—asparagus plants were showing up. Obviously, birds or wind had scattered the seeds, and some of these 'wild' plants are more luxurious than those in my regular asparagus bed."

Though we never attempted Stout's drop-them-and-mulch-them method of planting crowns, we did discover, as she had, that asparagus had no difficulty being fruitful and multiplying on its own. Volunteers began popping up around our original plantings and then started expanding outward until, today, the asparagus patch that originally occupied a scant quarter of our garden now inhabits a hefty third.

Asparagus isn't, after all, just any old garden-variety vegetable. Domesticated though it may be, it has a touch of the wild about it. It's spunky; it's botanical *joie de vivre* incarnate. Asparagus is a model of how to live, its spears sweet and tender, its roots tough and enduring. Among the first plants to nose their way into the light each spring, it explodes with vitality, often gaining an inch or more of growth a day. Then, when the weeks of our feasting on it are over, it spurts up above my head, its dense, frizzy foliage hovering over the garden in a soft green cloud. It's always beautiful. Even late in the fall when it stands brown and sere and its fronds become an incandescent, coppery filigree in November sunsets, asparagus reminds us it'll be back next spring, raring to go. I've always thought of it as Rita's totem vegetable.

Back in 1971, the chorus of *Hair* was proclaiming from the Broadway stage the dawn of the age of Aquarius, an era in human history when war would be a thing of the past, when a wave of brotherhood and sisterhood would sweep over all humankind, washing away the evils of racism, sexism, economic injustice, environmental degradation. We shared those worldwide Aquarian hopes and worked to realize them, doing our modest part to help bend the arc of history a little farther toward justice. And what dawned at the same time for Rita and me, in our personal lives, was our age of asparagus; not our salad days—we were well over thirty—but a richer, mellower era befitting our advanced years, a time in which we had recently promised to be loving and faithful to each other so long as we both should live. True to that promise we did indeed live. I wouldn't have missed our forty-six years together for all the world.

# The Tenacity of Trees

I marvel at the punishment trees manage to survive and the gallant attempts at survival they make, even when all the cards are stacked against them.

On our back porch this past June, I finally noticed something I should have noticed much sooner. The outermost deck board above the three steps that give us access to the porch was getting soggy from several years of rain and snowmelt, and in that same board, a broken-out knothole had let a sugar maple samara settle into a pocket of dirt and damp rot in the timber below, allowing a seed to germinate there. The embryonic maple that emerged was just far enough to the left of the steps to be out of the major traffic lane, but I was still amazed that a misplaced foot hadn't squashed this upstart long since.

I kept watering it with a sprayer, and when I got around to replacing that sodden porch board and several others along with it a few weeks later, I transplanted my foundling, which consisted of a stem, a couple of leaves, and a mere two-to-three-inch thread of a root, into a small bowl filled with a mix of compost and potting soil. I had visions of this infant plant growing into a robust seedling, a sapling, a tree that might eventually take the place of our aging dooryard maple that was most likely its parent.

But my fantasy didn't become reality. This small brave life had the bad luck to land in the hands of a bumbling horticulturist who didn't know what care and feeding his charge would need to grow and thrive. So my dream of raising a sugar maple from this seed that had literally fallen onto my doorstep came to naught. Disappointing as this experiment was, however, I can still rejoice over the lives of healthy adult trees that begin life in the wild, grow vigorously at locations even less hospitable than my back porch, and are still standing tall after forty or fifty or many more years.

One such is about halfway up the trail on nearby Bald Mountain, a yellow birch set in total isolation atop a glacial boulder about six feet high and eight or so in diameter. I can't imagine how this tree ever found enough soil up there to sustain itself in its early years, much less to let it send out exploratory roots that reached down the boulder on all sides and eventually sank themselves into the ground below. Now, those roots are great living ropes that both nourish the tree and bind it to its pedestal. This tree truly clings to its rock for dear life.

Much closer to home, on our woodlot across the road from our house, stands an aged white pine three and a half feet in diameter at breast height. Not long after Rita and I moved onto this old farm forty-seven years ago, the top quarter of this tree broke off and fell to the ground. That treetop, much worn down and sculpted by decades of weather, insects, fungi, and microbes, has become a dark brown snake wriggling its way across the forest floor and sporting brilliant green markings of moss on its back. Over these same years, this decapitated pine has worked steadily at replacing its crown. Two of its larger limbs have abandoned their original outward trajectories, turning instead in elegant swooping curves to shoot straight upward in their race to become the tree's new leader. Other smaller limbs haven't been able to break out so easily. One of them, blocked at first by its neighbors, had to make two right-angle turns before it could worm its way into the sunlight. And all this resurgence goes on despite a huge patch of rot hollowing out the first five feet of the trunk above ground level, proof that you can't keep a good tree down.

Is it any wonder, then, that we humans love and admire trees? Of course we're grateful to them for their fruit, for their wood we use to build our homes and furniture, for their wood we burn to warm us in winter, for their shade that cools us in summer, but even if they had no utilitarian value for us, we'd still love them for their beauty, for the music of the wind in their leaves, their companionship as we walk the face of this earth, the kinship we feel with them.

No matter how different from us they are, living their planted, rooted lives, how like us they are, too: so eager to live, no matter how inauspicious the sites that chance and circumstance have chosen for them, no matter the batterings they take, the weight of ice storms tearing them limb from limb, the ravages of spruce budworm and beech bark disease. Though hurricanes and wildfires can and do decimate them by the thousands, some are always left standing. Like us, they persist.

# Good Riddance

Whenever I walk in the back door and into the roughly nine-by-twenty-foot space in our ell that serves as part mudroom, part pantry, part general store, I vow once again to divest big time—to rid myself now and forever of all the accumulated clutter I see there. Taken in at a glance and in aggregate, that stuff would seem to call for a clean sweep. Just hire a bulldozer and shove it all out—everything—every last empty tube of sunblock, every pair of work gloves with holes in the thumbs.

But wait a minute. Not the chest freezer, please, with some venison steaks still in it—not to mention last summer's blueberries, green beans, zucchini bread, and, I'm sure, some soups and stews of Rita's making that I haven't yet dug deep enough to find.

And up against one wall, right next to the freezer, is a stove: a Modern Glenwood Wood Parlor, no longer modern but still serviceable and, in any case, not junk. Next to the stove come two cardboard cartons for recyclables: one for discarded magazines, advertising circulars, and last year's calendars; the other for mixed scrap paper like flattened graham cracker cartons and letters from politicians begging for money; and finally, a stack of newsprint for tinder and a five-gallon sheetrock compound bucket full of finely split cedar kindling.

In short, everything along that wall plays a crucial role in the everyday life of this household, with the exception of the Glenwood stove, but then you never know when you might need another stove.

The opposing wall presents a more complex picture. A bank of permanent shelves twelve feet long and divided horizontally into four-foot sections is built onto that wall. The first section, farthest from the door, was Rita's territory. It still is, and it is dedicated to food. On the floor and on all the shelves above it are glass jars. Some are the one-gallon variety that restaurants get their mayonnaise in and are now filled with pinto beans, kasha, cracked wheat, red kidney beans, black beans, long-grain rice, etc. Then there are one-quart Mason jars of canned tomatoes, one-pint jars of applesauce and stewed plums, half-pint jars of plum jam from the summer of 2015 when our two plum trees broke all records for fruitfulness. All these foodstuffs—along with Rita's treasures still in the freezer—are part of the legacy of love she has left to me and our son, Greg. These we will make use of, grateful to her for every last morsel. But what I can clear out are the excess empty jars, large and small, some here in these shelves and others we've never used at all upstairs in the attic.

The shelves in the section nearest the door are primarily mine. On them you will find a small basket full of cross-country ski waxes ranging from the gooiest Klister to the hardest cold-weather green; an empty Kleenex box close to overflowing with dead AA and AAA batteries; the owner's manual for my Kubota tractor; some basic tools of first resort: slip-joint pliers, lineman's pliers, needle-nose pliers, screwdrivers, an X-Acto knife; and a box of soba noodles that couldn't find space in Rita's shelf and has taken refuge here. Then there are no less than ten bottles of bug dope (from Ben's 100 to Green Ban), five quarts of motor oil, two large spools of nylon cord in ⅛-inch and ³⁄₁₆-inch sizes. I could go on, but I won't. You get the picture.

Thirteen years ago, I used that nylon cord to fill a pair of snowshoes—the heavier stuff under the feet, the lighter for the toes and heels. I haven't used any of that cord since. There you have the dilemma, both practical and ethical: how to create beauty and order in your living space without violating the commandment, "Thou shalt not be wasteful. Thou shalt not treat as trash anything into which others have invested their labor and ingenuity to make."

My attempts to rid my home of clutter always run up against things I'm no longer using but that someone else could use, or that I might use myself a year or two or three from now. I can't put that nylon cord in the trash and say, "Good riddance to bad rubbish," because it isn't rubbish; it's in perfect condition. The only justifiable riddance of it, the only good riddance, is to pass it on to someone who wants it. Fortunately, I can put these sorts of items out on the front lawn with a sign that says, "Free Stuff." Whether it's something like that cord or old car tires no longer fit for the road but passable for use on a farm trailer, often they will be gone within minutes of my setting them out. I call that a very good riddance: good for the ridder, good for the getter. The word "rubbish" never enters my mind. What I say to stuff I can pass on to some anonymous passerby is, "This is a good riddance—a good parting, old friend. You have served me well and faithfully. Happy landing, and good luck in your new home."

Would that good riddance were always so easy.

# My Topography as Autobiography

'm making no claim to land ownership here when I speak of "my" topography. That's a good thing because just about any place in New England—starting in the Berkshires and heading north through Vermont, New Hampshire, and Maine—I think of as "mine." The proprietary feeling I have for this huge swath of northern Appalachia has no basis in law; it is instead a claim of the heart, an affinity for this topography of hills, valleys, and intervales; of mountains, cols, cirques, and tarns; of high ridges thick with impenetrable krummholz; of bald granite peaks here in my adopted state of Maine where you can see Mount Washington off to the west on a clear October day. It's relief that draws me, the intricate web of small brooks picking their way between the hills and spilling into upland streams that in turn make their way down to the big rivers: the Kennebec, Penobscot, and Connecticut. It's the crowded, wriggling contour lines on topo maps that tell you, in increments of twenty feet, how steep a hill or mountain is and how high its trail or bushwhack will take you—two thousand, thirty-five hundred, five thousand feet, or more.

It wasn't until my college years that I got a chance to discover and indulge this near obsession. I grew up a flatlander in Mountain Lakes, New Jersey, a town about thirty miles west of New York City. We lived across the road from one of the small lakes that gave the town half its name. An extensive forested ridge on its northwestern border, topping out at 897 feet, accounted for the "mountain" half. Modest as that ridge was both in height and area, it was large enough to let me and my boyhood friend John Miller learn our way around in the woods and feel at home in them, an ideal training ground for what was to come in 1955, when my father quit commuting to work in Manhattan and bought a sporting camp in western Maine. I was a college junior then, delighted to no end with the prospect of working at Big Jim Pond Camps and of rambling not in mere hundreds of forested acres but in the thousands upon thousands in Maine's unorganized townships.

Over the next two summers, I spent my weekends climbing every major mountain within twenty-five miles of Big Jim Pond—Bigelow, Sugarloaf (before it was a ski mountain), Saddleback, Snow, Abraham— plus any number of no-name hills. I was permanently smitten, head over heels in love with this rugged country that rewarded every jaunt into it with another mountain view, another small pond to cast a fly into, the kind of country that invites the bear to go over the mountain—then over the next and the next—to see what he or she can see. Those mountains are Maine's highest after Katahdin, and here in Temple, where I've lived for the last forty-five years, we're within an hour's drive to the trailheads of most of them. Then, too, right at my doorstep, I have a whole township of my kind of topography: lots of crowded contour lines on the map and a trout stream in my backyard.

And nowadays, at least once a year, I have occasion to drive west on U.S. Route 2 into the farther reaches of my adopted home territory where, for example, after attending the Northern Woodlands Conference in Fairlee, Vermont, I might cross over the Connecticut River into New Hampshire to visit friends in Plainfield, then cross back for a sentimental journey to Grafton, Vermont, where Rita spent her first year in this country as an au pair from Switzerland.

Eventually, my long, looping tour often hits its southernmost point in a tiny hamlet in the Berkshires, where two of our old friends have retired. Their house is tucked into a tight, winding valley; across the road a small stream picks its way down to its confluence with the Deerfield River. The hills here are for the most part steep and bunched together, but then, nestled down among them are intervales and hollows and gently sloping hillsides where early settlers built their homes and cleared land for pasturage and hayfields. The complexity of this landscape sets limits to human enterprise and consequently keeps things on a human scale. There just isn't room here for sprawling industrial parks, mall complexes, or Kansas-style wheat fields.

About a mile up the road from our friends' house, a hillside graveyard affords a view that is intimate at first; the eye takes in the few homes and fields close by but is then drawn outward, onto the hills north of the Deerfield in Massachusetts and onto Vermont, onto the horizon, onto the sky above. It's easy—standing here in this place that ranks high on my list of the world's most beautiful places—to feel firmly planted on this earth yet a bit in touch with heaven as well, and to gratefully acknowledge how enlivening and inspiring for me the topography of my beloved Maine, my beloved New England, has been. I may possess several acres in Temple, but in the end it's the land that possesses me.

# Drury Pond: An Idyll

At the pond I imbibe both the sweetness of solitude and the sweetness of society. I also imbibe, on the porch of Wes and Diane's camp, an occasional beer, which adds a nip of hops to the largely mellow flavor of our conversations.

That Wes and Diane would be here, would in fact own this camp on the pond and by that owning add infinitely to the pleasure Rita and I take in this place that has long been one of our favorite places on earth, was not too long ago not at all certain.

They were in search of a place on water. I knew that, for I had visited with Wes several other places they were considering, none of which proved suitable. All those rejected places had neighbors too close or were intrinsically too tacky (interior walls of that plastic stuff that fakes wood paneling, accordion closet doors also of plastic), places located on little dirt roads at the head of which the visitor found six or a dozen or more signs nailed to a tree: Jones, Halleck, Dimbaugh, Crumpworth, Doodlebecker, Heep, Humbert, Smith, etc., each sign indicating that on this road Jones, Halleck, etc., each owned a camp, Halleck's camp cheek by jowl with Dimbaugh's and so on down the line.

Do we want this camp for peace and quiet, Wes and Diane had to ask themselves, or do we want to watch water skiers roar by behind their forty-horse Yamaha outboards? Do we want invitations to the Crumpworths' Fourth-of-July barbecue parties complete with firecrackers, sparklers, and hamburgers underdone on the propane grill? Do we want hearty laughter, conviviality, Reverend Whipsnack's account of climbing Pike's Peak with his lean, mean, twenty-six-year-old son and platinum blonde, long-legged daughter-in-law: "They thought they'd leave the old man huffing and puffing behind in the dust, but they had another think coming. Oh, I gave them a run for their money and then some. Ha, ha. Ho, ho."

How important, after all, is a flush toilet, electricity, a telephone? Isn't the point *not* to watch the TV, *not* to stay in touch with students, secretaries, deans, plumbers, electricians?

Of course that's the point, Wes agreed, but peace and quiet and plumbing and electricity don't have to be mutually exclusive, do they? So when Dick Vaughan told me he wanted to sell his camp on the pond—the most perfect camp, by the way, on this most perfect of ponds, a camp at the north end of the pond and so perfectly situated that, sitting on the porch, you can look south down the length of this small, barely half-mile pond onto the mountain rising beyond and can watch the sun come up over the eastern shore and watch it drop in the west, casting shadows of the tall white pines out onto the water as early as four on a summer afternoon; while here, at this camp, you can still bask in sunshine on the dock—when Dick told me he wanted to sell this camp, I told him I knew somebody who might be interested; but I was not hopeful. No flush, no electricity.

Wes and I went to have a look at the place one afternoon. Wes stands six foot three; this camp appears to have been built by the Seven Dwarfs. In the master bedroom upstairs there's barely room to walk around the double bed and fit in a dresser; the bedroom next to it is snugger still; and a third cubbyhole houses a double-decker bunk. Going downstairs, even I, at five eight, have to duck so I don't bang my head. Downstairs, living/dining room and kitchenette all share a space about twenty by twelve feet.

As self-appointed real estate broker, I put a positive spin on the camp's dimensions.

"Cozy, isn't it?" I observed, but I was thinking "cramped."

Wes nodded. He moved around cautiously, concerned, I imagined, not only about conking his head in the stairwell or on the wrought-iron chandelier over the table but also about banging his funny bone, shouldering candlesticks off the mantlepiece, barking his shins, stubbing his toes. Wes wears size fourteen shoes. Even his feet are too big for this place. Wes has written a poem about those outsized feet that have had to put up with a lot of ribbing in their time, as have the shoes that shod them—clodhoppers, platters, skis.

Unconcerned with fitting in,
all you have ever wanted was to take me in the direction
of my own choosing. Never mind the hands
getting all the attention as they wave to others
on the street, this is not their poem,
but only yours, steady vessels, who all along
have resisted my desire to be like everyone else,
who turn after the hands are done and carry me
with resolute steps into my separate life.

Where else, I wondered, but away from this small building would those resolute steps carry him? No plumbing, no electricity, and barely enough room for a big man to stand up or turn around.

What a pity, I thought; what a goddam crying shame. What wouldn't I give to have to have Wes and Diane our neighbors here, right next door to our own patch of land on this our favorite pond where, on just about every summer day, we come for a late-afternoon swim? Diane, who did not hesitate, when some creep in a Roman bus groped her daughter, to hit the guy over the head with her pocketbook; who brought us, one Easter, a little basket complete with frizzy cellophane grass, jelly beans, little yellow marshmallow chicks, and a couple of bunnies made of solid dark chocolate; Diane, whose red hair erupts from her head like molten lava, overflowing from her warm and fiery heart.

And instead of—or as well as—meeting Wes for beers in the brew pub in Farmington, we could meet on this very camp porch. Here, as the breeze died of a summer evening and the pond turned into a placid mirror and the hermit thrushes poured out their harmonies in the woods around us, we could raise our voices in celebration of the king-fisher's chattering flight, the word well chosen, the comma well placed, the yearling moose feeding in the lily pads, the murmur of Rita and Diane's talk down on the dock. We could also plot the downfall of all who deserve to fall down: Republicans, for example, and stuffed shirts and people who call too many meetings and write too many memos. Never mind that our plots will come to naught, that all the sonsabitches who ought to be in eclipse are instead at the zenith of their wretched powers. Never mind any of that.

Ah, Wes, you great ambling bear with feet to match the size of your soul, you old silvertip with your grizzled beard, your faded jeans, your Red Sox baseball cap, what a joy to think we might grow old together right here, walking these woods, sharing our loves and rages.

But after that first walk-through at the camp I was not hopeful.

"Well," Rita asked me when I came home, "what do you think?"

"Not a prayer," I said. "No plumbing, no electricity, and the place is too dinky. Have you ever watched a giraffe trying to get comfortable in a submarine?"

\*\*\*

When I call this pond the most perfect of ponds, I should add that its perfection lies largely, if not wholly, in the eyes of a very few beholders. Nothing here speaks of the high-value, upscale vacation experience. Fisherfolk will find no trout or salmon here, only sunfish and yellow perch and an occasional small pickerel, fish you can catch in any old warm-water pond anywhere. Tiny, tucked into the hills, hunched down, the pond is too small for even the smallest sailboat or motorboat.

Speed and power are useless here. There are no grand vistas, no broad panoramas, nothing at all for the wide screen. Like a porcupine, the pond is small, modest, unassuming, unglamorous, an unpretentious beast with prickly perimeter defenses that discourage most folks from seeking close association. Its entire west shore is so steep that even walking there, much less erecting any kind of structure, defies both gravity and common sense. At either end of that shore, a few semi-flat places not much bigger than a golf green harbor a few camps: John and Joanne Judson's, Jamila Vogel's, ours. The inlet bog forms an impassable moat at much of the north end. The outlet bog covers half the east shore and hooks around the south end. The remainder of the east shore is as steep as the west, except for a few hundred yards midway down the pond where the hillside flattens out enough to admit four camps.

Modest and unpretentious as the pond itself, these camps were built with a tact their present owners maintain. "We are here," these buildings say, "not to reshape this place in our own image but to let it shape us, not to teach this place a lesson but to let it teach us. We are here not to make noise but to be quiet, to listen and watch." Everyone who owns a camp on the pond adheres to that code. The only boats here are canoes and rowboats. There are no electronic horrors, no boom boxes. If you swim or paddle near Bill Meyer's place on a hot August afternoon, you might hear the Red Sox game drifting softly out to you through his open windows. The only other sounds generated by human beings are the comforting, companionable ones of kids splashing happily on the tiny beach at the Greens' camp, the *thunk* of an oar on a gunwale.

But to say the pond lacks glamour is not to deny it beauty. Its beauty is so clear and bright because it is not painted over—no lipstick, no mascara. Like a carrot pulled from the garden and eaten on the spot, it brings the tastes of sun, earth, and rain right to you unadorned. The pond is a miniature couched in its oval frame of hills. You can hold it in your two hands; the whole picture and every detail in it are visible at once. A patch of mist forms over the water, then dissipates. A swamp maple on the shore blazes up fiery red in mid-October.

At first glance, in other words, the pond may seem pleasant enough but no great shakes. At second glance, it starts to grow on you. At third and fourth glance, it really gets under your skin. At fifth and sixth and beyond, you realize you're undergoing a slow, osmotic process: The pond is getting into your blood. The prospect of living without the pond in your life is too awful to contemplate. Finally, you realize, you're in love.

\*\*\*

When Wes came back for a second look, then for a third and a fourth, I figured the place had to have gotten under his skin, too. We continued to have some pro-forma talk about electricity. Dick and Peg Vaughan, both being advanced in age and neither of them in the best of health, had not wanted to be without a telephone, so they had engineered a phone line that ran underwater across the cove from Bill Meyer's place to theirs.

"Couldn't we do that with a power line?" Wes asked.

"I don't see why not," I said, always the upbeat broker. "If Cyrus W. Field could get a telegraph cable laid across the floor of the Atlantic

Ocean from Ireland to Newfoundland, we can lay a few hundred yards of wire underwater from Bill Meyer's to you."

Wes had softened noticeably. I could already see the look of fond ownership on his face. This talk of submarine wire was academic. His eyes and mind were on other things. He was seeing the white pines towering up on either side of the porch, way too big in circumference for even a long-armed man like him to reach around. Inside, he was admiring the fieldstone fireplaces, one downstairs and one up in the master bedroom, each stone, like each word in a good poem, sharp and distinct in its own shape and grain yet tied in and linked to every other. He was listening to the clear, non-electrified silence surrounding the ovenbird's call. He was hooked.

"Gosh," Dick Vaughan said to me a couple of days later, "I hope your friends take the place. We can't imagine anybody we'd rather see have it."

"Nor can we, Dick," I said. "Nor can we."

\*\*\*

Summer is the time of society at the pond; winter, the time of solitude. The society we started with was our own—Rita; our son, Greg; our dog, Lucy; me—though without the society of the Judsons, we never would have come to know the pond ourselves. About twenty years ago, our postmaster told me the Judsons owned that tiny pond-side camp you could just barely see from the road. I found that an intriguing tidbit of Isn't-It-a-Small-World intelligence because some twenty years before, in 1965, I had met John and Joanne Judson at a dinner party in Waterville. But in the several years we had lived in Temple, we had never seen a sign of life at the Judsons' camp. They lived, the postmaster said, in Wisconsin and came to Temple only rarely. When I finally did see a car parked there one August afternoon, I didn't pass up the chance to reconnect.

"Sure, I remember," John said, "the Fullams' house, August 1965. You were just about to leave for Germany."

We reminisced, compared notes. John was teaching English at the University of Wisconsin/La Crosse, right smack on the Mississippi

River. For many years he and Joanne had been editing and publishing a little magazine called *Northeast*. John had been an all-around athlete in his youth: football, baseball, track. He still looked it, his graying black hair trimmed short to fit under a helmet, the compact, solid body of a quarterback who bounces off tacklers like a hard rubber ball.

"You guys should come swim," he said, "whether we're here or not. It'd be nice to know someone's enjoying the place."

And we did, we did. Late every summer afternoon we went there. We swam across to the great raft of lily pads that skirts the bog on the east shore; then we turned left and swam along the shore. Lucy—part black Lab, part spaniel, part seal maybe—was way ahead of us. Every day she charged out of the water at the little point where Bob Morris's camp sits tucked into a grove of big pines. She raced around in search of red squirrels, chickadees, chipmunks, anything to bark at. When we touched bottom at the point and headed back to Judsons', Lucy gave up her hunt, leaped into the water in a gleeful geyser, and chuffed out ahead of us again.

Somewhere out in the middle, immersed in the cooling but not too cold water warmed by the August sun, either Rita or I would repeat one of our pond mantras, something like: "It doesn't get any better than this, does it?" But, translated, all our mantras meant: "Ah, my beloved mate, have we not found the Earthly Paradise? So what if the house needs paint again and the clutch just went on the Subaru? Greg is a young man of kind and generous heart; Lucy, the world's prettiest, most sweet-natured black mutt. And here we are, all four of us, afloat in the world's most perfect pond."

As we neared the western shore, Rita cruised the blueberry bushes growing there. All through the season, she plucked the day's ripened berries and, still afloat, ate them. She was a shore bird feeding, an aquatic deer grazing.

\*\*\*

Poor Judsons! Only two, maybe three weeks a year they had free to spend here, and we dove off their dock every day from early June until

early September, sometimes even into early October in a really warm
fall. How could we possibly right that awful inequity?

The dock was pretty rickety, so I cut three big cedars on our place
and hauled them down to the pond, where my new pal, Bill Roorbach,
helped me assemble them into a new floating dock. Every fall, I pulled
the dock out of the water with a come-along. Every spring, I launched it
again and anchored it to the shore. Around Christmastime I called John
and Joanne out there on the banks of the Mississippi and reported that
all was well at their camp on the pond.

But of course there is nothing we can do for them that will ever
balance their gift to us of those many afternoon swims.

***

Six years ago, our neighbor Sandy Gregor told us she'd seen an ad in the
*Franklin Journal* for a camp and acre of land for sale on the pond. The
price was way too high. We didn't even want a camp. All we wanted was a
little piece of land on the water so that we could always, always, not matter what, have access to this tiny, unprepossessing, most perfect of ponds.

I cursed and bellowed about the camp. "Rita!" I said. "I can't stand
owning another building. I never want to saw another board! I never
want to pound another nail! Look at the roof!"

The roof—covered with ancient, dried-out, shrunken roofing
paper—leaked. I could see daylight through it. I could see rotting
boards in it.

"Will we ever again in this life," she said, "have a chance to buy a
piece of land on the pond? Camp or no camp? Leaky roof or no leaky
roof?"

"Most likely not," I had to admit.

"So?" she said.

So we bought it. And the next fall, I swung around on climbing
ropes, peeled the old roofing paper off, pulled four million roofing
nails, built scaffolding, dropped a scaffolding plank on my own dumb
head, yanked out rotting roof boards, nailed in new ones, laid tar paper,
climbed up and down ladders, laid row upon row upon row of green
three-tab asphalt shingles over the tar paper.

Lucy came with me every day, my sole help and support. She couldn't do much in a practical way, but her presence gave endless comfort. She rambled the hillside and settled down on the pine needles for snoozes.

When life up on the roof became too grim and wearisome, I would holler down to her: "Hey, Miss Dog! Hey, Ms. Lucy Poo!"

She would wag her tail and, along with it, her whole black, floppy-eared self. She would bark. "Come on down, man, and do something sensible. Let's take a walk. Let's go for a swim."

Now, some five years later, with the trials of the roof job faded into the past and dear Lucy, alas, in her grave, I have to say that roof gives me great pleasure. Every time we walk to the camp on the narrow, shaded trail that leads to it, I admire my own handiwork, those neat rows of green shingles I laid while Lucy cheered me up and cheered me on. By now, I'm totally reconciled to this building I didn't want. I'm downright fond of it. The screened-in porch reaches nearly to the water's edge, but pine, hemlock, and birch in front of the building and surrounding it make it nearly invisible from the pond. The place has the feel of a bird's nest, well camouflaged but affording a high, leafy vantage point for viewing the world.

The moral of this story? If you get a chance to spend too much money on a goofy, extravagant, self-indulgent enterprise, don't let a leaky roof stand in your way.

***

Owning our own place on the pond now, we extend open invitations to friends to come swim whenever they like, as John and Joanne did for us. Bill Roorbach and Juliet Karlsen and their dogs, Wally and Desi, come often but usually later than our four-thirty or five o'clock swim, so we usually miss them. If we do meet, most likely Rita and I will just be climbing up the dock ladder or on shore toweling off when Wally and Desi, the advance guard, come racing down the hill.

Desi, neat, trim, short-haired, black and white, has the air of a nervous middle-aged butler charged with keeping a hyperactive teenager out of trouble. Wally is no longer a teenager, but he still acts like one. A shaggy, long-eared spaniel and who-knows-what-else mix, he's all panting, pink-tongued exuberance. If you're not braced for him, he can bowl you over with his sixty-plus pounds of cannonball love. In the water, propelled by his broad retriever paws, he chugs along tirelessly, the image of unsinkable buoyancy. He's a furry aircraft carrier. You could land jet fighters on his back.

Water is not Desi's element. He approaches it cautiously, and only when it's clear that Bill and Juliet and Wally are heading out for a long, leisurely swim and that he'll be left behind does he overcome his reluctance and tiptoe in. For every one stroke of Wally's wide paws, skinny-legged Desi has to take three or four. Wally wallows and revels in the water. Desi churns frantically in it. He's trying to climb out and run on top. Go for a swim? He'd prefer a walk, thank you.

But sometimes we do all arrive together, and while Wally plops off the end of the dock and Desi frets at the watery prospect before him, we humans shed sneakers and shirts on the downed log that serves as our dockside bench. Bill wears raggedy cut-off jeans for swim trunks and his hair pulled back in a ponytail. He has a high, domed forehead, a downright Shakspearian forehead, lots of room in that brain for concocting ingenious plots, fashioning fine-tuned sentences. Bill is the guy every hippie ought to become when he grows up, just as open to the world and adventuresome as any youngster but with none of the flakiness that dogs most middle-aged hippies. He combines the élan of the amateur with the highly developed skills of the master. Whether he's remodeling his kitchen or writing a short story, his work is elegant in its conception, solid in its construction, flawless in its finish work.

But here at the pond, we're not working. Our medium is neither wood nor words but water. As all six of us—four humans, two dogs—swim out from the shade of the hill into the sunlight, we're like a school of dolphins or a family of otters. We're nowhere near as skillful swimmers as those aquatic acrobats; but water seems to affect us as it does them, making us more sociable and playful. Blood is thicker than water, but water is thicker than air. In the kind of non-competitive swimming we do in the pond, water conducts the currents of our friendship back and forth between us. We converse silently through the ripples and wakes our fins and flippers and paws trail behind us, and if we do speak, our words sound a bit like the murmuring gabble of a raft of ducks or, if we're clowning and boisterous, the hooting of loons.

\*\*\*

Swimmingly—that's how summertime goes at the pond. The summer of 2000 proved one of fresh starts that all went swimmingly, the summer when Wes and Diane deliberated about the Vaughans' camp, bought it, and settled into it with all the chattering glee of house wrens building a nest, also the summer when Juliet was pregnant with Elysia, who would be born in September.

Slim, blonde, and lithe, Juliet the swimmer has always reminded me of Venus in Botticelli's most famous painting, which I now retitled in my own mind as "The Birth of Venus about to Give Birth." If outside influences—the music an expectant mother hears, the tranquility or agitation of her days—do in fact help determine an infant's temperament, then it seemed to me Elysia was destined to be the most cheerful of children. Not only were her prenatal days filled with the voices of adults eager to welcome her into the world; but, on nearly every summer afternoon, she would also be doubly upheld, afloat in the womb and in the pond. Juliet remarked more than once what a pleasure swimming was to her in those late months of her pregnancy, how light she felt in the water.

Okay: The sunny, even-keeled disposition Elysia has displayed in her first years of life owes much more to her parentage than it does to her mom's prenatal swims, but I like to think that being cradled often in these friendly waters contributed in some small way to Elysia's buoyant nature.

\*\*\*

The first inklings of solitude come in September. Early frosts cool the water. The four camps across the pond are buttoned up for the coming winter. Wes and I begin our polar-bear contest: Which one of us will be dumb and stubborn enough to keep swimming until ice starts forming between our toes?

It's about three o'clock on an October afternoon and unseasonably warm even for this stretch of mild Indian summer days. Our place on the west shore is already deep in shadow that extends well out into the pond. Where there is no sun, the water is noticeably cooler, so I swim off Wes and Diane's dock, which is still drenched in sunshine. But still, after only about ten minutes in the water, time to swim across the inlet cove and back, my fingers are icy and white. When I climb out, the heat of the sun is a blessing.

I didn't expect anyone to be here, and no one is. I leave a note stuck in the camp screen door at about eye level. "October 12," the note says. "The bear was here."

***

In the summer, we drive the mile and a half from our house to where we park the car, then walk the quarter mile through the woods to our camp and small dock at the north end of the pond. But once ice forms, the south end is just twenty minutes away from home by foot, even less when there's enough snow to travel on skis.

I love being at the pond, but I love going to it too. After a few days and nights of clear, sharp cold in early December, I can cross Temple Stream right behind our house on the inch or two of ice there, swing north through our big hayfield, then into the now nearly snowless woods where the deer can still ramble and feed at will, then across the Mitchells' woodlot and onto the landing where Toby and Weikko Hellgren yarded the wood they cut here, then up over the little hill on the short stretch of truck road that goes from the landing out to the town road. From the little metal grill bridge that crosses the pond outlet, I can see the beaver dam that has raised the water level of the pond about six inches this year. That slightly higher water makes the going from the road into the pond much easier than it usually is before heavy snow comes to level things out. Usually I have to fumble along, feeling my way between hummocks of marsh grass. Now, threaded between the hummocks, is a smooth path of ice I can follow the hundred yards or so to the edge of the outlet bog.

And there, on the pond itself, is ice not perfect for skating but almost perfect for rambling. This ice has been subject to rain and thaws, so it is not that smooth black ice of an uninterrupted deep freeze. It's milky with trapped air bubbles but still clear enough that the cracks in it show up like thin white walls, and I can read how thick the ice is—a good six inches.

I can also read what I take to be spring holes in the pond, too. What else would make these irregular stars or starfish or octopi in the ice? The springs send warmer water to the surface, forming perfect round nuclei from which arms of varying length, number, and writhing complexity radiate, registering how the warmer water spread out when it hit the ceiling of ice forming above it. Or such is my theory. It's lovely what the mind, unfettered by knowledge, can come up with.

There are patches of dry snow here and there, windblown remnants from the occasional light flurries we've had. They make for perfect trot-and-skid ice. I use the patch of snow to trot and get up a little speed; then, when I reach the edge of the snowpatch, I skid out onto the ice. And so—trot, trot, skid—trot, trot, trot, skid—I trot-skid the length of the pond, heading for Wes and Diane's camp.

There, at the north end, the light snow has gathered into a continuous crescent around the end of the pond, and in it are coyote tracks patrolling the water's edge and stopping to investigate the old beaver lodge built right on the edge of the inlet bog.

Later, when ice and woods and hills all lie under a thick blanket of snow, I ski the length of the pond from south to north, then turn around at the mouth of the inlet stream. The landscape lures vision skyward. My eye rambles down the length of the pond and, toward the far end, picks up speed, then races up the ramp of hillsides until, like a ski jumper in reverse, it launches itself from the rounded peak of Derby Mountain and into thin air.

If summer is down-to-earth time, a time when we are preoccupied with everything that grows, swims, runs, and flies down here in the little bowl of hills that holds the pond, then winter is sky time, a time of heavenly preoccupations.

In these darkest days of winter right around the solstice I usually head for the pond about 3:45. The work day is over. Whatever I meant to do today is either done or undone, and now it's time to go see what wonders the fading light will be working at the pond. There's nothing wrong with being out there on the ice at noon, soaking up the sun's heat on a below-zero day, but the experience is static: The sun shines and shines and shines. Or if the sky is overcast, it is gray and gray and gray.

But at sunset, there's no telling what will happen from minute to minute. Tonight, in late December, clouds hanging low in the south-western sky are picking up patinas of red and gold from the sun already below the horizon. Shadows thicken down here under the pines, but above the string of clouds the sky is clear, and Venus is bright high in the south-southwest. A bit below her and slightly to the north is just the faintest sliver of moon. I can't recall ever having seen one so fine, a slender cantaloupe rind of a moon, a nearly transparent cedar shaving. To call it a "waxing crescent" would be an absurdity, so fine and deli-cate it is, and fleeting too; for no sooner do I notice it there, just barely skimming the treetops, than it begins to drop below them and is out of sight by the time I reach home.

***

And twelve days later: a rim of clouds around the horizon the color of wild trout belly, a deep, fleshy red, nothing flaming about it, cold-blooded, winter red, and the moon almost directly overhead and bulg-ing out of its first quarter, well on its way toward puffed up full.

Venus is still higher and brighter tonight. At this point in my life, I tend to see lone stars in duplicate or triplicate or with rays of light projecting from them. This, my optometrist tells me, is the result of astigmatism, the eyeballs sagging out of shape after being hauled around in my head for sixty-five years. Well, whatever the reason, Venus, my favorite star, my favorite goddess, is always welcome in triplicate. Who can ever get too much of Venus?

Mild, quiet. What bloody noisy creatures we humans are even at our most silent. Here I am, sliding along on wooden skis, and the racket is intolerable. I'm hauling my bubble of noise along with me like a snail his shell or one of those spiders with a big balloon on behind. The only way I can escape the crunch of my poles and skis in the snow, the creak of my leather boots against the metal of the bindings, my own breath, the movement of air in my ears, is to stand stock-still. When I'm moving, I'm my own deafening noise machine.

***

Tonight, even the most skilled of watercolorists would go mad. He couldn't concoct washes subtle enough to capture all these shades. There's broken cloud cover letting patches of blue sky through, but along the horizon, that rich, deep-sea blue fades into an icier, paler blue. Overhead, tinges of red, pink, and mauve edge into royal purple where the clouds are thickest. Embers glow in the southwest as gray starts settling out of the clouds to the north, and in the fifteen minutes it takes me to go up the pond, turn, and start heading back, gray has covered the northern sky, obliterating the color. By the time I'm off the pond and in the woods, the whole sky is gray. The watercolorist could not have kept up with these rapid shifts, each of them so fleeting that it's impossible to speak of "each of them." What I saw was a continuum. No static art could catch its reality. No motion picture could either because even the widest screen is too small a frame. Art, that poor old stumblebum, just can't catch up with nature.

***

Over the twenty or more years of my winter visits to the pond at dusk, it has shown me all its moods. The wind may be howling, whipping spindrift up into my eyes, or the air may be clear and still with stars starting to spark way up in the sky as the temperature heads down toward twenty or thirty below zero. But if there is any image that is most like the pond in winter, an image like a characteristic expression on a beloved face, then it is what I see on this evening in late January.

The day warmed slowly after a night near zero. Smoke from the chimney has been heading north all day. The cloud cover has been thickening, as if someone were pulling up one blanket then another on a cold night until, now, the temperature is just a bit below freezing, and the air seems filled with fine goose down.

Standing on my skis in the middle of the pond, I look back onto Derby Mountain, and it is no more than a hazy outline. The air is palpably soft; sky above and snow below shade into each other as the light fades. Which is heaven? Which is earth?

Molly, our neighbor Sandy's dog, is with me tonight and standing now at the edge of the outlet bog. She's troubled by something there yet fascinated by it. My fading eyes cannot penetrate the thickening darkness. I suspect she has scented some creature that gives her pause rather than invites her to the chase. What it is I can only guess. She turns away and bounds across the ice to run ahead of me in my ski trail as I head for home.

How unlike Lucy who always stuck close by me in the last few years of her life. She was my constant companion on these daily winter outings, and I felt bad about them only when the snow conditions were miserable for her. Like one time in her last winter when the snow was slightly crusted and my skis broke the path up into chunks she fell between. She came home lame but was ready to go again the next day. Or when her paws kept filling up with packed snow she would stop to chew out.

I think of her as I ski home, her grave under a red maple down near the garden. Rita has said she would like her ashes buried on Lucy's grave. Why not? And if Rita's and Lucy's are there, where else would I want mine?

***

Then, some evening in early or mid-February, when I make my turnabout at the inlet bog and head back down the pond, I feel faint breath of warm air on my face; and the sky in the south is soft and dark, a huge, water-laden sponge ready to start wiping winter away. The sun rides a little higher each day. I can ski out here as late as 5:30 and still have plenty of light to get home.

Temperatures ride up into the forties in the daytime. The lovely, silky powder snow of winter goes to hell in a handbasket, thaws and freezes, turns grainy and icy in the overnight cold, pulpy in the warmth of day. Out on the pond, water wicks up so fast in my ski track that I can't go back on the trail I made coming out.

In March the wind out of the northwest, picking up water from the melting snow, is no longer dry. It smells like laundry hung out on a breezy spring day, sun soaked and wind drubbed. In April I have to go to the pond in the morning before the sun turns the whole surface to a treacherous mush I sink in over my ankles. To get out onto ice that will hold me, I jump across the narrow moat of meltwater all around the shore of the pond. Soon the water will take over, soaking up through the snowpack like coffee in a sugar cube. The surface of the pond will be black and immobile. We can't get on it with skis; we can't dive into it. If we launch a canoe, we can't go anywhere. The ice is too thin to bear our weight and too thick to let the canoe pass. If we are alert and pay close attention day by day to what sun and wind work here on the pond, we can catch that moment when the sheet of ice disintegrates into candle ice. Then we can paddle everywhere, each stroke setting those clear, hard candles tinkling like a million crystal chandeliers.

*** 

But for a few weeks there will be no skiing, no ice fishing, no snowmobiling, no swimming, no boating. Neither we nor anyone else will be able to *do* anything on the pond. Or, rather, all we'll be able to do is contemplate it, which is the most important thing we do here anyway, regardless of whatever else we're doing. Before and after each swim, we stand and look. Even in the middle of each swim, right from water level, we look. In the middle of each snowstorm or each brilliantly clear December evening, we stop and look.

And in May, when the sun has warmed Wes and Diane's porch by late afternoon, we can again settle into the rocking chairs there for beers and conversation. Wherever else our talk may take us, it inevitably circles back to where we are, to what we are seeing. We know that here—on this pond, at this moment, for as long as it lasts—we are living an idyll. Idylls are not a hot literary item these days. They celebrate the peace and simplicity of pastoral existence, things most people can hardly conceive of, much less hope to experience. The very idea of an idyll seems rather quaint and cute, a theme for a costume party maybe, shepherds and shepherdesses cavorting on the green.

But chase a word back far enough and you find there's more to it than meets the eye. In the third century B.C., Theocritus called his short poems about rural life *eidyllia*, or "little pictures." *Eidyllion* is a diminutive of *eidos*, meaning "form" or "picture," and that noun goes back in turn to the verb *eidein*, "to see," which is also the root of "idea" and of the Greek *eidenai*, "to know." What the idyll is really about, then, is not a masquerade ball but about seeing and knowing the natural world, living in it and in harmony with it. At Drury Pond the human and the natural coexist in a near perfect balance. The size and topography of the place have set limits on human presence and activity; and, so far anyway—knock wood—the people drawn to the pond have understood those limits as benefits, not drawbacks, of this landscape and been more than content to live within them. So to say we live an idyll at Drury Pond is as literally true as the truth of a word can get, not so little a picture after all but quite a big one, a vision of what could be in the world beyond the pond, if only that world would let it.

# Country Singing

'm struck time and again by the power group singing has over me, not singing I am audience to, but singing I take part in, singing that is, I suppose, not very "good" from a musical point of view. It's the singing you do in churches or at the end of the high school Christmas concert when the audience is invited to sing along, and it just plain bowls me over.

When it starts, I make a firm resolve that this time I will not be a sentimental old fool. This time I will sing "Rock of Ages" or "We Shall Overcome" or "O Little Town of Bethlehem" just like any other solid citizen—dry-eyed, full-voiced, no nonsense.

But resolves be damned. After a few bars, the tears are about to leak down my face; the lump in my throat swells to watermelon proportions, and because it is difficult to sing around a watermelon, my otherwise unexceptional baritone begins to squeak, then gives out altogether.

The song does without me while a stern inner voice says, "Stop your blubbering. You're an embarrassment to us all."

"Oh, I know," I say, "I *[sob!]* know."

I get hold of myself and climb back onto the flow of song: "The hopes and fears of all the years . . ." But before I've made it through "are met in thee tonight," I've wiped out again.

It *is* an embarrassment, and I often wonder how many people have gone home from musical events in Farmington, Maine, and told their wives or husbands, "Gee, you know, I sat next to this guy at the concert tonight who cried all the way through 'Rudolph the Red-Nosed Reindeer.'"

I also wonder how many other closet weepers there are out there in the singing public. For years I've been asking myself that question, and for years I've been coming up with the same answer: "None, you maudlin sap."

Then just this past Christmas, after the community chorus concert, I was talking to a guy who is a superb violinist, a violin maker, a musician of the finest sensibility, in short, a man in whose musical judgment and instincts I put the utmost faith. After we had exchanged a few remarks about the afternoon's performance, he said to me: "But you know what just bowls me over? It's when everybody sings at the end. That whole auditorium full of people—all those voices, not trained singers or anything but just people singing—it chokes me up like nothing else I know."

"Sob sister," I said. "Aren't you ashamed?"

And then I fessed up.

I don't mean to claim any special powers for country singers and country singing. There are plenty of people living in cities who will know what I mean when I talk about that almost palpable blow to the midsection I feel when the voices of "my" people begin to sing, people I have lived with, against, and alongside of for years, people I'm fond of and not so fond of, people I positively can't stand today but may admire tomorrow, people I seek out and people I studiously avoid, all the people who are the color and fabric of this place that is my place in the world. As the Shaker hymn says, "'Tis a gift to come down where we ought to be." For some, that may be an urban neighborhood. For me, it's this patchwork of fields, ponds, forests, and hamlets in the foothills of the White Mountains, and singing began to assume the place it has in my life only after my wife and I made our permanent home here many years ago.

In our first winter we found ourselves part of a group of about a dozen people who met on Sunday afternoons to sing and play recorder together. We were all relative newcomers, all "from away," and the music we made together had a community-building effect, the kind it has for all immigrant groups that still have more in common with where they came from than with where they are. Our musical leader was Eric Leeber, a transplant from New York City, who, with a Renaissance-music consort he called The Red House Circus, brought some wonderful evenings of music to western Maine.

It was an article of faith for Eric that audiences were not at concerts just to sit and gawk and listen, but to participate, too, and every

Red House Circus concert included a lot of audience singing, mostly of rounds, which Eric loved to get rolling through an auditorium in eight parts. Those rounds would gather in the distance like a summer thunderstorm, slowly building to their full power as each new voice came in. Then, after one voice after another had dropped out again and the storm passed away down the valley, we would be left sitting there in the clean, fresh silence, the air positively dripping with the music you hear when the music stops. And Eric would grin and look around and nod his head and say, "Yeah, yeah."

When I was still a teenager, there was a French singing group that called itself *Les Compagnons de la Chanson.* I grant you it's a tacky name, both to the mind and the ear, but it suggests something of the companionability of songs and of the power of singing to make and maintain society, a power that came home to me recently on a wilderness canoe trip in Labrador. The singing our party did almost every night around the campfire was a ritual celebration of our small human community of nine where we were the only community there was, but it was also a celebration of our membership in the families and communities we had left behind and to which we would return. The singing was like the river itself. It was not something we "did." It was there, constantly flowing along; and in the evening, we would launch ourselves onto it, just as we set out on the river in the morning. It was a link to our past, both personal and communal, and it was a link to our future. It carried us out, and it would carry us back. It was both line and circle.

But for all the delights and illuminations that have come my way in singing with family, friends, and fellow wayfarers, that small, closed-circle context is not the one in which singing affects me so powerfully that I sometimes wonder if my mental and emotional underpinnings are not giving way altogether. The essential condition for that experience is a large group that includes your whole local world, not just the people you invite to your house for dinner or the ones who invite you to theirs.

As for the singing itself, it is unrehearsed, ragged, far from perfect. People are off key. The back of the room may be lagging a bit behind the front, but still, it all works. There is an audible unity of purpose, and the voices that may not be doing just what they ought to do are heard as impromptu embellishments rather than unwanted disturbances. The able singers who are the soloists and stars of church choirs, operettas, and close-harmony groups continue to stand out here too, not alone, but as bright threads in the fabric, their voices blending in with everyone else's; and voices that are rarely or never heard in other circumstances, the ones that are too shy to speak up at town meetings or in public debates, are in full voice.

It doesn't matter if one of us stumbles or even falls silent for a few bars. I can choke up as much as I want. The singing goes on, and the stumbler is carried along with it. Here the halt and the lame are not halt or lame at all. No one has to be persuasive, knowledgeable, coherent. There is no budget to be approved or cut, nobody on your side and nobody on my side. Perhaps the greatest miracle about a hall full of people singing is that we all speak and we all listen at the same time. Faces soften. Scrooges are transformed. We are not performing; rather, we are celebrating what we could perhaps be if we would only let ourselves. When we sing, we all become citizens of Utopia, of the Kingdom of God, call it what you will. When we walk out the door, we'll still be up against the same old stuff we're always up against; but for now and for as long as the singing lasts, we can hear clearly where it is we want to go, and every time I hear that song, it chokes me up like nothing else I know.

# References

Essays in this book were previously published in the sources listed below.

"Asparagus." *Northern Woodlands* 23, no. 3 (Autumn 2016).

"Baffling Beavers." *Northern Woodlands* 19, no. 3 (Autumn 2012).

"Bailey." *Northern Woodlands* 16, no. 2 (Summer 2009).

"Big Jim." *The Missouri Review* 31, no. 1 (Spring 2008): 34–52.

"Buying a New Fridge at Sixty-Five." *Fourth Genre: Explorations in Nonfiction* 6, no. 1 (Spring 2004): 47–50.

"A Chance at the Mythical Buck." *Northern Woodlands* 14, no. 3 (Autumn 2007).

"Citizen Scientists." *Northern Woodlands* 22, no. 1 (Spring 2015).

"Clunker." *Northern Woodlands* 20, no. 4 (Winter 2013).

"Comfortable Winter Camping." *Northern Woodlands* 14, no. 4 (Winter 2007).

"Consolation Prizes." *Northern Woodlands* 16, no. 3 (Autumn 2009).

"Country Mice, City Mice." *Northern Woodlands* 22, no. 3 (Autumn 2015).

"Country Singing." In *Upcountry*, 161–66. Camden, ME: Down East Books, 1991.

"Deep Cold, Deep Snow, Decent Winter." *Northern Woodlands* 13, no. 4 (Winter 2006).

"Dish-Fed Retainers." In *Living Wild and Domestic*, 85–103. Guilford, CT: Lyons Press, 2002.

"A Dog's Life." *Northern Woodlands* 23, no. 4 (Winter 2015).

"Drury Pond: An Idyll." In Robert Kimber, Wesley McNair, and Bill Roorbach, *A Place on Water*, 1–43. Gardiner, ME: Tilbury House, 2004.

"A Fine Woodworker." *Northern Woodlands* 17, no. 1 (Spring 2010).

"Firewood from the Sky." *Northern Woodlands* 27, no. 4 (Winter 2020).

"Flummy." *Northern Woodlands* 21, no. 4 (Winter 2014).

"Footwear." *Northern Woodlands* 17, no. 4 (Winter 2010).

"Good Riddance." *Northern Woodlands* 24, no. 2 (Summer 2017).

"A Great Garden Glut." *Northern Woodlands* 18, no. 2 (Summer 2011).

"Griff's Camp." *Northern Woodlands* 20, no. 3 (Autumn 2013).

"The Ice Cutter's Song." *Northern Woodlands* 19, no. 4 (Winter 2012).

"In the Interior: Your Not-So-Typical Suburb." *Maine Times*, October 15, 1998.

"Larix Laricina." *Northern Woodlands* 27, no. 1 (Spring 2020).

"Late-Summer Fishing." *Northern Woodlands* 14, no. 2 (Summer 2007).

"The Lawn." *Northern Woodlands* 26, no. 4 (Winter 2019).

"Leaf-Peeping Season." *Northern Woodlands* 24, no. 3 (Autumn 2017).

"A Legacy Maple." *Northern Woodlands* 21, no. 2 (Summer 2014).

"A Local Hero." *Northern Woodlands* 24, no. 4 (Winter 2017).

"Lost But Found." *Northern Woodlands* 7, no. 2 (Summer 2000), as untitled "A Place in Mind" column.

"A Kitchen with a View." *Northern Woodlands* 19, no. 2 (Summer 2012).

"Meanders." *Northern Woodlands* 13, no. 2 (Summer 2006).

"A Mean Winter." *Northern Woodlands* 26, no. 3 (Fall 2019).

"My Topography as Autobiography." *Northern Woodlands* 25, no. 2 (Summer 2018).

"A Navigational Muddle." *Northern Woodlands* 17, no. 2 (Summer 2010).

"No Bugs." *Northern Woodlands* 18, no. 1 (Spring 2011).

"Northern Jungle." *Northern Woodlands* 22, no. 2 (Summer 2015).

"November Epiphany." *Northern Woodlands* 15, no. 3 (Autumn 2008).

"Of Skis, Moose, and Climate Change." *Northern Woodlands* 27, no. 3 (Fall 2020).

"The One That Got Away." *Yankee* (October 2000).

"Our Butterfly Net." *Northern Woodlands* 26, no. 2 (Summer 2019).

"Our Drought." *Northern Woodlands* 23, no. 4 (Winter 2016).

"Paddling with Young Guys." *Northern Woodlands* 19, no. 1 (Spring 2012).

"The Perfect Canoe." *Northern Woodlands* 28, no. 1(Spring 2021).

"Prologue: Porcupine Stew and Asparagus." In *Living Wild and Domestic*, 1–10.

"Raising Rocks." *Northern Woodlands* 16, no. 1 (Spring 2009).

"A Raspberry Diary." *Northern Woodlands* 25, no. 4 (Winter 2018).

"Remote Ponds, Wild Trout." *Northern Woodlands* 15, no. 2 (Summer 2008).

"The Ripeness of Deadwood." *Northern Woodlands* 13, no. 3 (Autumn 2006).

"Rita's Memorial." *Northern Woodlands* 23, no. 2 (Summer 2016).

"Rites of Spring." *Northern Woodlands* 15, no. 1 (Spring 2008).

"Saint John Memories." *Northern Woodlands* 24, no. 1 (Spring 2017).

"Sandy's Painting." *Northern Woodlands* 28, no. 2 (Summer 2021).

"Sheep in the Parlor." In *Upcountry*, 8–17.

"Sightseeing." *Northern Woodlands* 18, no. 3 (Autumn 2011).

"Silent Nights." *Northern Woodlands* 16, no. 4 (Winter 2009).

"A Slipping-Down Farm." In *Upcountry*, 48–57.

"Squirrel Brains." *Northern Woodlands* 21, no. 3 (Autumn 2014).

"String Fever." *Down East* (April 1991).

"Summer's Boomerang." In *Upcountry*, 67–69.

"Survey." *Northern Woodlands* 25, no. 3 (Autumn 2018).

"Swiss Canoe Trip." *Northern Woodlands* 17, no. 3 (Autumn 2010).

"Table Manners of Birds." *Northern Woodlands* 27, no. 2 (Summer 2020).

"A Tale of Tall Snows." *Northern Woodlands* 15, no. 4 (Winter 2008).

"The Tenacity of Trees." *Northern Woodlands* 25, no. 1 (Spring 2018).

"Three Tractors." *Northern Woodlands* 18, no. 4 (Winter 2011).

"Trees and Dendrons." *Northern Woodlands* 14, no. 1 (Spring 2007).

"Unexpected Gifts." *Northern Woodlands* 23, no. 1 (Spring 2016).

"A Visit Down Country." *Northern Woodlands* 20, no. 1 (Spring 2013).

"The Weather." *Northern Woodlands* 20, no. 2 (Summer 2013).

"Of Wind, Water, and the Best of Friends." *Northern Woodlands* 26, no. 1 (Spring 2019).

"Winning the Ice Out Prize." *Northern Woodlands* 21, no. 1 (Spring 2014).

## OTHER REFERENCES

Lopez, Barry. "Searching for Ancestors" (1983). In *Crossing Open Ground*. New York: Vintage, 1988.

Lorenz, Konrad. "Part and Parcel in Animal and Human Societies." In *Studies in Animal and Human Behavior*, translated by Robert Martin. Cambridge, MA: Harvard University Press, 1971.

Nelson, Richard. *The Island Within*. New York: Vintage Books, 1991.

Oliver, Mary. "A Few Words." *Blue Pastures*. New York: Harcourt Brace, 1995.

Roze, Uldis. *The North American Porcupine*. Washington, DC: Smithsonian Institution Press, 1989.

Shepard, Paul. "On Animal Friends." In *The Biophilia Hypothesis*, edited by Stephen R. Kellert and Edward O. Wilson. Washington, DC: Island Press, 1993.